IMAGES
of America

GREATER CARPINTERIA SUMMERLAND AND LA CONCHITA

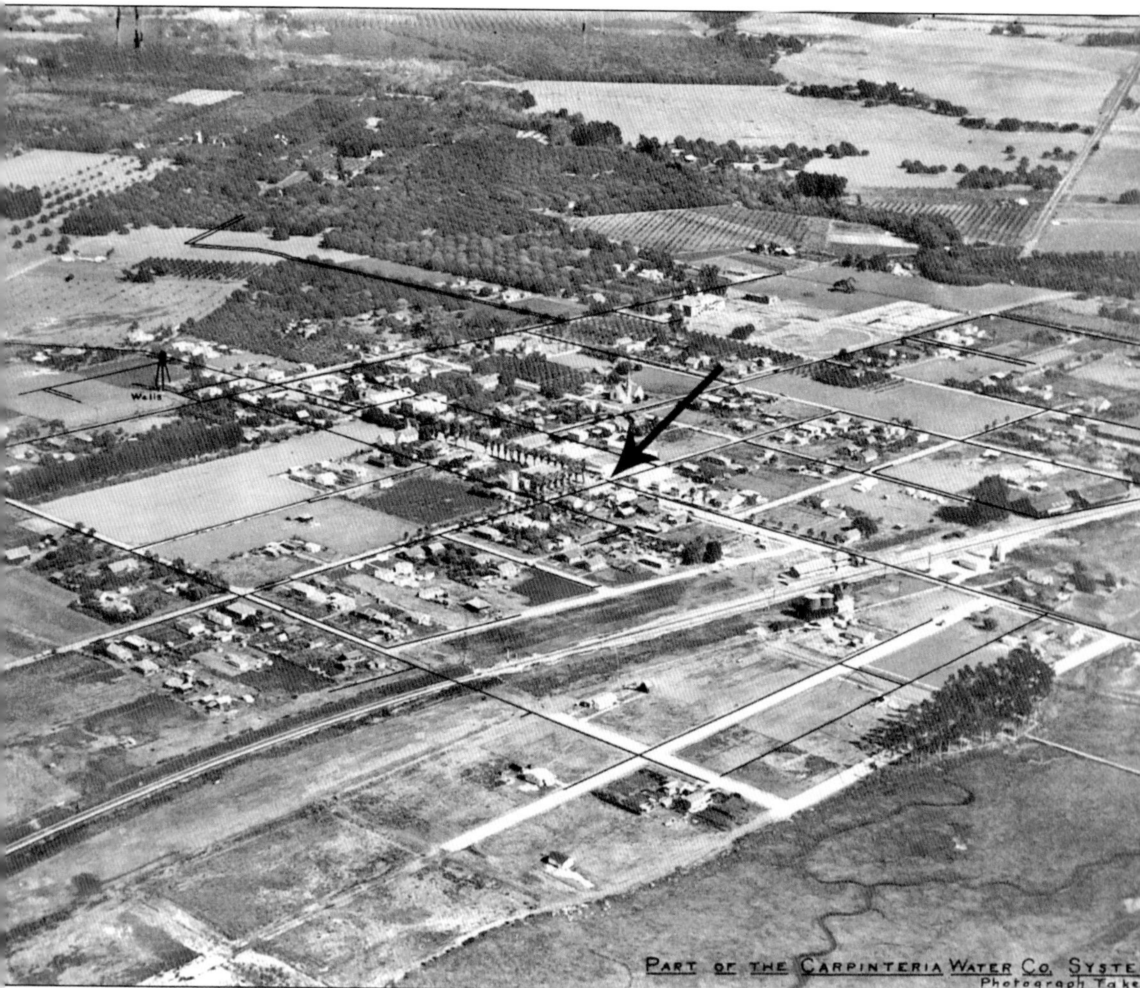

Don't be misled by the penned-in water company lines and notations in this 1924 aerial view of Carpinteria. The arrow in this shot is pointing to the corner of Linden Avenue and Seventh Street, which then, as now, is boxed in by towering palms. There are two ways to dissect this remarkable photograph—by looking for what's in the picture, or what isn't. (Courtesy Carpinteria Valley Museum of History.)

ON THE COVER: A panoramic view of Carpinteria Beach at the foot of Linden Avenue in 1927 attests to the fact that the tenor of the beach scene in Carpinteria remains largely unchanged some 80-plus years later. If it ain't broke, don't fix it. (Courtesy Carpinteria Valley Museum of History.)

IMAGES
of America

Greater Carpinteria
Summerland and La Conchita

Jim Campos, Bonnie Kelm,
Dave Moore, Tom Moore, and the
Carpinteria Valley Museum of History

ARCADIA
PUBLISHING

ISBN 978-0-7385-7098-3

Published by Arcadia Publishing
Charleston, South Carolina

Printed in the United States of America

Library of Congress Control Number: 2009925465

For all general information contact Arcadia Publishing at:
Telephone 843-853-2070
Fax 843-853-0044
E-mail sales@arcadiapublishing.com
For customer service and orders:
Toll-Free 1-888-313-2665

Visit us on the Internet at www.arcadiapublishing.com

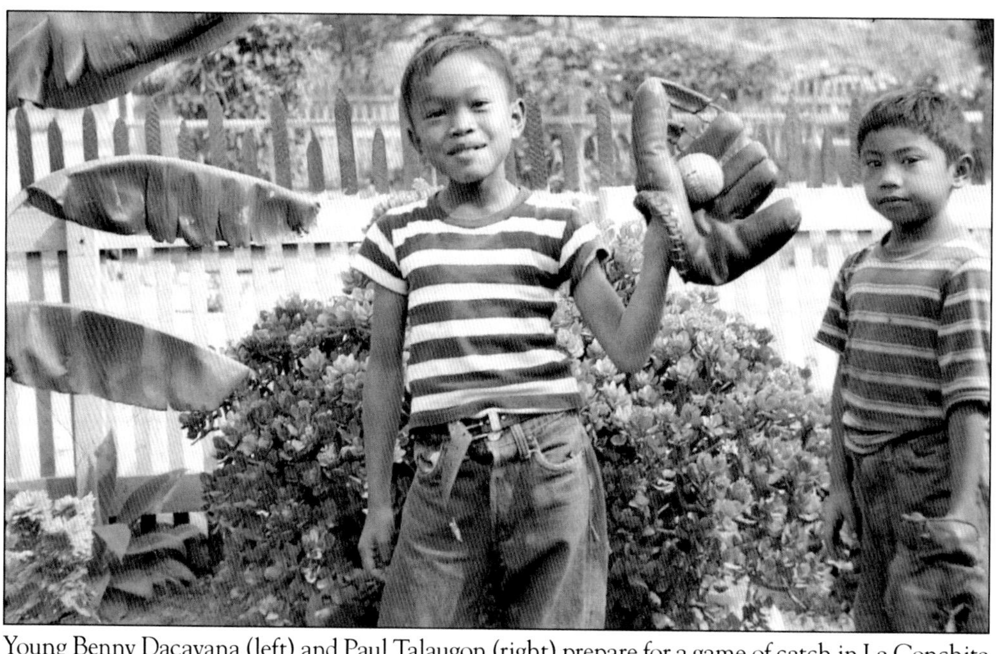

Young Benny Dacayana (left) and Paul Talaugon (right) prepare for a game of catch in La Conchita in the late 1940s. La Conchita became the home of a thriving Pacific Islander community beginning in the early 1930s. Many of the Dacayanas, Talaugons, and Alpenias, among other prominent families, began their lives as Americans in La Conchita and enriched the cultural fabric of the central California region. (Courtesy Ben Dacayana.)

Contents

Acknowledgments

Louise Moore and Herman Zittel deserve a hearty round of applause for their tireless efforts on behalf of this project. Louise again managed to piece together our well-intentioned scribblings and randomly arranged photographs into a volume that looks and reads even better than we imagined it might. It wouldn't have happened without Louise. Herman provided a gift of equal value, as he led us through the Carpinteria Valley Museum of History's spectacular photographic archive. Many thanks, Herman.

Thanks again to David Griggs, director/curator of the Carpinteria Valley Museum of History, and Patty Manuras for cheerfully repairing our garbled grammar, imperfect punctuation, and historical inaccuracies.

The La Conchita chapter presented a special challenge, since so little of its history has been archived. Grateful appreciation is expressed to Jeff Ross, Eleanor Gallardo Ramey, Chet Dacayana, Bill Mingus, Federico (Dick) Talaugon Jr., Allen and Ray Blackwell, the late Pete Richardson, and Robbie Hutto for helping to tell the story of this unique community.

The kindness extended to us during this adventure was, once again, remarkable. If we overlooked anyone in what we hope is a comprehensive listing, please accept our apologies.

Thanks also go to Michael Alden, the Alvis family, Andrew Barnes, Shari Barnes, Jerome Behnett and the Nugget, Vera Bensen, Jonathan Brown, Bruce Campbell, Sal and Delia Campos, Valerie Campos, Carpinteria High School, Cate School Archives, Mary Alice Coffman, Fran Davis, Larry and Bonnie Donovan, Kirby Duncan, Jean M. Fox, Lee Hammock, Ken Hazlewood, Kelly Hill, Mary Holzhauser, Ernie Johnson, Kathe Klock, Stewart and Mary Kelly, Sey Kinsell, Patricia A. Latham, Rod Lathim, Rob Malone, John McCafferty, Linda Merrill, Marny Middleton, Bill Malis, Bruce Morden, Jacqueline Morse and the Summerland Presbyterian Church, Maggie Munro, David Myrick, Donna May Ogan, Claire Thurmond Roberts, Jim Rockwell, John Rodriquez Jr., Jimmie Roseboro, Gar Salzgeber, Harold and Nancy Smith, Lisa Stone, Mildred Treloar, Doug Treloar, Rene and June VanWingerden, Fran Vos, Jeff White, Elizabeth Woodworth, and Roger and Judy Zisman.

INTRODUCTION

A local Woman's Club member had this to say about Carpinteria some decades ago, "This is the paradise where I shall spend the rest of my days." This line has been co-opted by the vast majority of Carpinteria's locals. Carpinterians, as of 2009, are generally in it for the long haul, which is why they have stubbornly refused, repeatedly, to barter away their spectacular surroundings. In fact, the citizen-supported purchase of the Carpinteria Bluffs and its subsequent designation as a nature preserve would suggest that Carpinterians are consciously tacking away from any type of growth that compromises the magic of their valley.

Locals tend to simply let Carpinteria's nearly indescribable beauty speak for itself. Not surprisingly, this understated approach to the valley's attributes has segued into a template for Carpinteria's heavy lifters—the folks who've made it their business to enrich Carpinteria with the best they have to offer while remaining well under the radar of notoriety. A classic of this genre is Del Kent.

Kent, Carpinterian of the Year in 1977, lived a life of service that strains the limits of credibility. He served as city treasurer, school board member, historical society president and treasurer, Friends of the Library volunteer, Meals on Wheels driver, recorder for the blind, Humane Society member, scout treasurer, and Carpinteria Community Church pillar—and this, it should be noted, is the short list. His financial philanthropy, amazingly, merits another whole discussion. Cres de Alba, Vera Bensen, Dorothy Campbell, Dr. Bill Carty, Dr. Horace Coshow, Lou Grant, Rev. John Imbach, Ed Macias, Fr. Francis Roughan, Lois Sidenberg, and Emma Wood have also, with little or no fanfare, left their indelible mark on Carpinteria. Carpinteria tends to bring out the best in most every Carpinterian relative to their support of each other and their valley.

The net result has been the creation of a tightly knit, uncluttered, down-home community that has synthesized timely and timeless, a condition that locals assume as a given and visitors applaud as a breath of fresh air. Carpinteria, for all intents and purposes, is a workingman's Carmel, although most Carpinterians would probably argue that Carmel has a long way to go to be in Carpinteria's league.

Harry McKown, a Carpinteria teacher of some reputation, routinely informed folks that Carpinteria (population 15,000) is located "Halfway between La Conchita and Summerland." This nugget, while seemingly aimed at facetiousness, does embody a hefty dose of truth. In terms of mind-set, Carpinterians, almost from the beginning, have shown a greater affinity for the communities that bookend their valley geographically than for Santa Barbara and Ventura, their more cosmopolitan neighbors.

Approximately 5 miles southeast of Carpinteria, near the base of Rincon Mountain, is La Conchita, a small coastal community of nearly 400 people. In the beginning, La Conchita was a small piece of a parcel called Punta Gorda, which in turn was part of an even larger area known as the Rancho El Rincon. This rancho included all the land between today's Rincon Creek and Sea Cliff. From 1880 to 1916, Punta Gorda and its U.S. post office were stops for both the stagecoach, which routinely traveled on the beach at low tide during this era, and the railroad. Interestingly enough, La Conchita was part of Santa Barbara County until 1873. From that point on, flying in the face of all logic, La Conchita took up residence in Ventura County.

La Conchitans are justifiably proud of their cultural heritage. A rich mix of Anglos, Hispanics, and Pacific Islanders has populated La Conchita from 1890 right up to the present day.

The blasting that prepared a shelf for the Southern Pacific railroad tracks was the precursor of a roadway built to connect Carpinteria and La Conchita around 1910. The first incarnation of this causeway was a 16-foot-wide wooden trestle cooperatively built by Ventura and Santa Barbara Counties. This wooden construction became part of the state highway system in 1912 and was replaced with a concrete structure in 1926.

It was the Ramelli brothers who really got La Conchita's residential ball rolling in the 1920s. While Edward was tending to his hotel, the Mussel Rock Inn, which was situated on the beach at Mussel Shoals, brother Milton was hatching plans for residential sites. The first 19 homes of his La Conchita del Mar Development were only the beginning. The following May, he laid out 327 lots on the mountainside of the highway. The Punta Gorda Land and Oil Company had arrived on the scene in 1900, a fact that didn't escape Milton as he peddled his parcels. One of these properties could be had for $200, and he reminded buyers who considered his price excessive that oil rights were part of the package, although this proved to be a meaningless enticement. La Conchita proper has never produced any oil.

Lack of water, a continuing problem in La Conchita's early years, made farming, the occupation of choice in the area through World War I, problematic to say the least. In the 1930s, the Matilija Water Company did its best to alleviate La Conchita's continuing water woes by delivering water at 25¢ per 5-gallon jug. In 1959, Casitas Dam was completed, and La Conchita was included in its distribution system—water was no longer a problem.

In the 1950s and 1960s, La Conchita became a popular vacation spot for folks from the San Fernando Valley. Travel trailers and small cottages sprouted across the community during these years, and soon afterward, larger custom homes appeared on the scene.

The two tragic mudslides of 1995 and 2005, while certainly defining moments, don't begin to tell the story of a vibrant, supportive family whose resilience and devotion to their community and each other is much admired locally. La Conchitans look forward to a freeway widening project and the installation of a state-of-the-art beach undercrossing for pedestrians that will be completed as part of the freeway enlargement plan of 2010 or thereabouts. Locals are confident that these improvements will enhance their reputation as the spectacular beachside community they've become.

Summerland residents are equally enamored with their seaside abode. This hillside haven started percolating in 1883 with the arrival of Henry Lafayette Williams, a wily entrepreneur, and his wife, Katie, a dyed-in-the-wool Spiritualist. H. L. was a pragmatist, and when plans for raising pigs on his 1,050-acre property faltered, he simply shifted gears and eased into a career as a real estate entrepreneur. The result was a town adjacent to the Southern Pacific's beach route and lots—lots of lots—for sale. These tent-sized 60-foot-by-25-foot parcels sold for $25 each, a mere pittance (even if one bought four of them) compared to Milton Ramelli's building sites, which were going for the princely sum of $200 just down the road in La Conchita.

H. L. and Katie dedicated themselves to establishing the new community as a home for their Spiritualist brothers and sisters. In 1889, this Spiritualist sanctuary was christened Summerland, which, not coincidentally, was the name of the Spiritualists' heaven. A local temple was built where social gatherings and séances, part and parcel of the Spiritualist experience, became an integral part of community life. Intolerant contiguous neighbors, who were unnerved by Spiritualist activities, were quick to dub Summerland "Spookville."

Beginning around 1890, natural gas was piped to many Summerland homes for lighting. More importantly, at least from a youthful perspective, gas was available for lighting up the neighborhood during nocturnal baseball games. This was accomplished by tapping pipes into the ground and lighting them. The dangers inherent in this enterprise apparently eluded the folks who, one would have assumed, were providing adult supervision.

Smith Cole's accidental discovery of oil while probing for gas in 1894 led to widespread drilling. The building of derrick-laden wharves on Summerland's beach was quick to follow. This visionary effort established Summerland as the inaugural offshore oil field in the Western Hemisphere, and arguably, with the possible exception of some drilling sites in the Caspian Sea, the first such field in the world. Not surprisingly, "black gold fever" gave Summerland an "Alaska-ish" gold rush feel for a brief moment. The population spiked. Hotels, rooming houses, and saloons proliferated, and Summerland's religious temperament was steamrolled by baser pursuits, much to the chagrin of the Spiritualists. It was even rumored that Summerland's new look and odor inspired roaming bands of Montecito hooligans to sabotage its oil-related infrastructure. Drilling at reduced levels continued right on into the 1930s, but with oil deposits dwindling in the immediate area and piers and derricks deteriorating, this chapter in Summerland's history came to a close.

Additional growth in Summerland was hamstrung by water issues, and much of the community fell into a relatively dilapidated state, which led to affordable housing that was snapped up by the artists, surfers, and hippies who held down the fort during the 1960s and 1970s. This was an era that many of Summerland's more traditional locals were delighted to see fade into memory. Happily for the disgruntled old-timers, the resolution of Summerland's water problems redirected the community's residential portfolio, helping to propel Summerland, at least in the view of many, from raffish to respectable. Contemporary Summerland (population 1,500) is decidedly well-heeled in terms of housing, businesses, and, most importantly, outlook. One would suspect that H. L. and Katie Williams would be much pleased with where their coastal creation has landed, although they might be a might miffed about the lack of a Spiritualist medium to connect the community with its pioneering forefathers.

"Be True to Your School," a Beach Boys anthem from the early 1960s, nicely sums up the mind-set of the folks who reside in Carpinteria, La Conchita, and Summerland. The locals seem to believe that if you're fortunate enough to land in paradise, you should dig in, embrace it, and above all, not tinker with the perfection you've been handed. As of 2009, this is the locals' story, and they appear to be sticking to it.

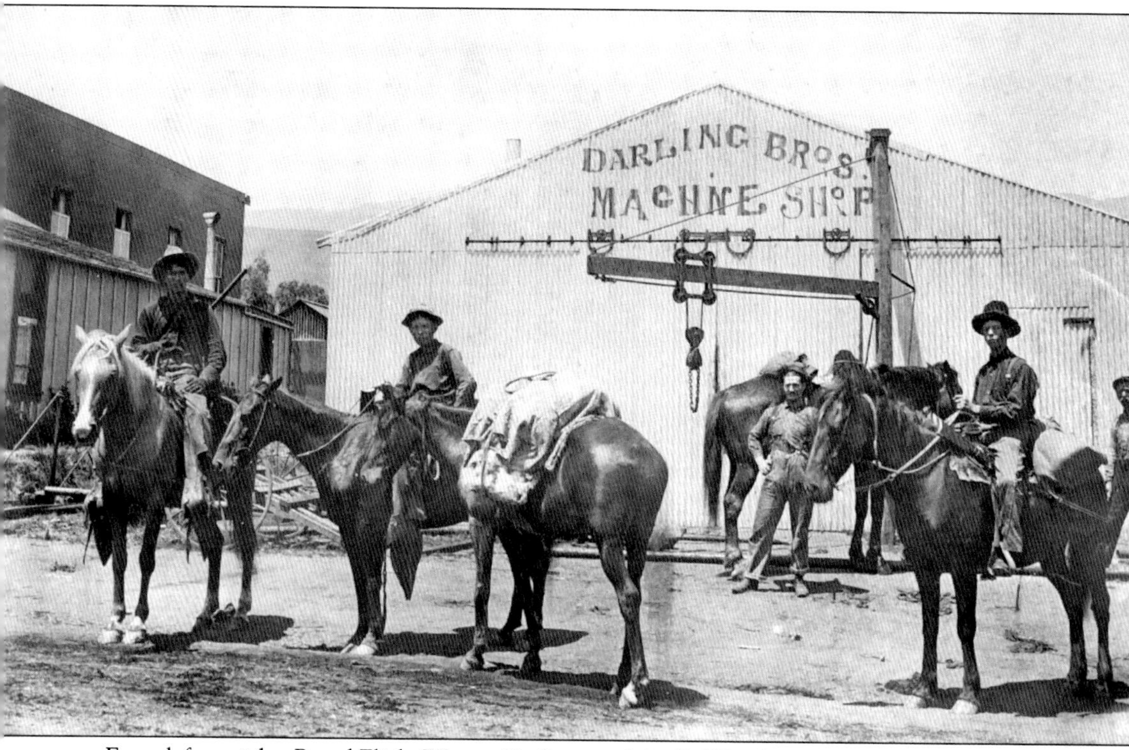

From left to right, Byard Flick, Wayne Darling, and A. G. Wood are mounted on horseback and equipped to go hunting in the backwoods of the Carpinteria Valley. Their point of departure is the Darling Brothers Machine Shop in Summerland around 1897. (Courtesy Carpinteria Valley Museum of History.)

One

The Carpinteria Valley's Wild West

At the time that American frontiersmen entered the Carpinteria Valley, it was covered with a dense growth of oak and willow trees. The Americans also found trout-filled creeks that bisected the green valley from Ortega Hill to the Rincon. Because of its water resources, and despite the density of the oaks and willows, the valley was attractive to the frontiersmen, just as it had been to the Spanish and Mexican families of Santa Barbara County, who used it primarily for grazing livestock. According to James Heath, who was raised in Carpinteria in those frontier times, "There were a few Spanish families, lots of Mexicans, and a great many Indians" living in the valley. Heath elaborated further, "It was pretty rough and wild, and there was little law."

In Carpinteria's Wild West days, a station for the overland stagecoach line stood in what today is called the "old town" of Carpinteria along Santa Monica Creek. Stagecoaches traveled the beach shore route to get in and out, as the tide would allow, until 1878, when a surer path inland through the Casitas Pass replaced the ocean route. News of the surrounding world came into Carpinteria via stagecoach and was disseminated at the nearby saloons. In 1887, the Southern Pacific Railroad placed a train station along Linden Avenue, bringing more news and visitors from the outside world and opening agricultural markets for Carpinteria's developing class of farmers to explore.

Lawrence Bailard, descendant of one of Carpinteria's pioneer families, says he used to wonder why early resident Dr. Walter Biggs had sold the large Rancho Arellanes on the Rincon to his family and others, leaving the lush paradise that was the Carpinteria Valley to move to Chile. He concluded that it had to do with the fact that in the late 19th century, cities like Valparaiso and Santiago were cosmopolitan, much like San Francisco. What, on the other hand, was the Carpinteria Valley? It was a paradise, yes, but it was undeveloped, and there was a lot of hard work ahead.

In the 19th century, hunters, trappers, miners, farmers, schoolmarms, entrepreneurs, displaced Southerners following the Civil War, and the occasional hard cases with six-guns came into the Carpinteria Valley. Welcome to Carpinteria's Wild West days!

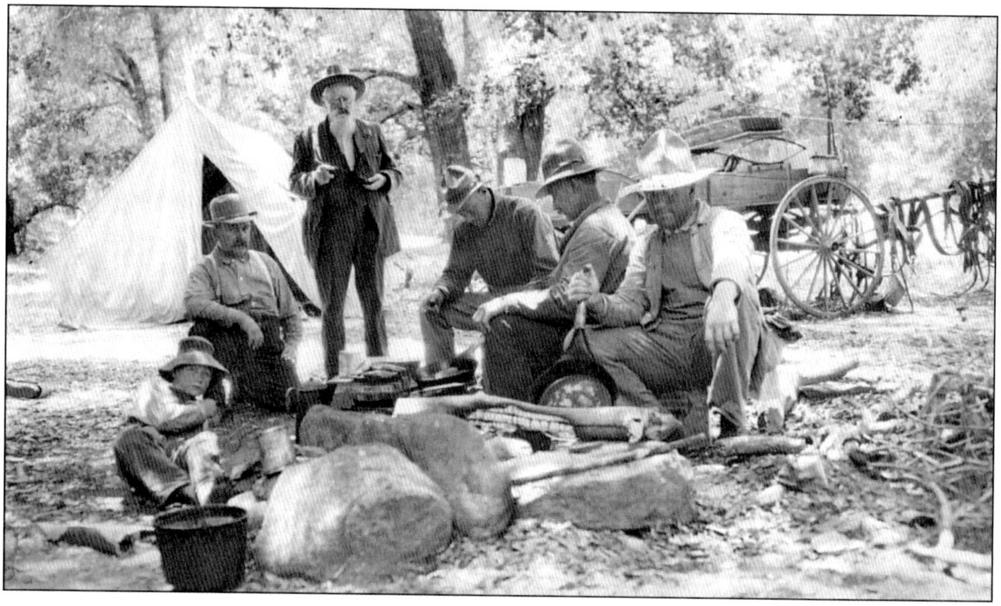

The frontiersmen who settled in and around the Carpinteria Valley were a hardy lot. The first to come were traders and trappers who married into Californio families, like Capt. George Nidever, who gained fame by discovering the lone woman of San Nicolas Island. The incident was romanticized in the novel currently read by every fourth-grade student in California, *The Island of the Blue Dolphins*, by Scott O'Dell. Next were adventurers, epitomized by the gold miners, most of who had failed in the goldfields and were looking for riches elsewhere. The beauty of the Carpinteria Valley did not escape these frontiersmen's eyes, and wagons west converged here, bringing families with dreams of establishing shops, ranches, and farms. Captain Nidever's brother, John, for example, later settled in the valley. The early photograph above of the foothills of Carpinteria captures the spirit of the frontier west, as does the picture below, both taken around 1880 to 1900. (Both courtesy Carpinteria Valley Museum of History.)

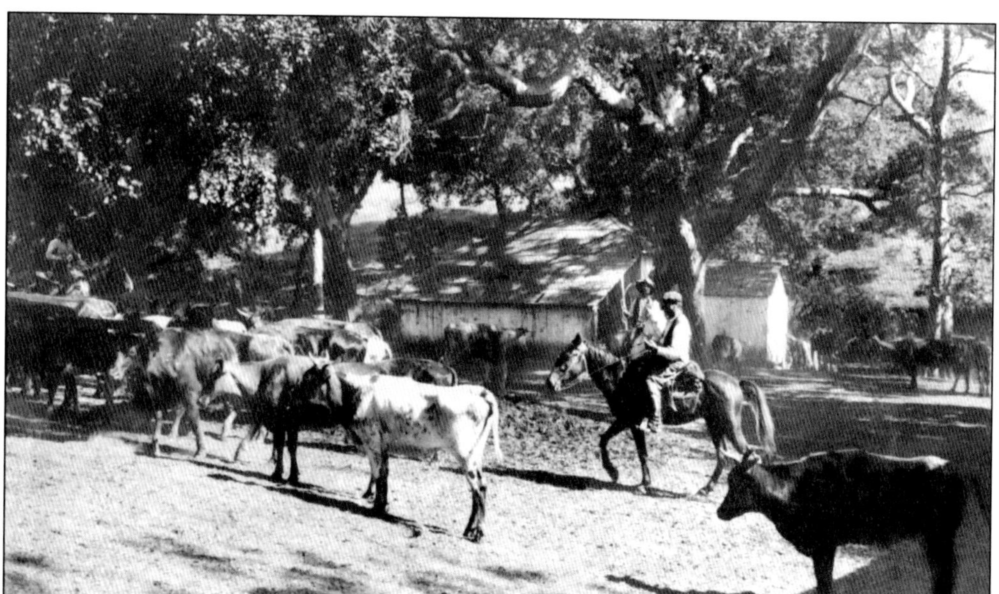

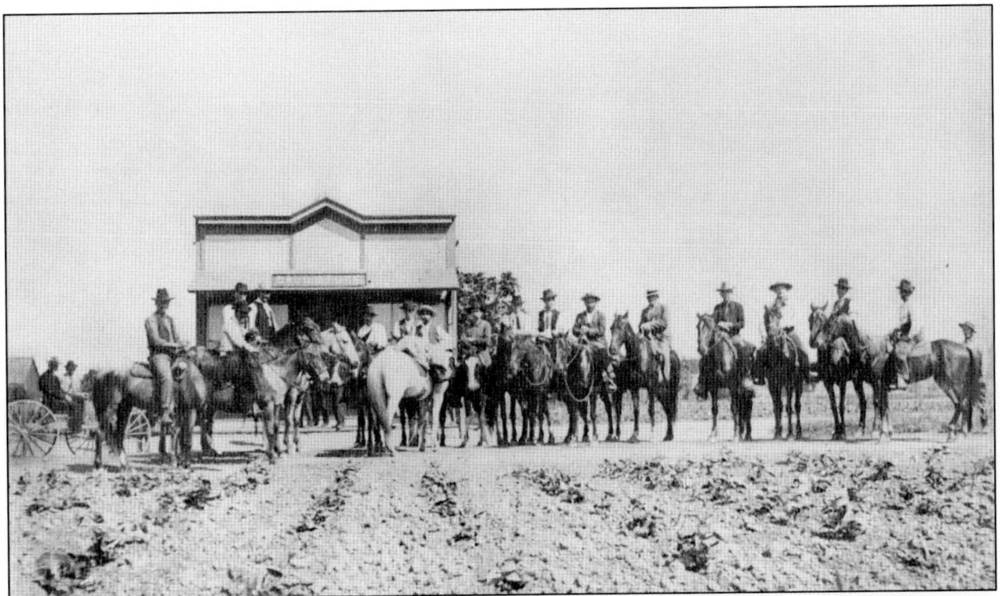

This *c.* 1885 photograph, taken facing west between Sixth and Seventh Streets, attests to the wide-open spaces of Carpinteria's early history. The men atop the horses, mules, and carriage also suggest the era of livestock ranches that predated the agricultural period. The structure behind the riders is the drugstore of Dr. William Marquis, Carpinteria's first physician. Note the lima bean field in the foreground. (Courtesy Carpinteria Valley Museum of History.)

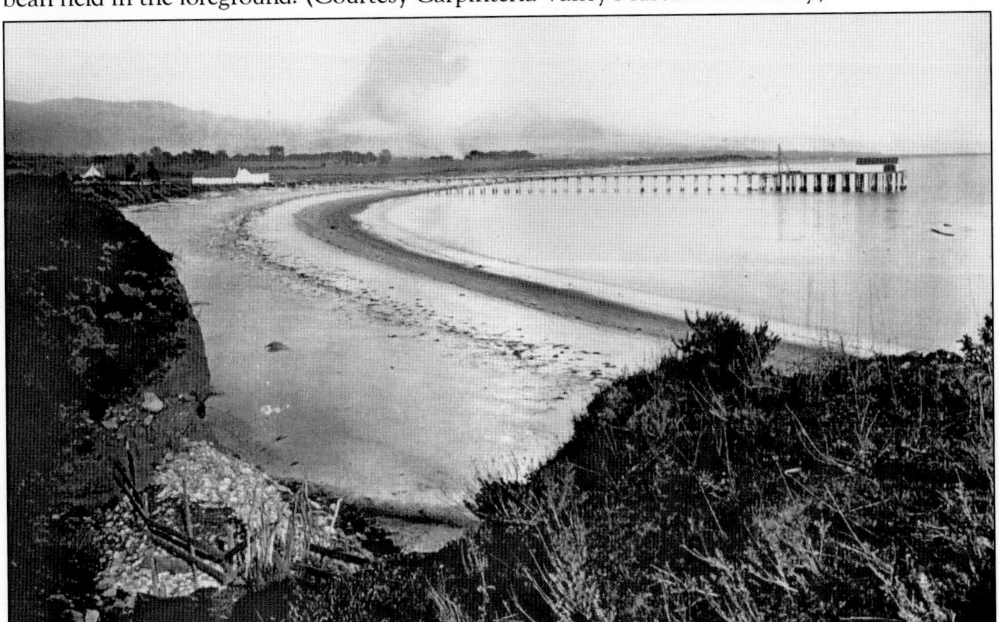

The close of the ranching period was accelerated by the rains of 1861, which flooded the valley. A two-decade drought followed. It forced ranchers to move their livestock to moister areas or simply slaughter them for market. The beach areas near Santa Claus Lane and Ortega Hill were known as *matanzas*, or slaughterhouses. Cattlemen butchered their livestock on them. Later on, Serena Wharf, seen here around 1880, was built near the sites of the matanzas. (Courtesy Carpinteria Valley Museum of History.)

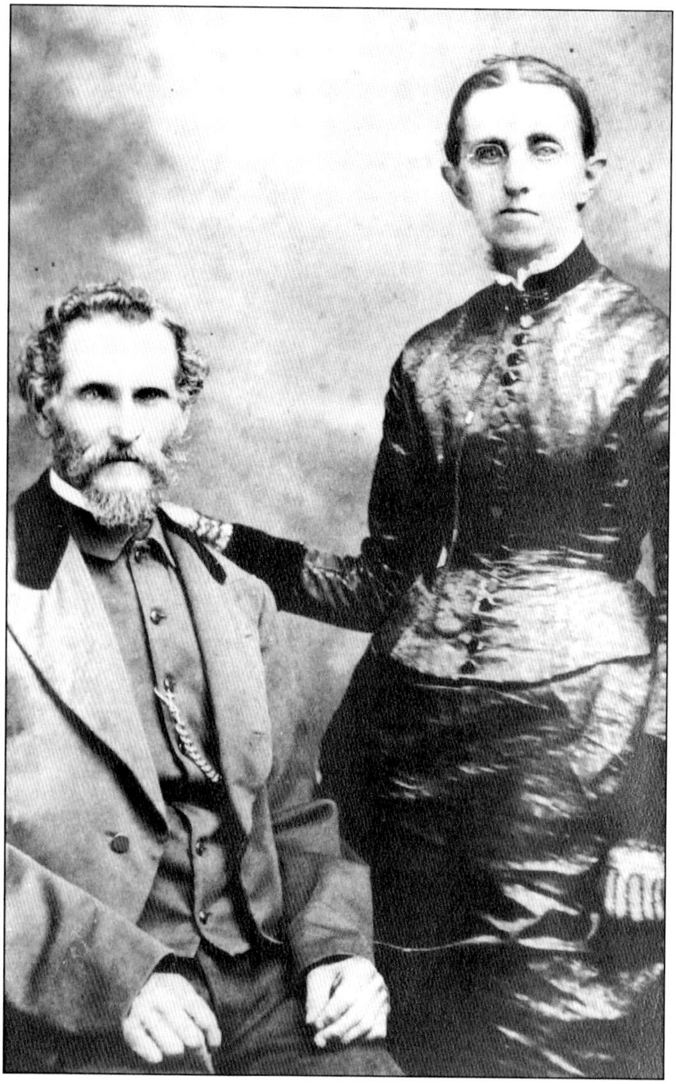

The Cadwells arrived in the Carpinteria Valley about 1868. The posed stills represent several walks of life in Carpinteria's frontier days. Oren, seen above at left with his wife Rosina, was the most illustrious member of the family in Carpinteria's history. He is recognized for horticultural innovation, developing a wide variety of fruits and vegetables in the valley, including the avocado. His brother, Erastus Jr., on the left below, is dressed in a hunter's buckskins with his kill. His son Andrew (center) poses as a dashing gambler. Finally, at the bottom right is Oren's son Arthur, leaning on a rifle with a steely glare, a bowie knife, and six-guns at each side. Sadly, Arthur and Erastus Cadwell were both left out of the family's will, in Arthur's case possibly as a result of his rumored alternative life style, which was taboo in the Old West. Despondent, both committed suicide. (Above, courtesy Carpinteria Valley Museum of History; below, courtesy John Rodriguez Jr.)

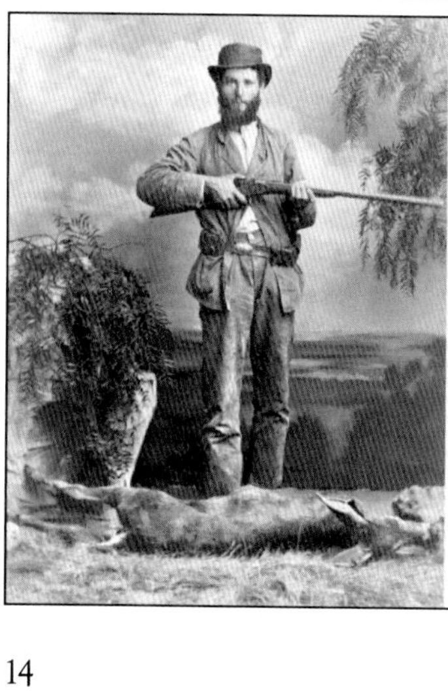

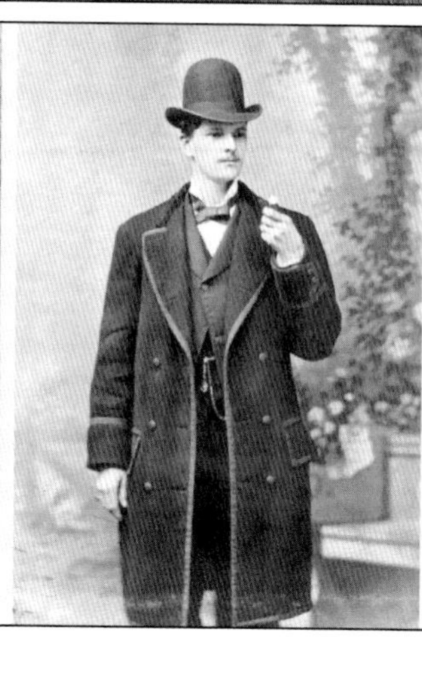

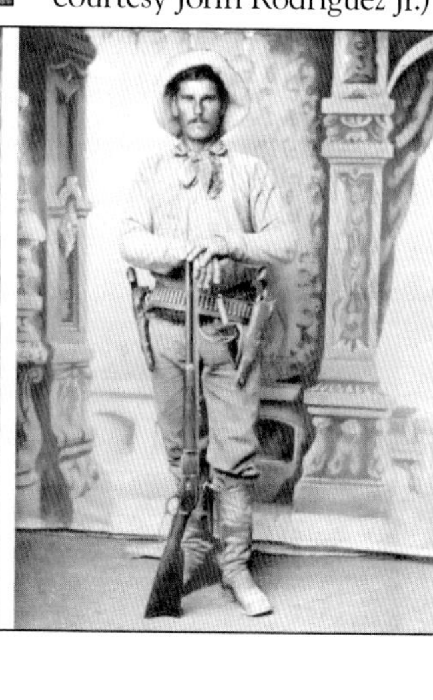

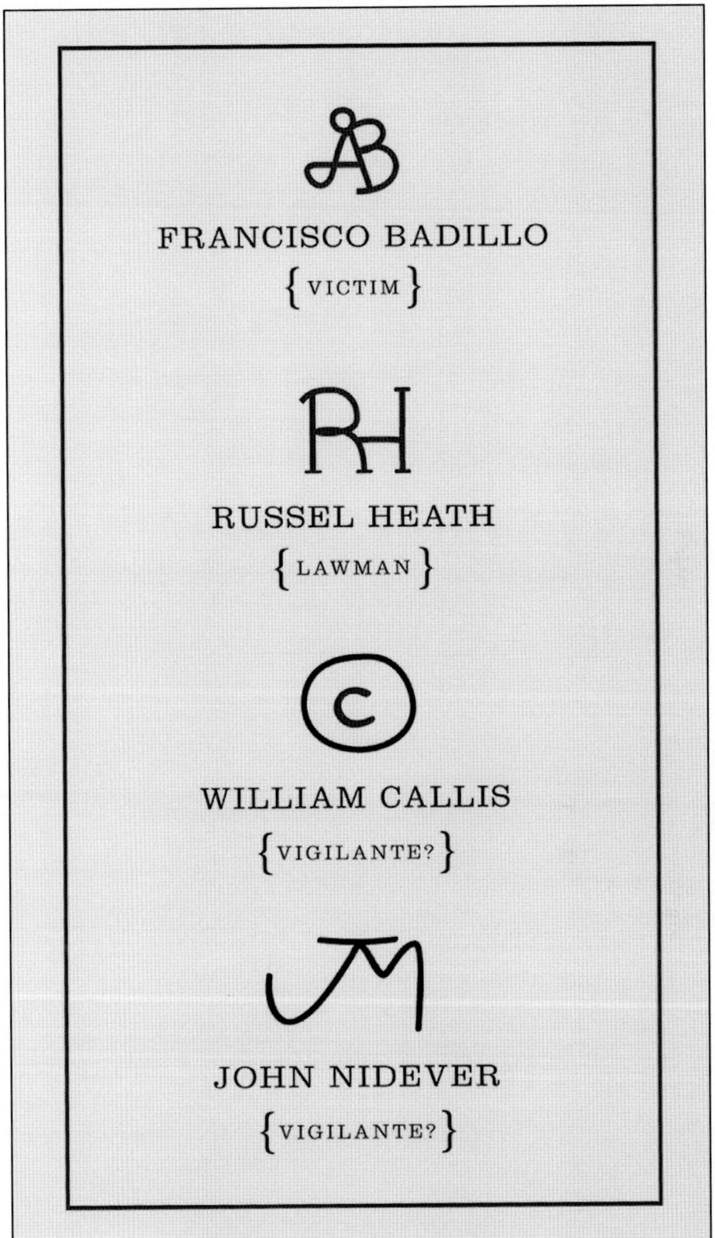

Carpinteria's Wild West demonstrated its ugly side with the vigilante hanging of Francisco Badillo and his teenage son in 1859. The illustrated cattle brands belong to the principal players of the drama that unfolded. The lynching party was allegedly led by John Nidever, his sons Ebenezar and George, William Callis, John McKeon, and M. Coates. Badillo, a suspected horse and cattle thief, had an unsavory reputation in both the Mexican and American communities in the Carpinteria Valley. His hanging, however, flamed tensions between the two ethnic groups. The U.S. Army, stationed in Fort Tejon, was summoned to quell the situation. It has been postulated by some Carpinterians that the fact that Badillo owned beachfront property from the original Rancho El Rincon may have been a factor in his removal from the local scene. (Sketches by Andrew Barnes.)

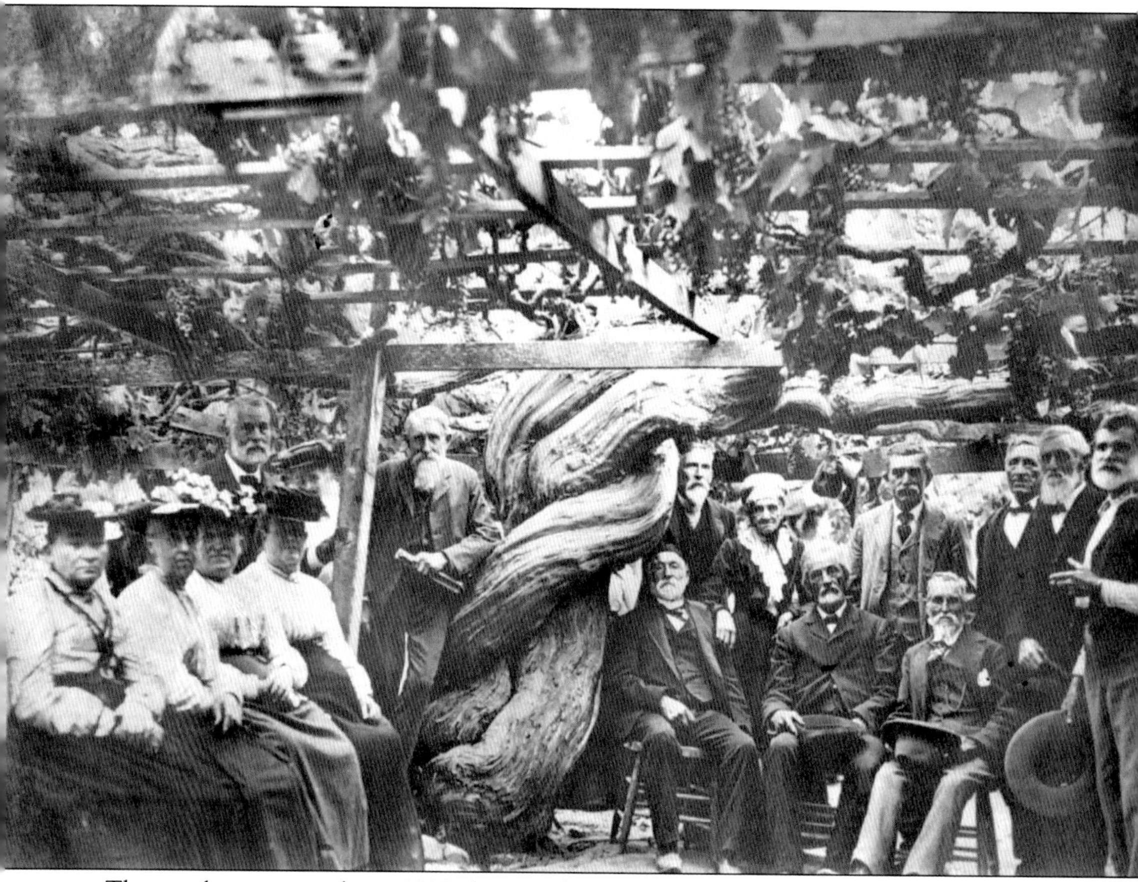

The people posing in this *c.* 1888 photograph under the largest known grapevine in the world, the Ayala grapevine, are a veritable who's who of the founders of the town of Carpinteria. Pictured from left to right are (seated) Mrs. John Bradford, Katherine Bailard, Christina Pyster, and Elizabeth Jane Cravens; (standing) the Reverend T. G. McLean and Stephen H. Olmstead; (seated at right) James Blood, Mathew J. Moore, and Oren N. Cadwell; (standing at right) Ed Thurmond, Cornelia Blood, John Pyster, Jake Wilson, Harlow D. Woods, and Juan Carrillo. The Ayala grapevine, the largest enclosure in the Carpinteria Valley, stood in Old Town between Santa Monica Road and Cravens Lane and served as a principal meeting place for valley residents. It was 9 feet in circumference and produced 10 to 12 tons of grapes each season. (Courtesy Carpinteria Valley Museum of History.)

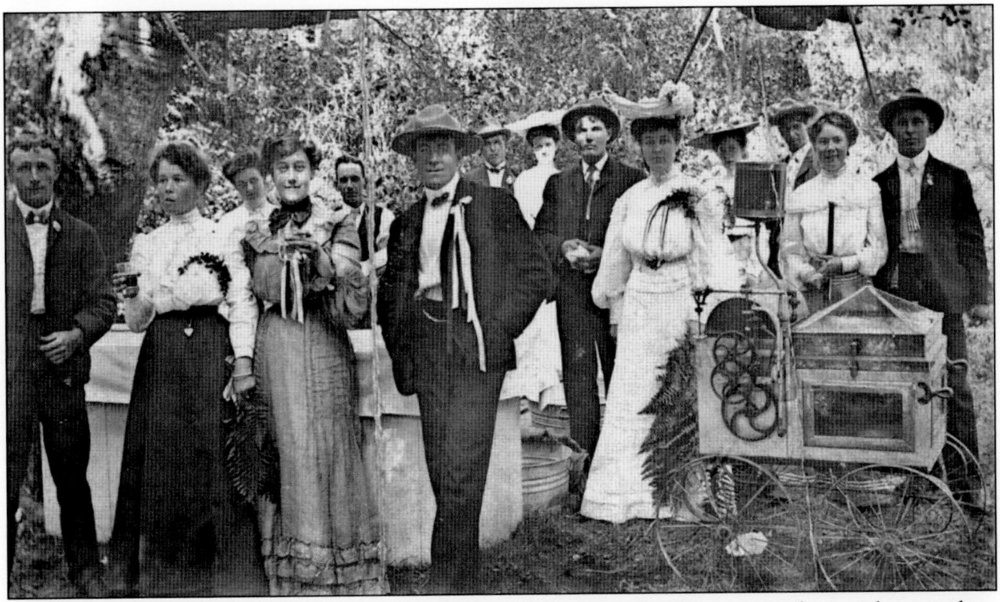

In 1869, the first site of worship services for Protestant pioneer families was under a wide-spreading oak tree on the ranch of Oren and Rosina Cadwell. Churches were built in the ensuing years in Carpinteria, but the Sunday school oak tree remained a popular place for community events. In this c. 1905 photograph, a Fourth of July celebration appears to be taking place. From left to right towards the forefront of the photograph are Forest and Ora Treloar, Maybelle and Charles Treloar, and Clarence and Carrie Sawyer. (Courtesy Mildred S. Treloar.)

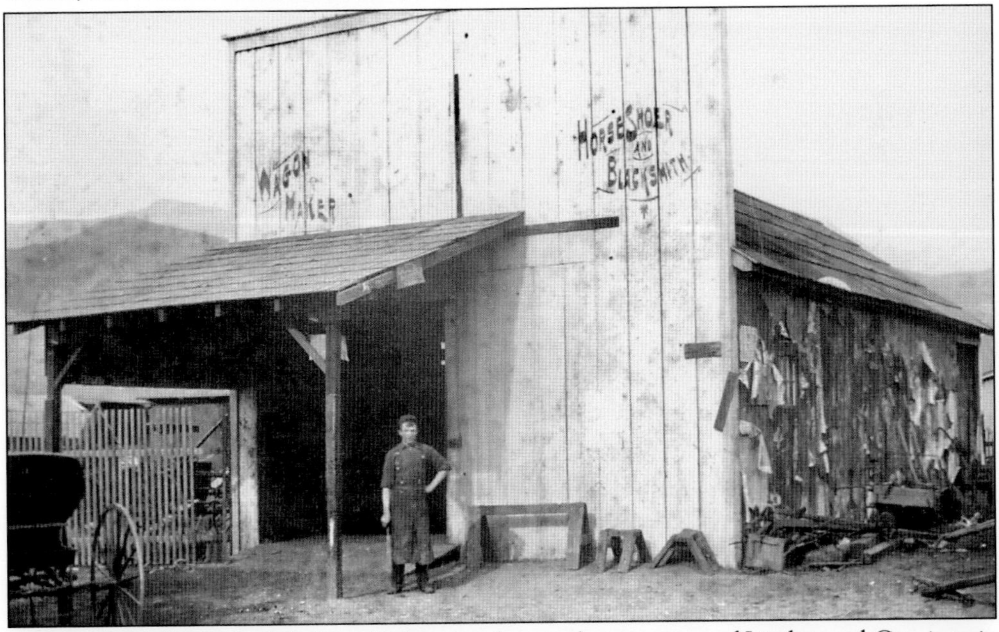

J. M. Burleigh built this blacksmith shop on the northeast corner of Linden and Carpinteria Avenues in 1887. The building of the railroad depot on Linden Avenue shifted the center of town there that year. Burleigh had a perfect location to begin his business. Pictured is Billy Treloar, who later took over the shop and remained until 1898, when he left for the goldfields of Alaska. (Courtesy Doug Treloar.)

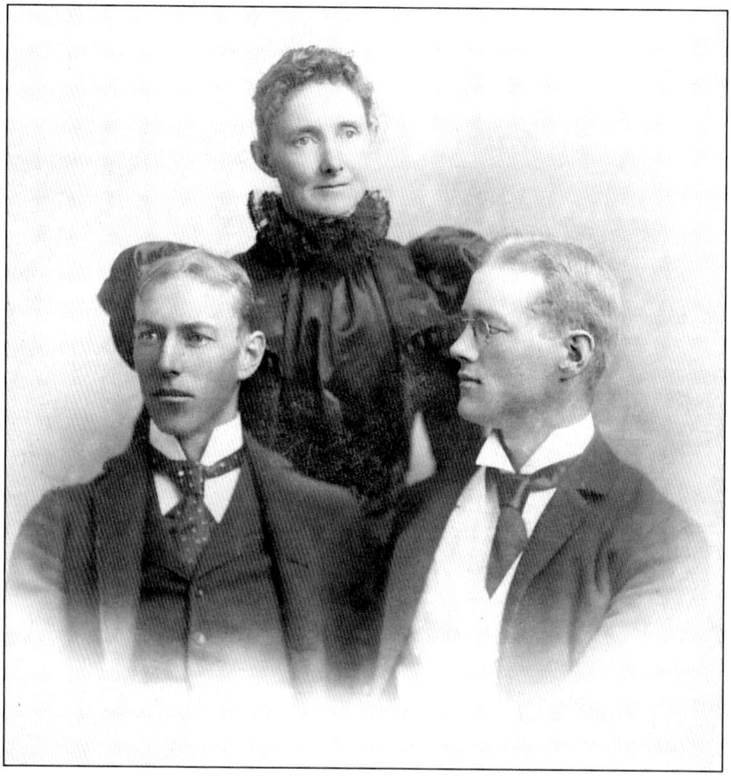

Belle Oglesby Franklin, flanked by her sons, Gideon and Jessie, is credited as the guiding force in establishing an organization for women in the Carpinteria Valley. In 1894, she and several other women started the Carpinteria Literary Society, also known as the "Shakespeare Club." In 1910, they opened the first branch library in California. In 1924, as members of the Carpinteria Woman's Club, they purchased land on Vallecito Road for a future clubhouse. (Courtesy Carpinteria Valley Museum of History.)

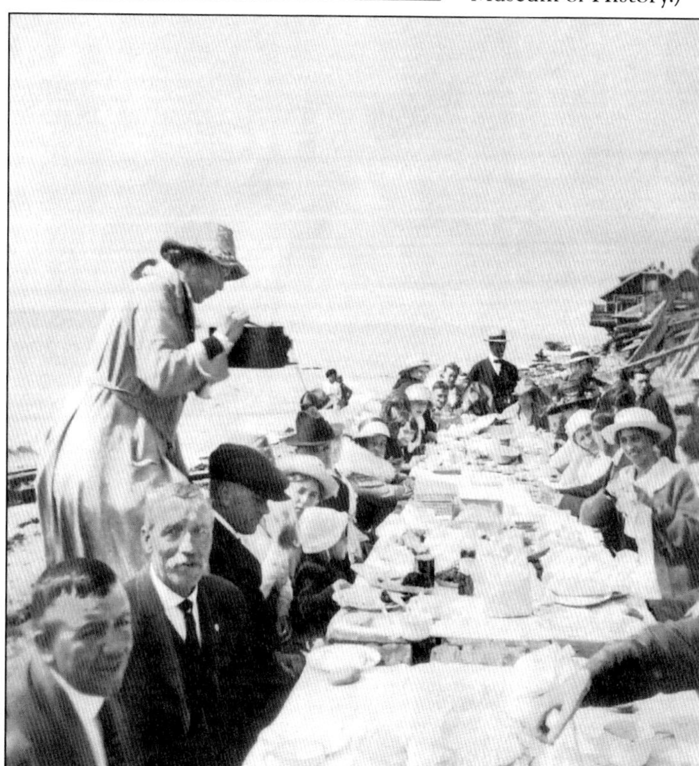

The Carpinteria Woman's Club sponsored annual picnics, usually at locations in Franklin Canyon and on the beach of Serena Park, as in this photograph. The events drew as many as 200 of the Carpinteria Valley's leading citizens dressed in their Sunday best, even on the sandy venue shown here. The fund-raising events propelled them to quickly achieve their goals of establishing a town meeting hall, a public library branch, and their own Carpinteria Woman's Club building, completed in 1934. (Courtesy Harold and Nancy Smith.)

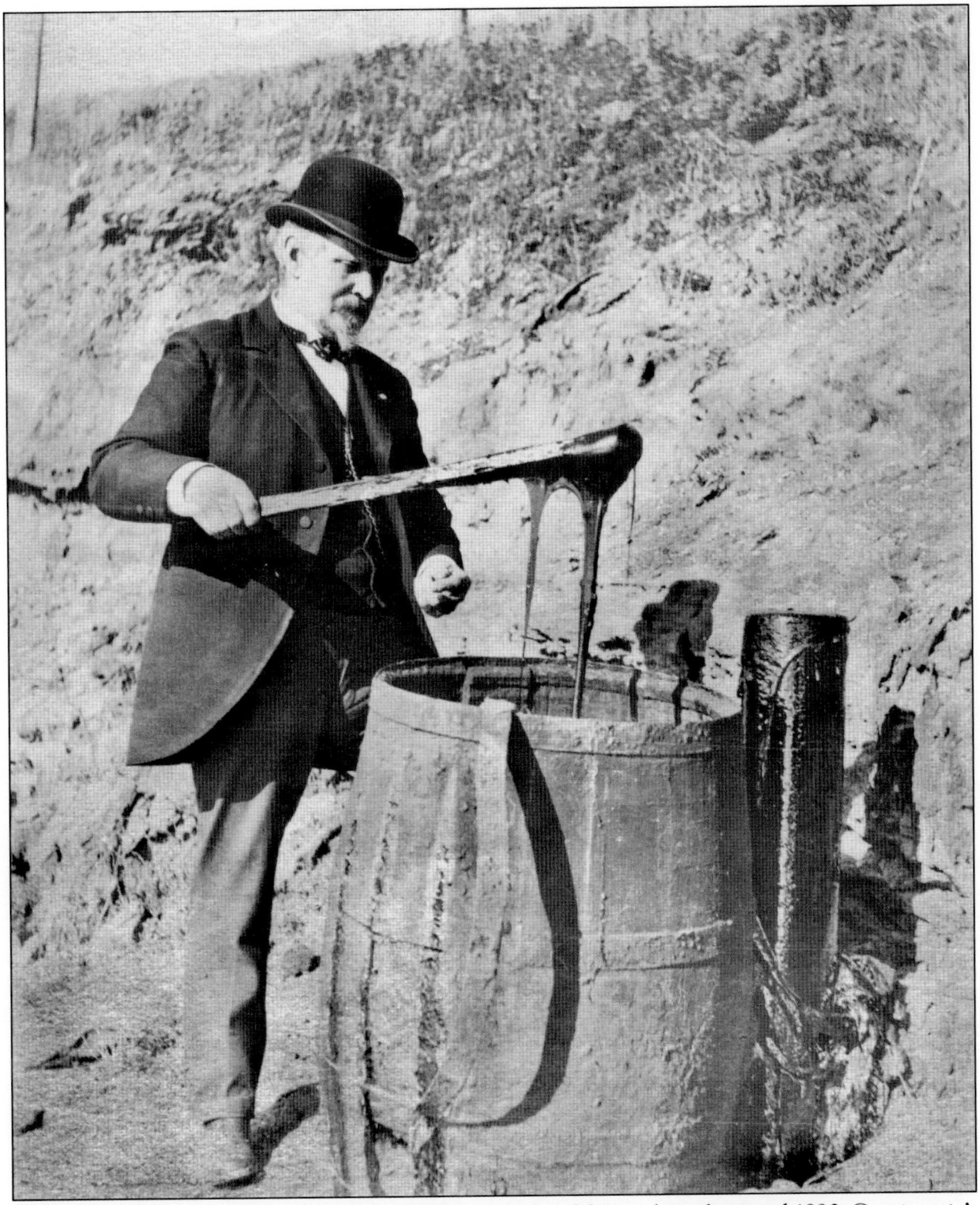

Phineas C. Higgins is seen scooping a ladleful of crude oil from a barrel around 1890. Carpinteria's asphalt mines lacked the fine grade of oil that made Summerland famous for its onshore and offshore wells. However, the lower grade of oil proved satisfactory for paving roads. Carpinteria lore has it that Higgins was a powerful opponent of moving the coast road from Carpinteria to Santa Barbara off Padaro Lane to the north side of the railroad tracks. The road through Carpinteria to Santa Barbara veered south towards the beachside at Santa Claus Lane and veered back towards the mountainside along Padaro Lane, four railroad crossings in all. Fate can be cruel—Higgins was killed along this stretch of road when the Lark Train hit his automobile at one of the crossings in 1913. Santa Barbara County First District supervisor and Carpinteria resident Howe Deaderick had no trouble after that having the highway changed to a safer route. (Courtesy Carpinteria Valley Museum of History.)

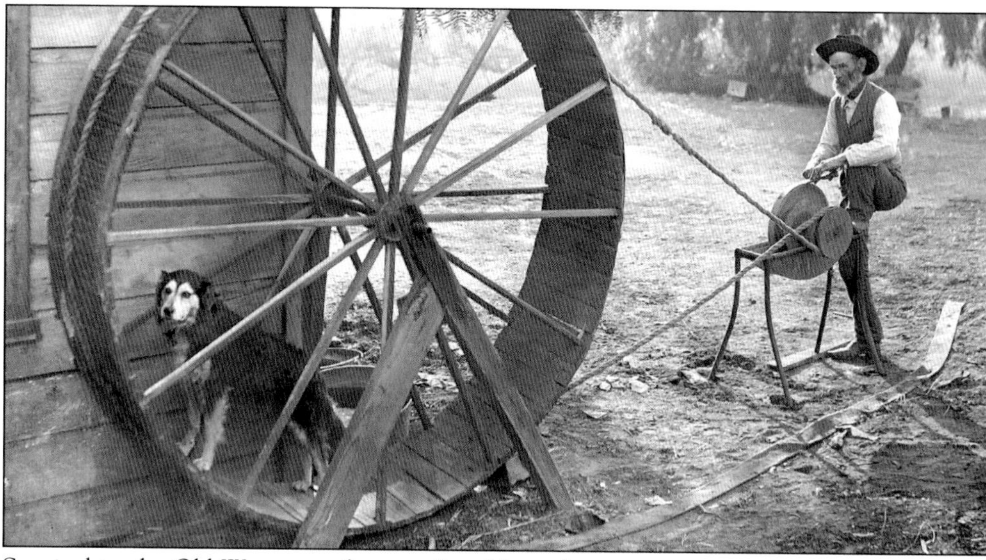

Survival in the Old West was often attributable to frontier ingenuity. James Dane, pictured around 1900, was up to the task of generating energy for his home by using "one-dog power" to run the grindstone to sharpen his tools. According to his granddaughter, Phyllis Dane Carter, Dane also rigged the dog, Old Gyp, to power the wood-barrel washing machine for his wife. Old Gyp supplied the power to turn the pulleys that powered the agitator in the machine by keeping a steady trot. (Courtesy Carpinteria Valley Museum of History.)

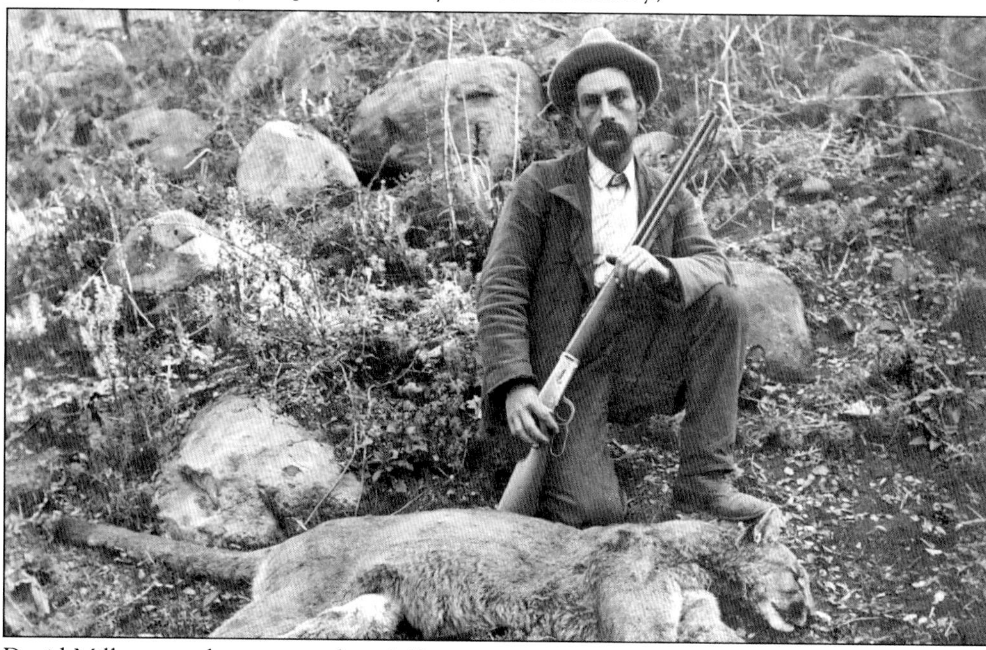

David Miller owned a goat ranch in Lillingston Canyon. He sold goat's milk and meat to the residents of the Carpinteria Valley. The goats also attracted attention from mountain lions in the hills and canyons above Carpinteria. In this 1903 photograph, Miller has eliminated one of those predators. Carpinteria teacher George Metcalf wrote in his diary, "Mr. Miller killed a mountain lion on Lillingston's ranch. Children have to go see it"—not your typical field trip by today's standards! (Courtesy Carpinteria Valley Museum of History.)

Historian Stephen Ambrose writes, "In nearly every western railroad town, there used to be a Chinatown." An early pioneer account appears to place a cluster of Chinese apartments—a Chinatown—on the west side of Linden Avenue along the Coast Highway (Carpinteria Avenue). In this *c.* 1900 photograph, James R. Heath stands beside a group of Chinese men. The Chinese at the Heath Ranch served as domestics—cooks, laundrymen, housekeepers, and gardeners. (Courtesy Carpinteria Valley Museum of History.)

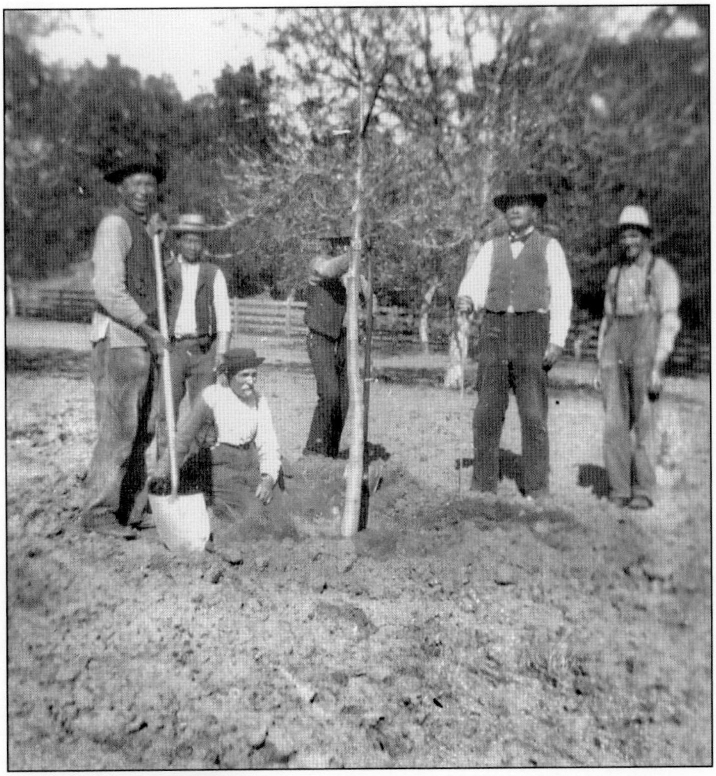

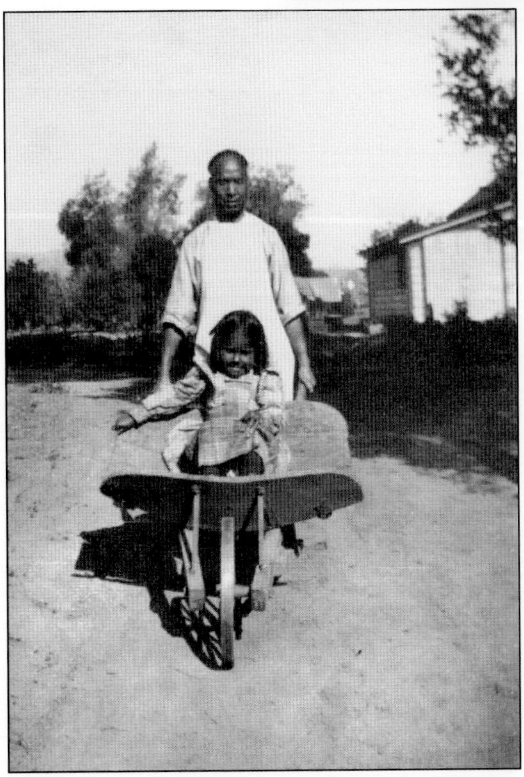

Poi is pictured here around 1900 with another resident of the Heath Ranch, the Chumash girl Ruth Cordero. The Chinese quarters on the ranch can be seen on the right. Albertina Rodriguez, a chronicler of Carpinteria's early days, remembers Poi baking cookies for her and other children of the valley. According to Carpinteria lore, after he returned to China, Poi fondly looked back on his time in Carpinteria as the best years of his life. (Courtesy Carpinteria Valley Museum of History.)

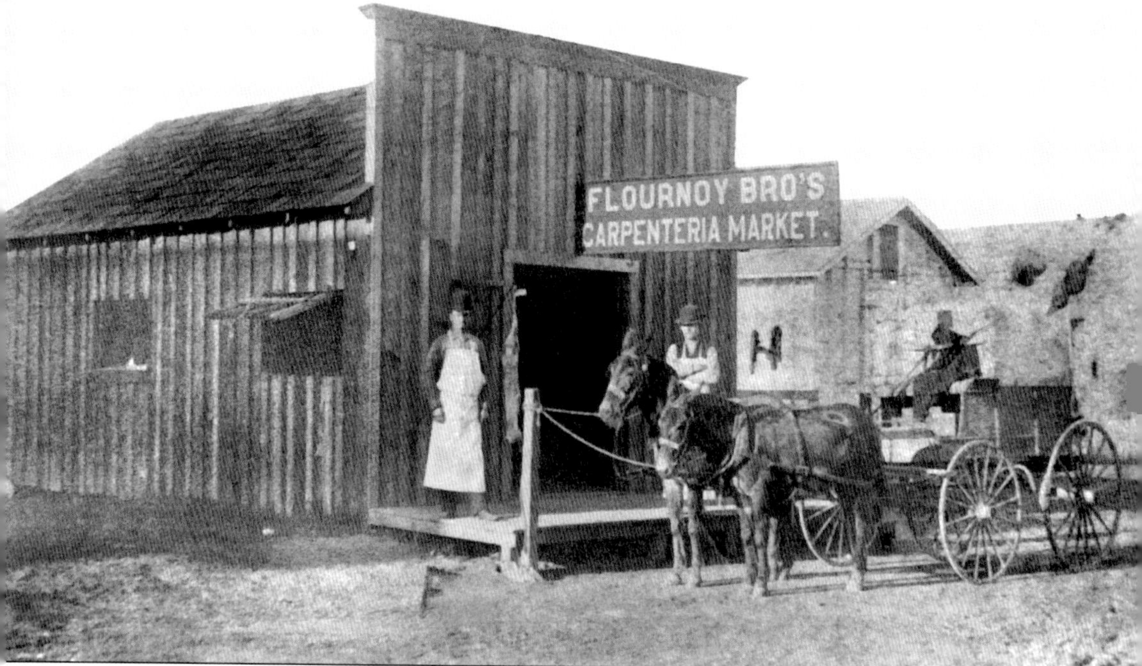

The Flournoy Market was established in 1879 and closed in 1882. The sign bearing the store's name spells the town's name "Carpenteria," an Anglicized misspelling of the Spanish word *Carpinteria*. Carpinteria was named by the Spanish soldiers of the Portola Expedition in 1769, after they observed skilled Chumash canoe builders at work in what looked like a *carpinteria*, that is, a carpentry shop. The chronicler of the expedition, Fr. Juan Crespi, usually gave a Catholic saint's name for each new site found; in Carpinteria's case this was to have been San Roque, but history deemed otherwise. In 1867, the U.S. Postal Service made the spelling mistake. Carpinteria thus became Carpenteria for the next 33 years. In 1900, the U.S. Postal Service welcomed the new century by correcting the misspelling. Spelling confusion, however, remains, and it is not uncommon to see a document or poster with the incorrect spelling to this day. (Courtesy Carpinteria Valley Museum of History.)

Eureka! The Reverend John W. Dorrance has made an artesian well strike in this *c.* 1900 photograph. Artesian wells in the Carpinteria Valley were sometimes only 10 to 40 feet below the earth's surface. They were often capped because of their powerful upward flow. The artesian well used at the Palms Hotel was said to be so powerful that it supplied water to its second story without the use of a pump. (Courtesy Carpinteria Valley Museum of History.)

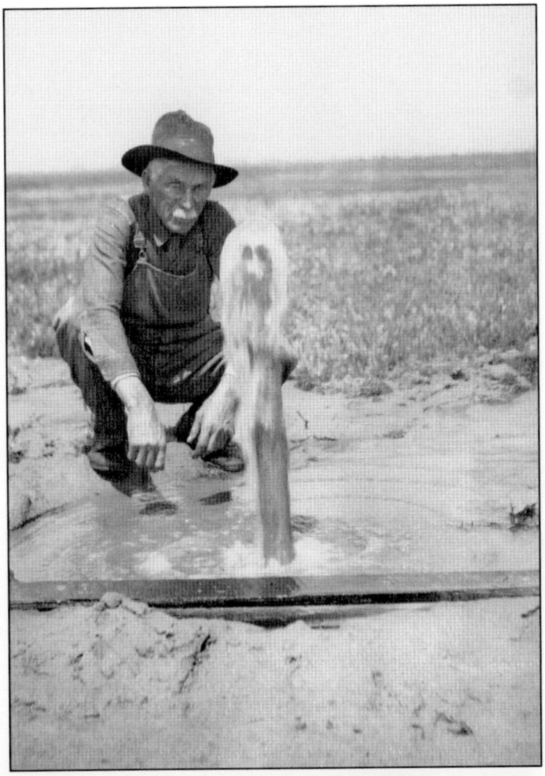

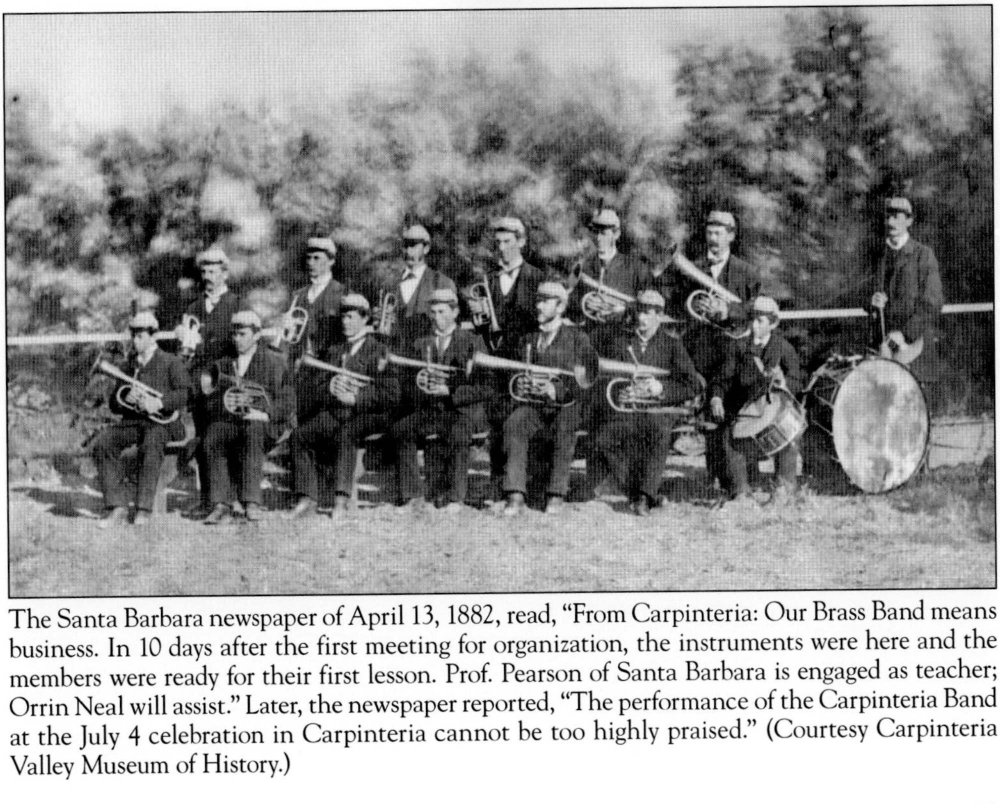

The Santa Barbara newspaper of April 13, 1882, read, "From Carpinteria: Our Brass Band means business. In 10 days after the first meeting for organization, the instruments were here and the members were ready for their first lesson. Prof. Pearson of Santa Barbara is engaged as teacher; Orrin Neal will assist." Later, the newspaper reported, "The performance of the Carpinteria Band at the July 4 celebration in Carpinteria cannot be too highly praised." (Courtesy Carpinteria Valley Museum of History.)

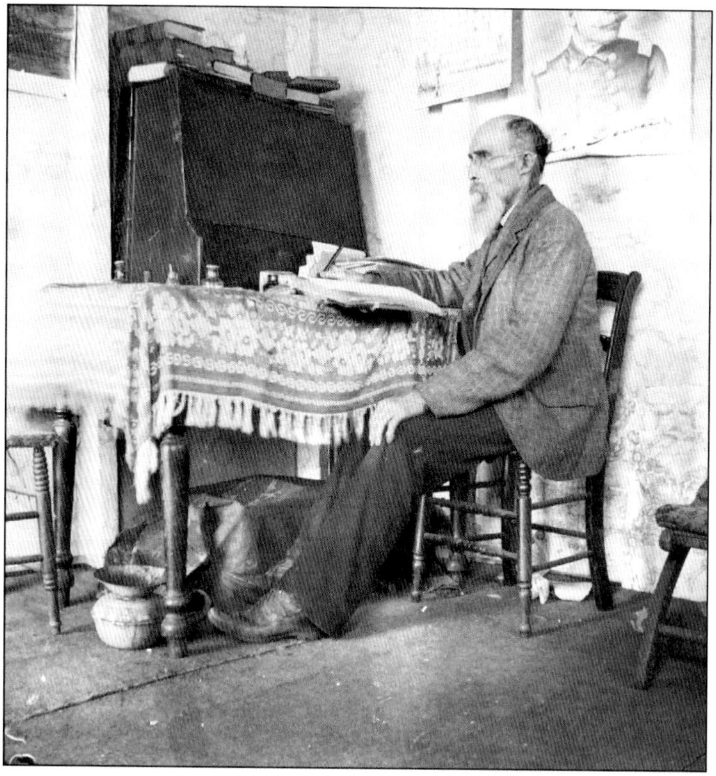

There were numerous judges in various parts of the Carpinteria Valley during its Wild West days. Melvin Snow presided in Summerland. James Miller presided in the Casitas Pass area. Judge Solon Smith, pictured around 1890, presided in Serena Park. He is writing at his home office desk, with law books, inks, and a wax seal at his disposal. (Courtesy Harold and Nancy Smith.)

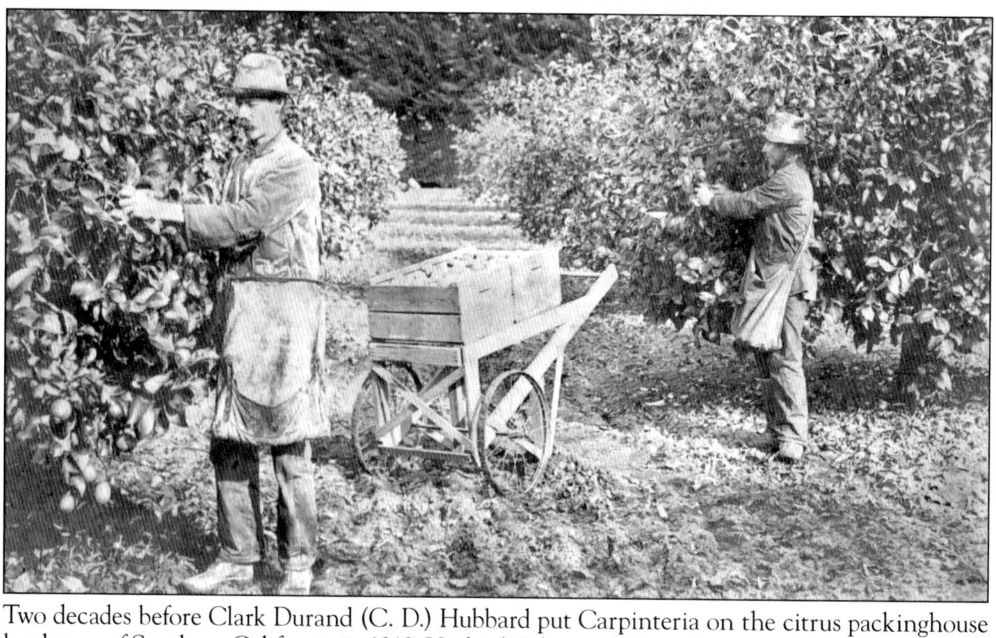

Two decades before Clark Durand (C. D.) Hubbard put Carpinteria on the citrus packinghouse landscape of Southern California in 1912, Harleigh Johnston's Fruit Company, based in Montecito and Santa Barbara, did the job of harvesting and packing Carpinteria citrus products. Note that in the photograph above, the lemon pickers are Anglo men. Use of immigrant labor in orchards and vegetable fields became necessary with the advent of World War I. (Courtesy Carpinteria Valley Museum of History.)

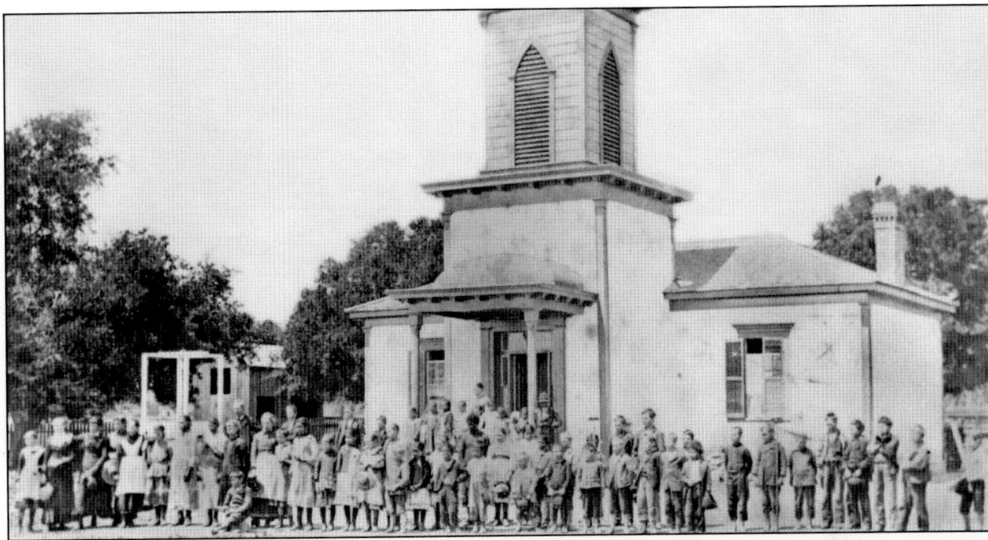

The Carpinteria School on Upson Road was the first public school in the valley, built in 1858. It is the two-room adobe structure above. A new wood-frame school, pictured below, was built next to the adobe one and later replaced it. Two other schools—the Rincon School and the Ocean View School—were established in the 1870s. These three Carpinteria Valley schools were about 3 miles apart: Ocean View in Serena Park to the northwest, the Carpinteria School in the middle of town just off Santa Monica Road, and the Rincon School to the southeast on Casitas Pass Road. It appears that no child in the Carpinteria Valley was more than about a mile and half from a public school. (Both courtesy Carpinteria Valley Museum of History.)

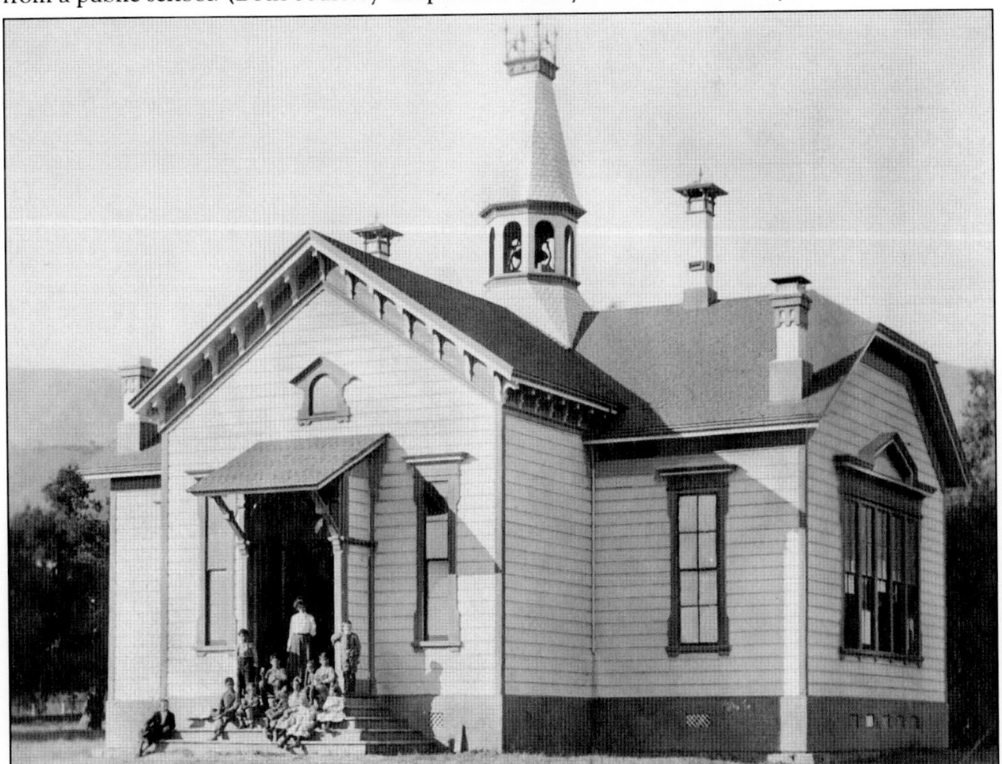

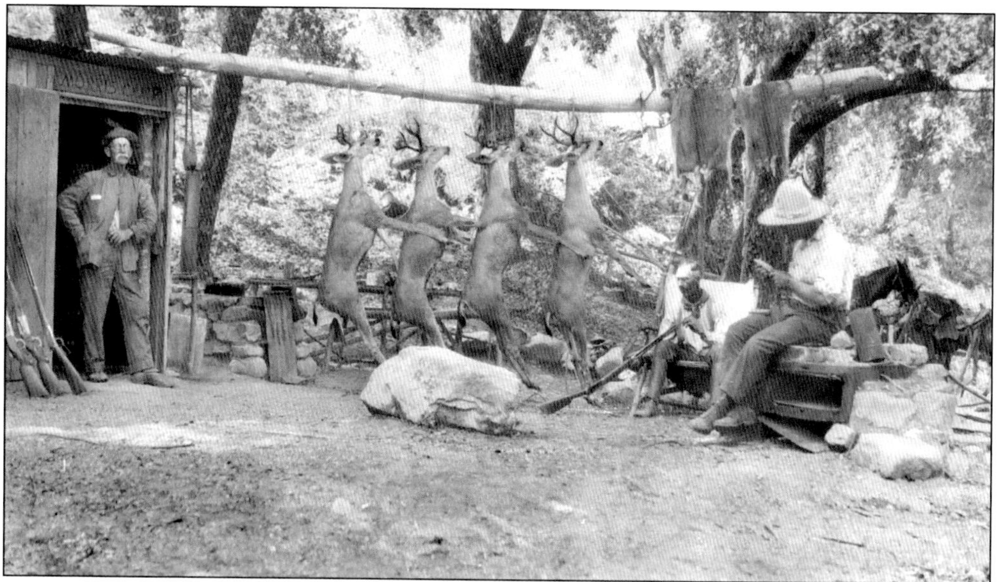

Men hunting in the Carpinteria Valley were aided by a number of camps in the foothills equipped with cabins and other amenities. Some of the popular ones were the Bailard-McCloskey Camp, the Romero Camp, and the Morris Camp. Dick Morris, the namesake of the Morris Camp, is on the far right of this c. 1900 photograph, in the company of Tim and Rolland Ogan. While the men were away, their wives would entertain each other with knitting parties while the children played. (Courtesy Donna May Ogan.)

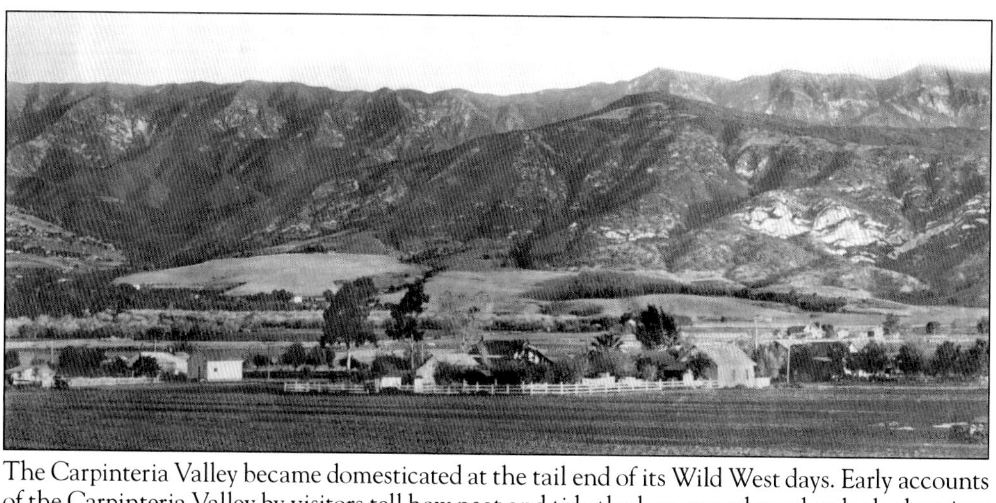

The Carpinteria Valley became domesticated at the tail end of its Wild West days. Early accounts of the Carpinteria Valley by visitors tell how neat and tidy the homes and ranches looked against the landscape. This c. 1910 photograph is a testament to those accounts. (Courtesy Jonathan Brown, Thomas Fish photograph.)

Two

Business as Usual

Carpinterians have generally refrained from shopping anywhere other than Carpinteria. A multi-paged insert in an ancient *Carpinteria Herald* unwittingly distilled the essence of the locals' enthusiasm for homegrown commerce. Each entry in this guide featured a photograph of a hometown business and its owner(s). It turns out that the typical Carpinterian's devotion to the local product was, in reality, simply loyalty to neighborhood proprietors, a connection that trumped any temptations folks might have had for the more comprehensive and often less expensive products offered by retailers in Ventura and Santa Barbara.

Vernon Graham at Graham's Market, Dick Dailey at Dailey Chevrolet, Jesse Skinner at Carpinteria Frozen Food Lockers, Marc Latham at Carpinteria Valley Lumber, Ralph Walsh and Jim McWhirter at Ralph's Market, Don Groves at the Seaside Gas Station, Dorothy Schlotter at Schlotter's Restaurant, Sal Campos at Sal's Shoe Repair, Tom Cundith at Carpinteria Cabinet Shop, Creel and Doris Husted at Husted Plumbing, Margaret Mills at Mills Drugs, Rudy Cervantes at Cervantes' Groceries, and Fred Risdon at Risdon's Service Station—these were some of Carpinteria's business folk, and anything less than total loyalty to them was frowned on, to put it mildly.

Over the years, Carpinteria's downtown entrepreneurs have artfully adapted nationwide trends for local consumption. Take, for example, the Carpinteria street fair in the 1920s that introduced locals and tourists to the automobile. The Avocado Festival, an annual favorite of tens of thousands of Californians, is but the latest in a long list of events that local businessmen and women have orchestrated in a well-calculated effort to keep the crowds coming to one of California's last great beach towns.

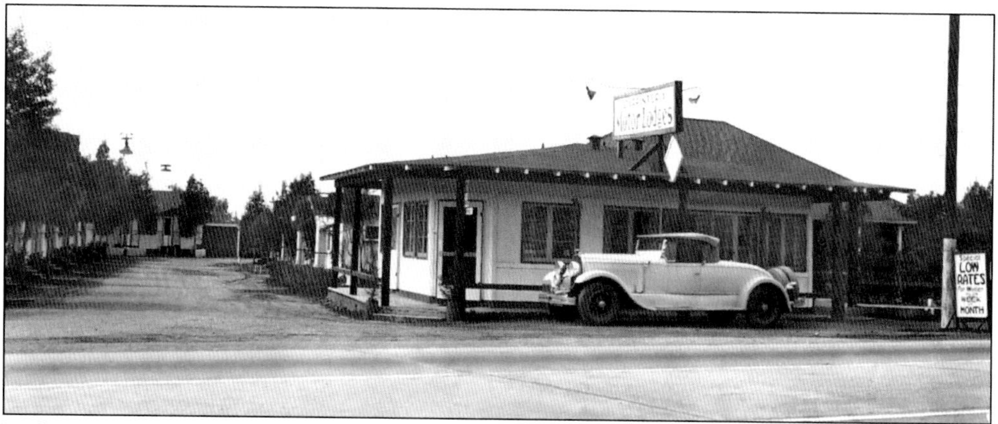

Walter Kenyon's Carpinteria Motor Lodge was on the Coast Highway, the current Carpinteria Avenue, where Sun Coast Rentals stands today. The rental cabins were tended by family members Alice Kenyon, Dutch Munn, Pat Dehnke, Ruth McIntyre, and Marny Middleton. The lodge was sold to the Carpinteria Mutual Citrus Association in the early 1940s for use as migrant labor housing. (Courtesy Marny Middleton.)

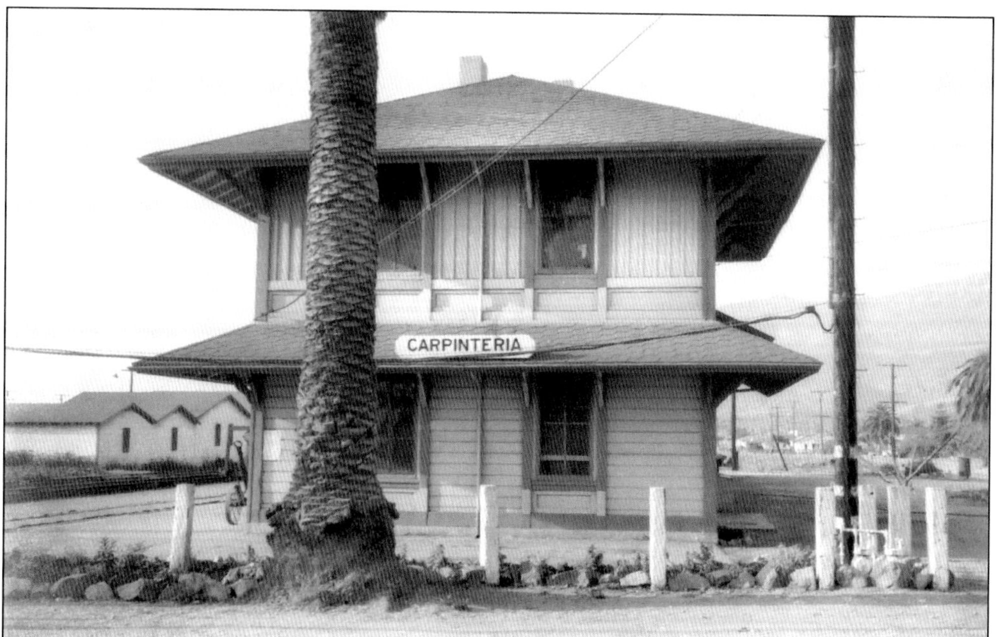

The train depot on the corner of Fifth Street and Linden Avenue, pictured around 1948, was an unwitting player in the recruitment of local car club members. The uninitiated were required to drive over the loading dock both forward and backward, followed by a sprint onto the beach at the foot of Linden Avenue, where wannabe members had to perform a perfect donut. The depot was closed in 1958 and razed in 1967. (Courtesy Carpinteria Valley Museum of History.)

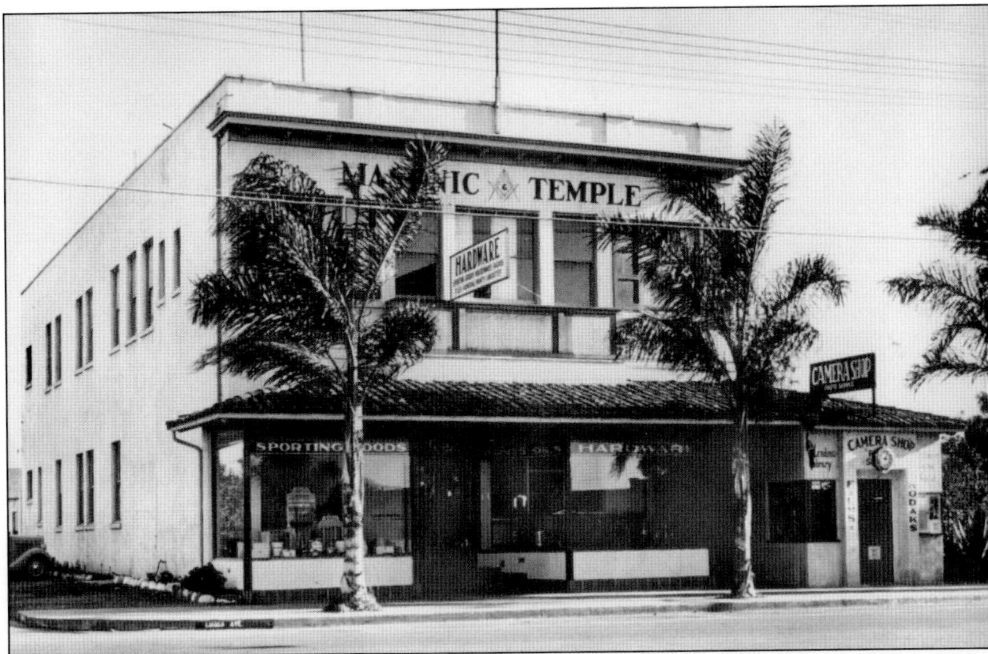

The 800 block of Linden Avenue was the Masonic Temple's home from 1914 to 1964, when it moved into its new site on Carpinteria Avenue next to what is now the middle school. It shared this building with a hardware store and a camera shop. (Courtesy Carpinteria Valley Museum of History.)

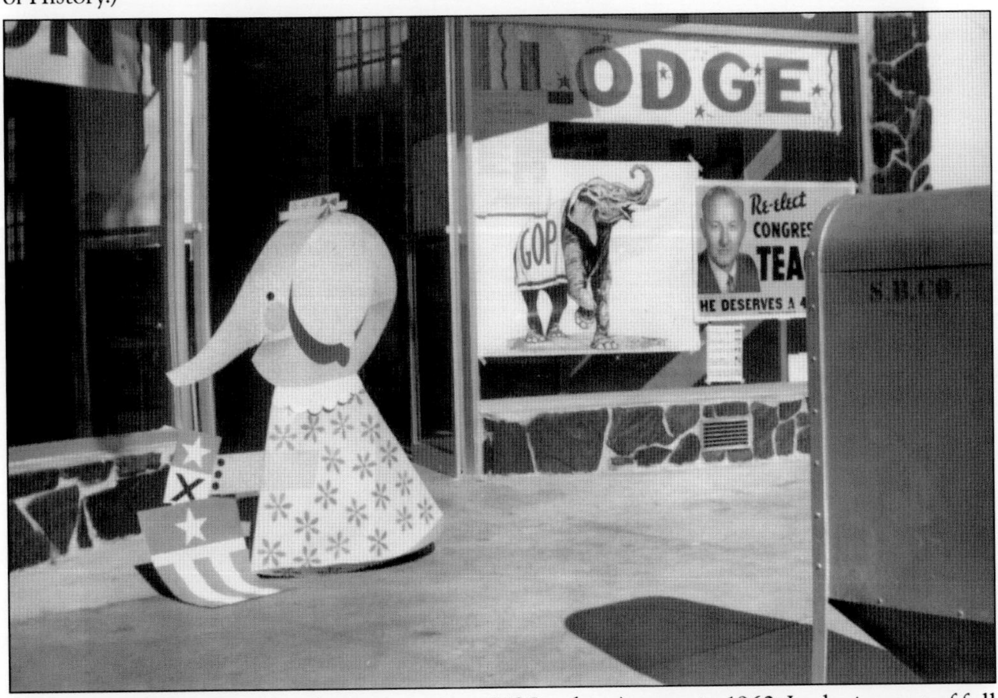

Carpinteria's Republican headquarters were at 943 Linden Avenue in 1960. In the interest of full disclosure, it should be noted that the Kennedy/Johnson ticket prevailed in the general election that year. (Courtesy Carpinteria Valley Museum of History.)

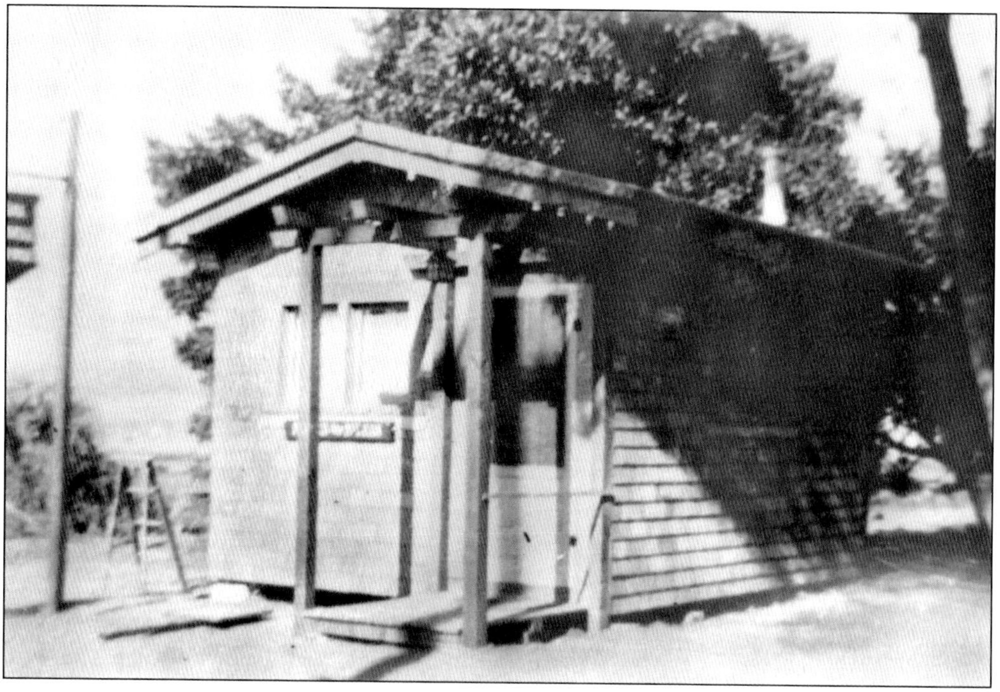

The picture above is of Carpinteria Realty in 1916. The view below was taken by Bert McLean, Carpinteria's answer to Ansel Adams, in the 1940s. This particular edition of the Carpinteria Realty office was located in the 5000 block of Carpinteria Avenue. (Both courtesy Carpinteria Valley Museum of History.)

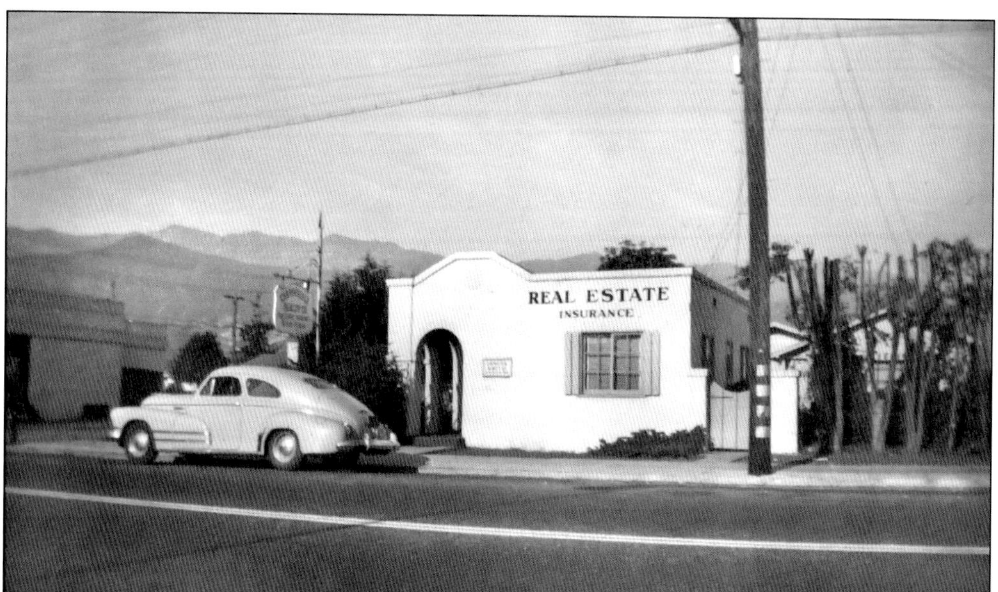

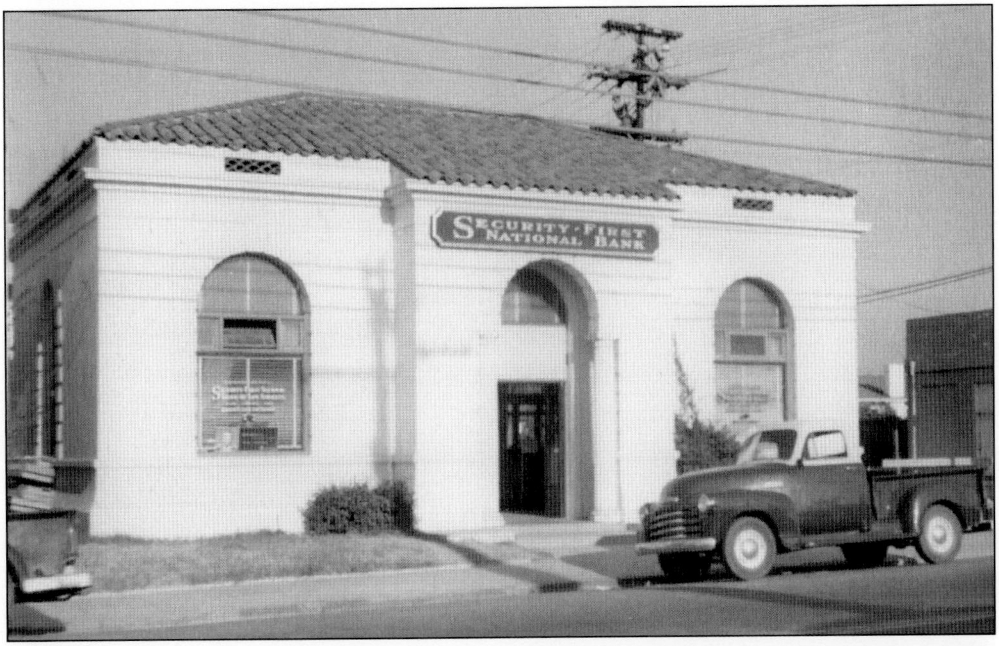

Now you see it, now you don't. Hopefully, this refers only to the Security First National Bank and not to the truck that's pictured in the top photograph. (Both courtesy Carpinteria Valley Museum of History.)

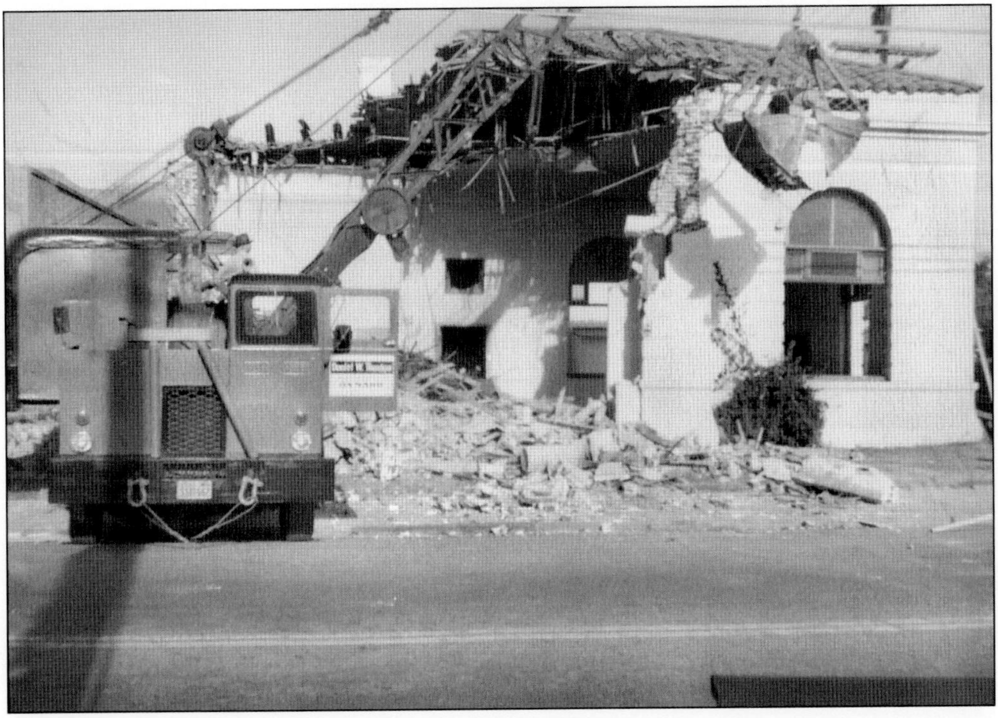

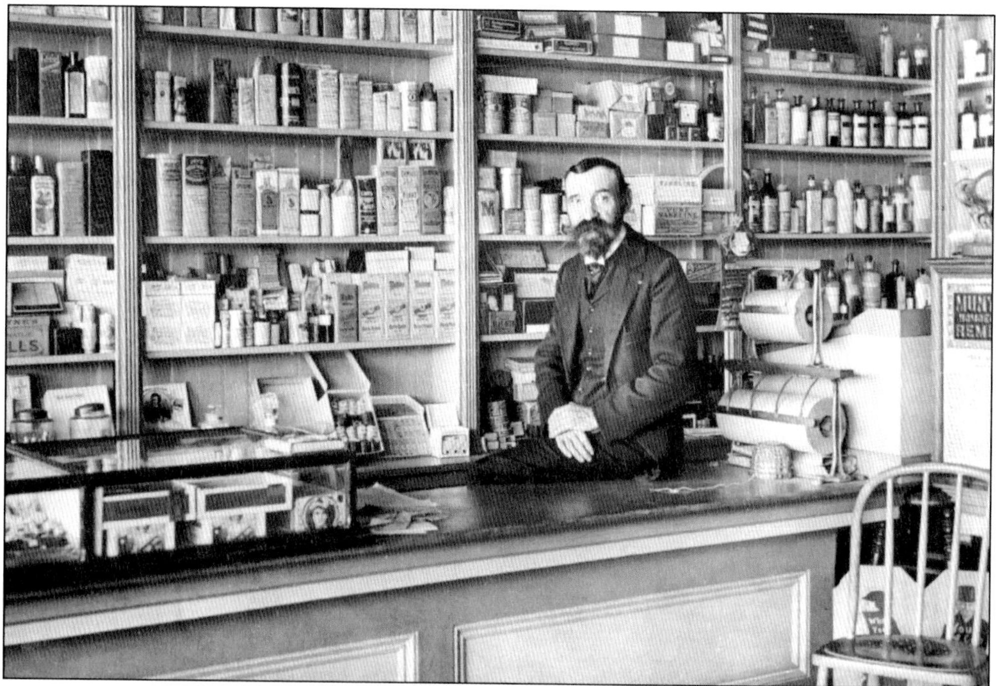

Dr. C. L. Downey, looking suspiciously like one of the Smith Brothers of cough drop fame, ran this drugstore in the 600 block of Linden Avenue at the beginning of the 20th century. (Courtesy Carpinteria Valley Museum of History.)

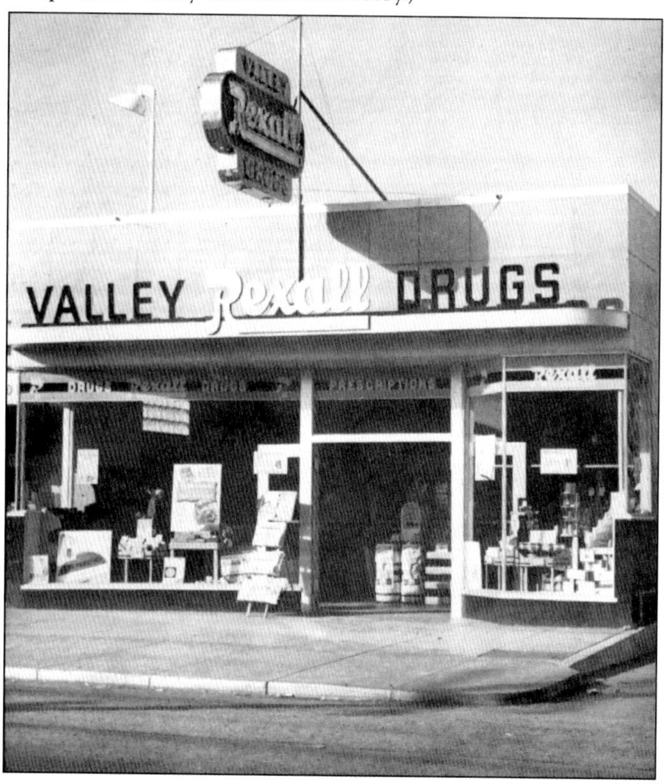

The folks employed at Valley Rexall Drugs could look across the intersection at the Coast Highway and Linden Avenue and almost see the whites of the eyes of their major competitors at Mills Drugs in 1948. The big winners in this rivalry were Carpinterians, as both drugstores were a class act. (Courtesy Carpinteria High School.)

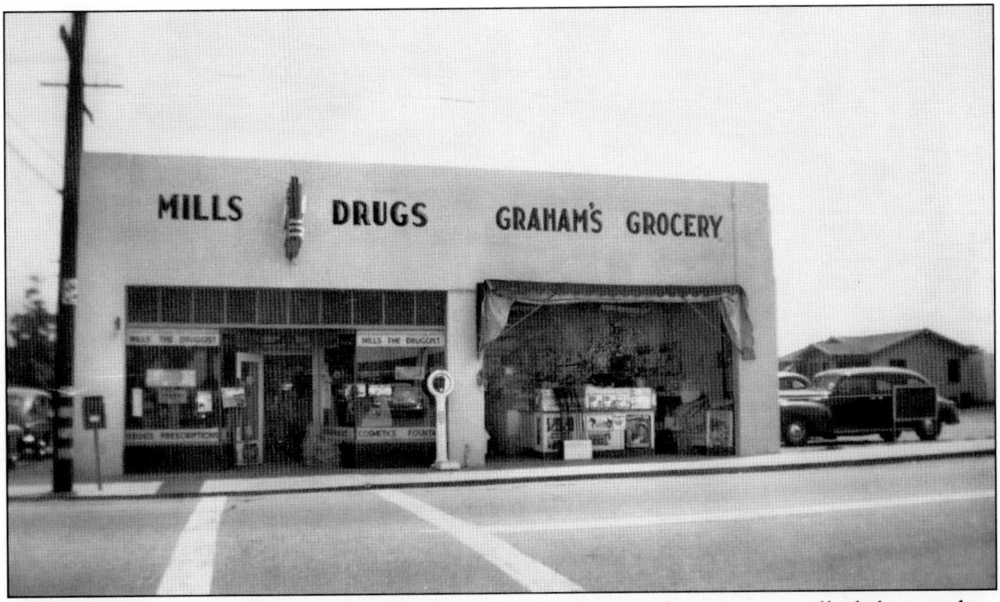

Mills Drugs and Graham's Grocery, pictured around 1940, shared a common wall while providing locals with one-stop shopping on the corner of Linden Avenue and the Coast Highway. During the early years, Mills featured a soda fountain, guaranteeing that Carpinteria's younger set was never overburdened with loose change. (Courtesy Carpinteria Valley Museum of History.)

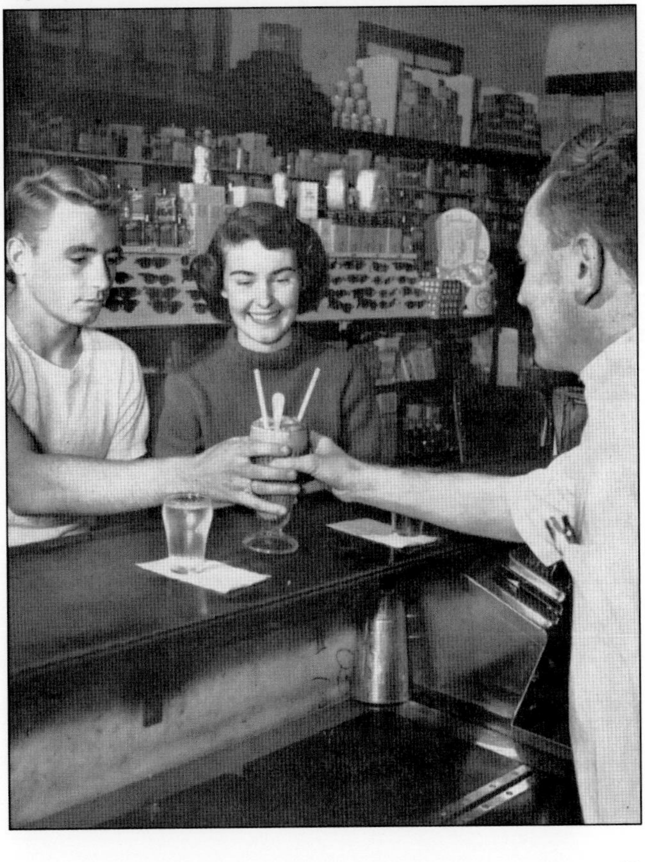

Mills Drugs' appeal, as mentioned above, wasn't exclusively pharmaceutical. As far as Burgie and Eleanor were concerned around 1948, there was never a bad time, never mind mom's mantra on spoiling whatever meal was coming up next, for one of Mills' tasty soda fountain concoctions. (Courtesy Carpinteria High School.)

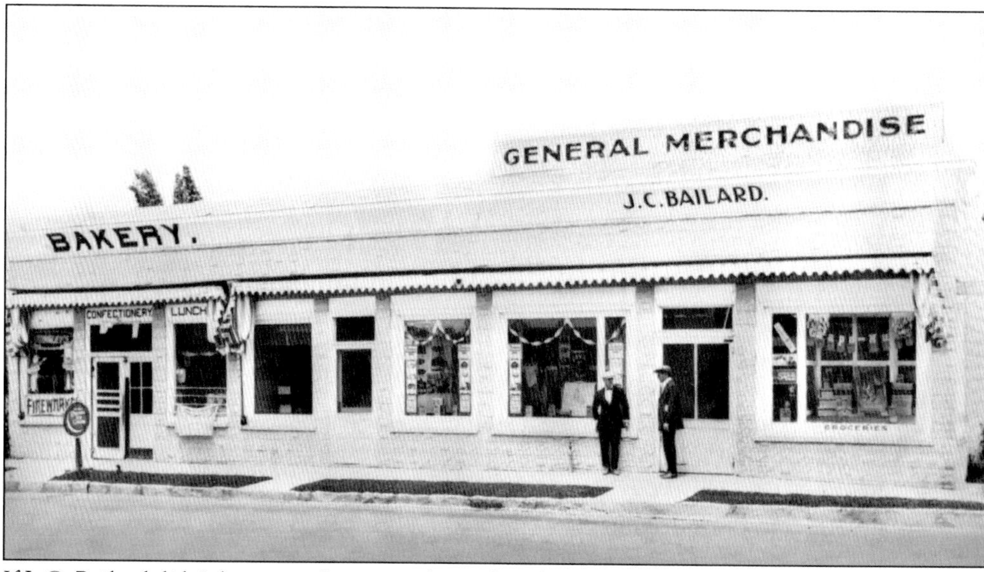

If J. C. Bailard didn't have it at his general merchandise store on the southwest corner of Linden Avenue and the Coast Highway, you probably didn't need it. This picture was taken around 1920. (Courtesy Carpinteria Valley Museum of History.)

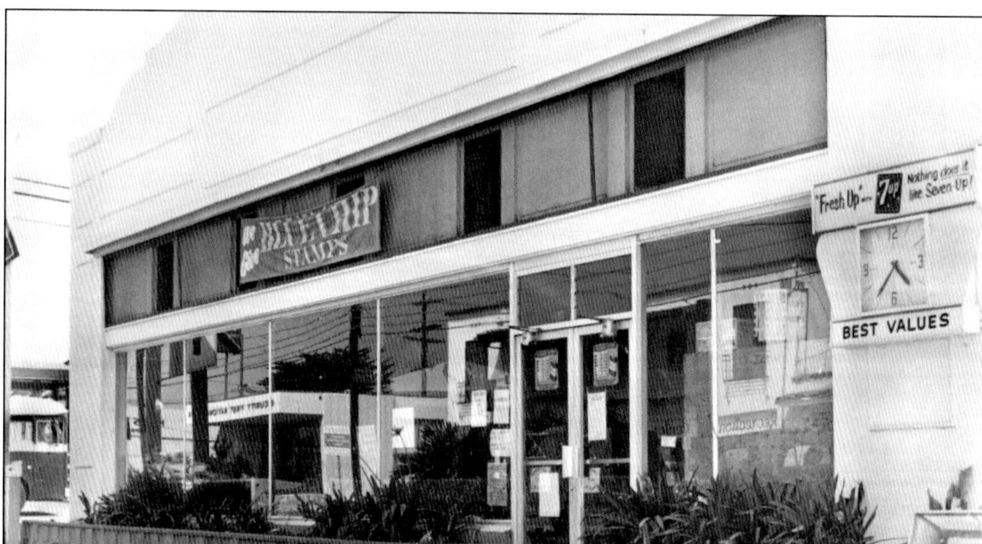

When Safeway turned the corner onto Linden Avenue with their operation in the 1960s, the building they'd called home on Carpinteria Avenue was quickly taken over by local grocers. Most shoppers remember the name of the store that was up and running when their teenagers worked there. Many recall it, with some enthusiasm, as the Hi-Lo Market. (Courtesy Carpinteria Valley Museum of History.)

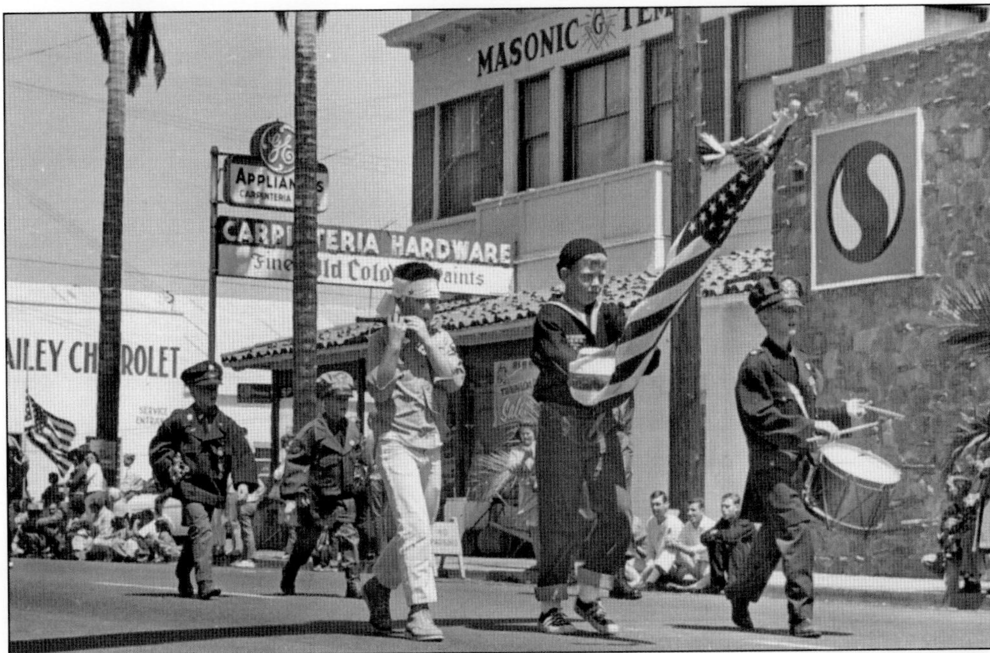

Carpinteria's finest—its youngsters—march down Linden Avenue in a reenactment of some of America's finer historical moments in a 1962 Loyalty Day Parade. The big "S" on the wall next to the Masonic Temple stands for Safeway, which was initially located on the street where the Vons' parking lot sits today. (Courtesy Carpinteria Valley Museum of History.)

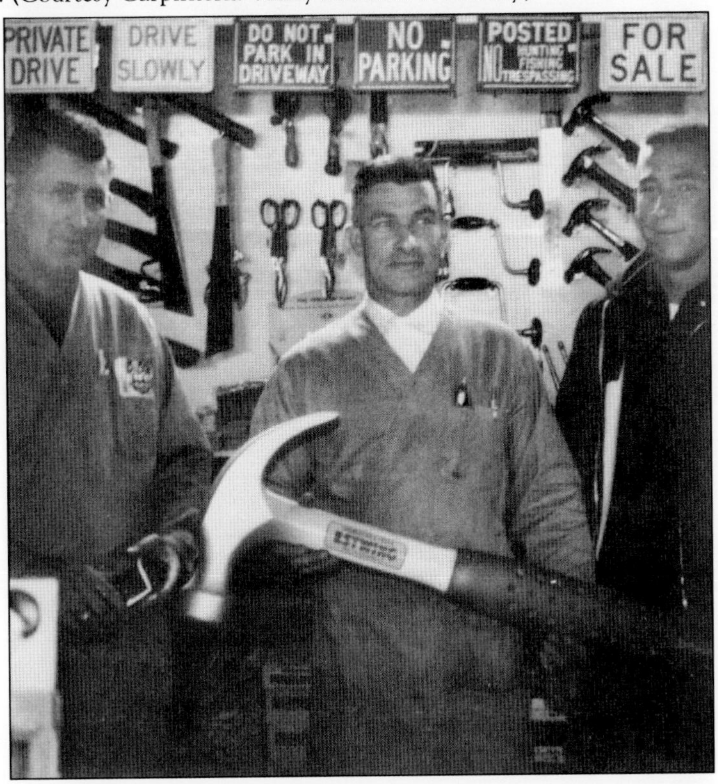

Carpinteria Hardware wasn't kidding around in 1963 inventory-wise. The owners were apparently fans of an old Teddy Roosevelt line that they reworked for Carpinteria: "Walk softly and carry a big hammer." From left to right are Ray, Chuck, and Doug at your service. (Courtesy Carpinteria High School.)

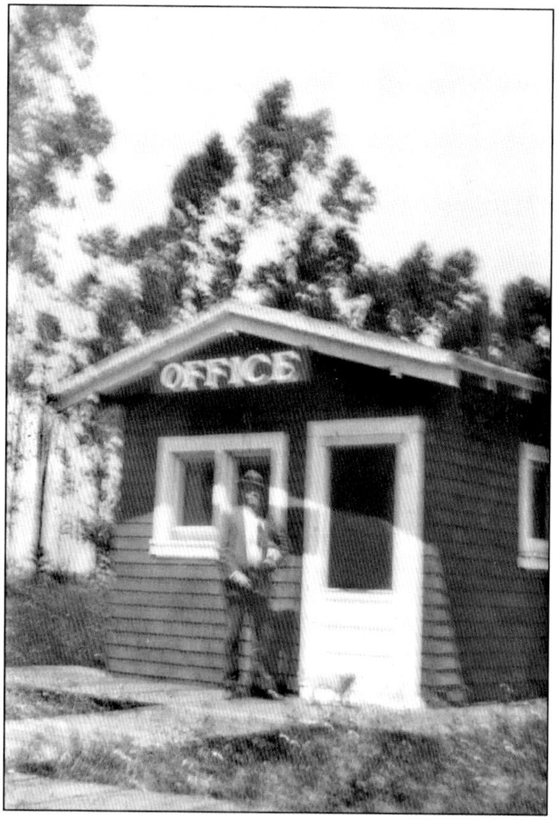

"Wanna' buy some land?" This gentleman was the man to see. Buyers could either step inside his office in the 300 block of Elm Avenue and look at the subdivision map or simply take a walk around the Dorrance tract, pictured below in the 1920s. (Both courtesy Carpinteria Valley Museum of History.)

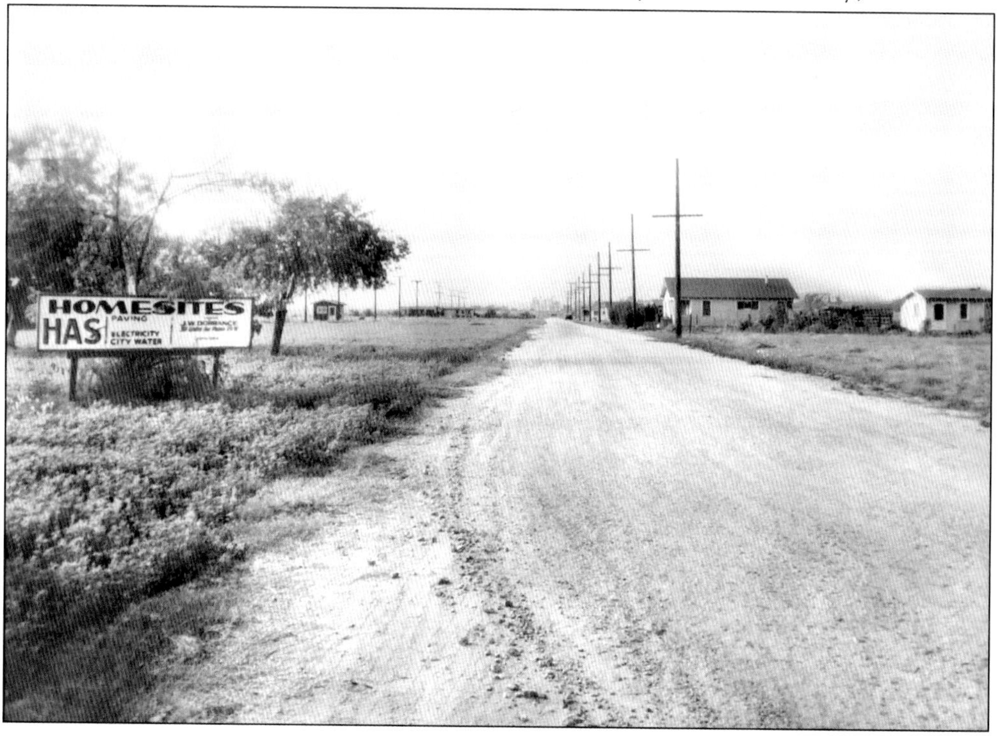

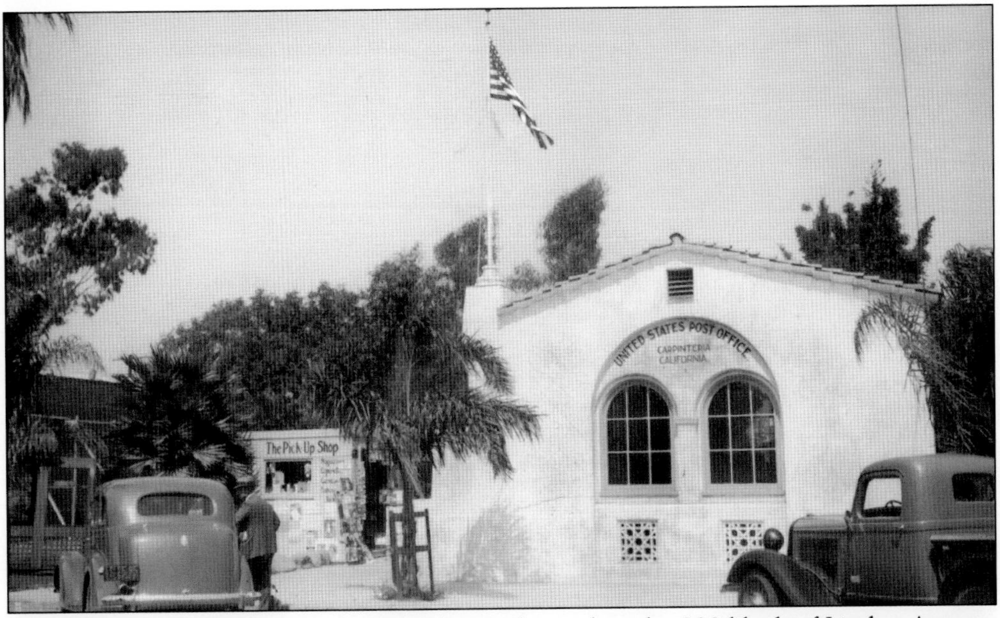

In 1937, the post office, minus a zip code, was located in the 900 block of Linden Avenue. (Courtesy Sey Kinsell.)

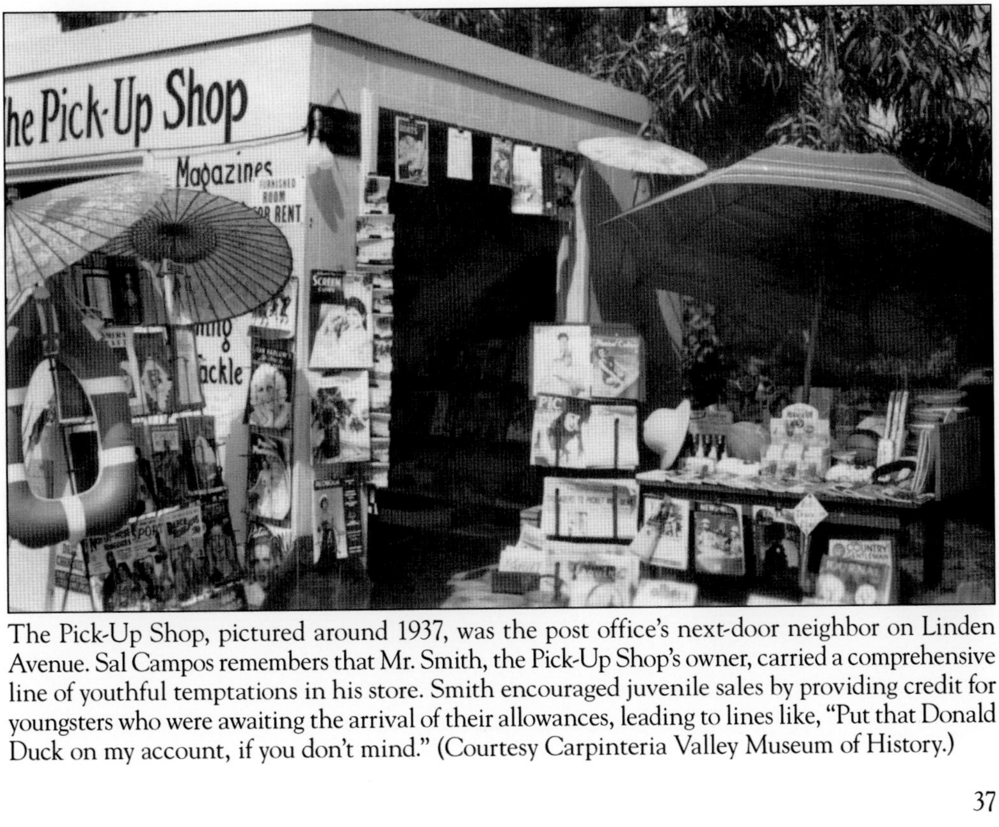

The Pick-Up Shop, pictured around 1937, was the post office's next-door neighbor on Linden Avenue. Sal Campos remembers that Mr. Smith, the Pick-Up Shop's owner, carried a comprehensive line of youthful temptations in his store. Smith encouraged juvenile sales by providing credit for youngsters who were awaiting the arrival of their allowances, leading to lines like, "Put that Donald Duck on my account, if you don't mind." (Courtesy Carpinteria Valley Museum of History.)

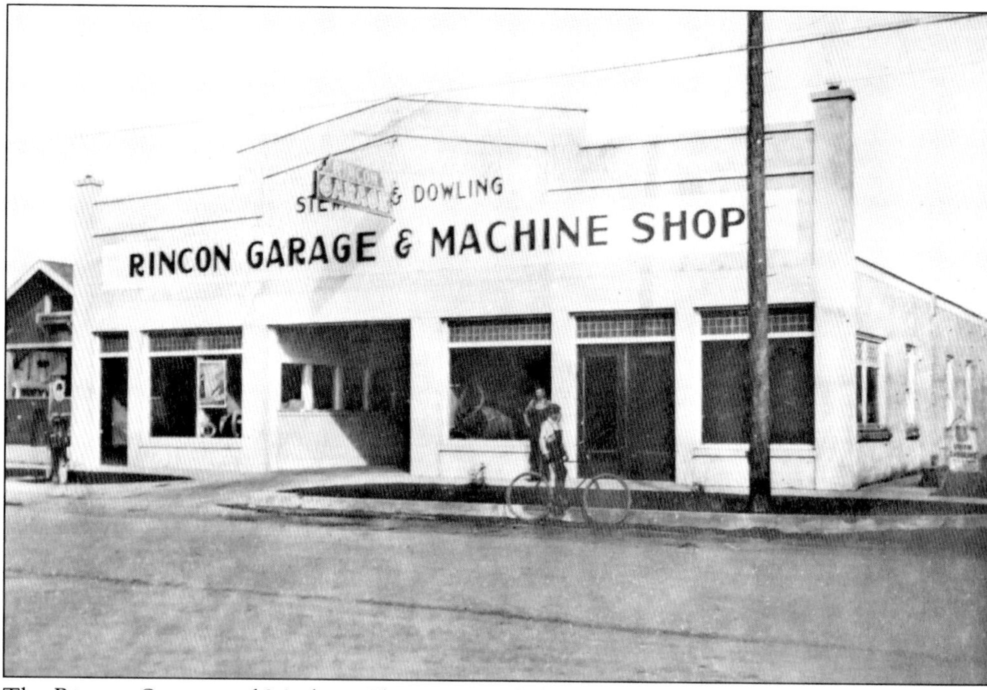

The Rincon Garage and Machine Shop, pictured above around 1918, helped get Carpinteria's automotive industry in gear at this location on Linden Avenue where Robitaille's Candy and the CorkTree Cellars reside today. The interior of the Rincon Garage in the early 1920s is seen below. The gentlemen pictured from left to right are Walter Dowling, Frank Stewart, Jack Crother, and Elza Oberholtzer. (Both courtesy Carpinteria Valley Museum of History.)

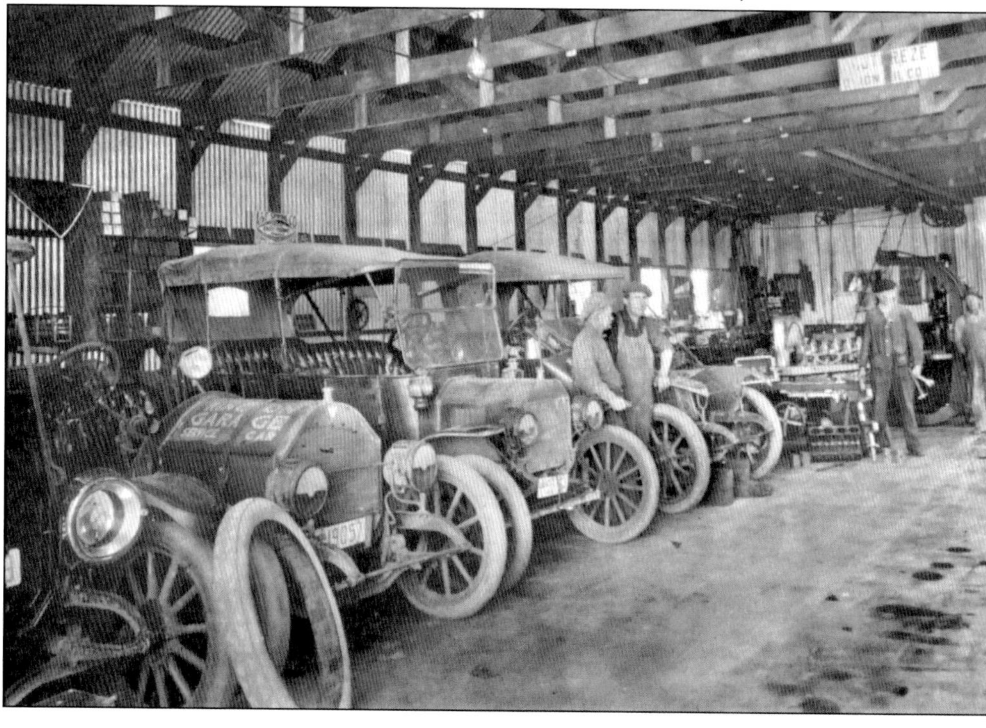

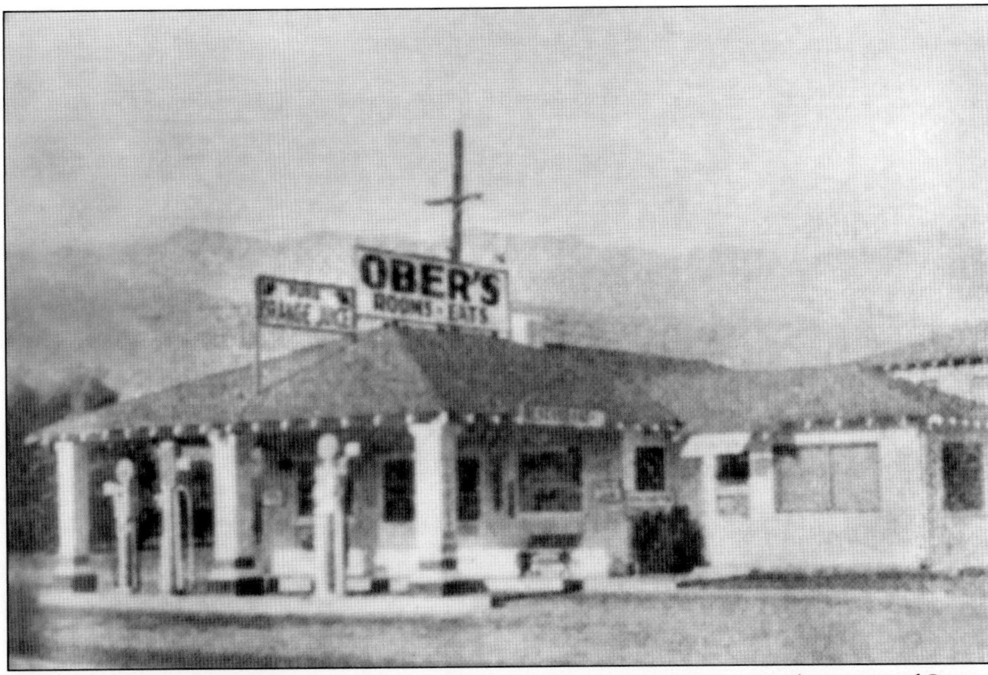

Ober's Gas Station and notions outlet was dispensing 7-11-type inventory on the corner of Casitas Pass Road and the Coast Highway long before convenience stores had started being convenient. (Courtesy Carpinteria Valley Museum of History.)

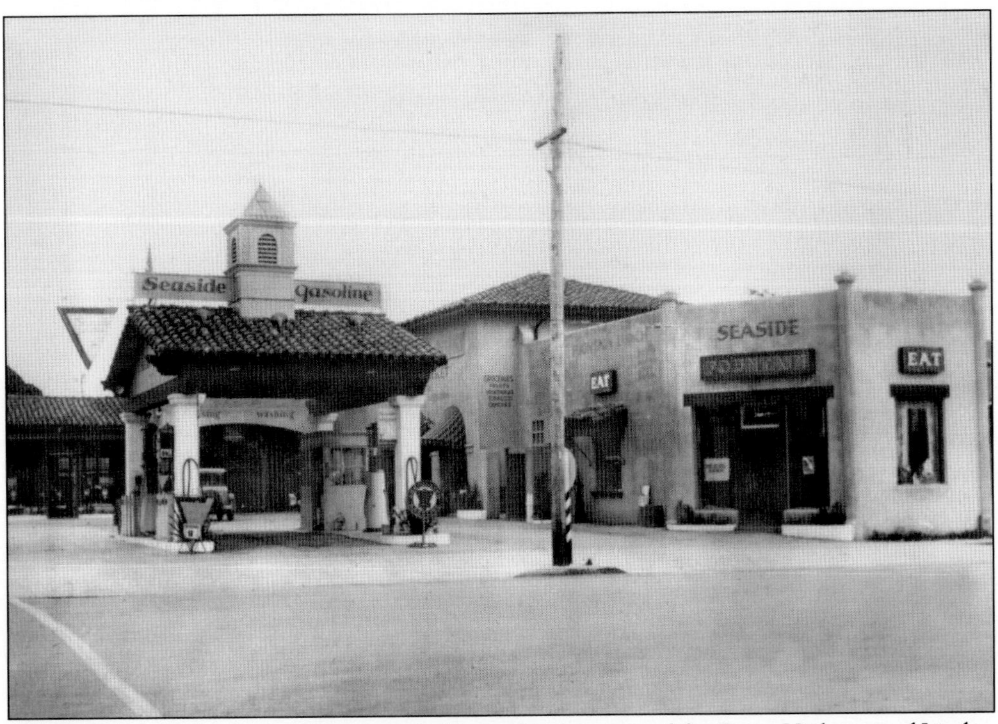

The Seaside complex pictured here sat on the southeast corner of the Coast Highway and Linden Avenue in the 1920s. (Courtesy Carpinteria Valley Museum of History.)

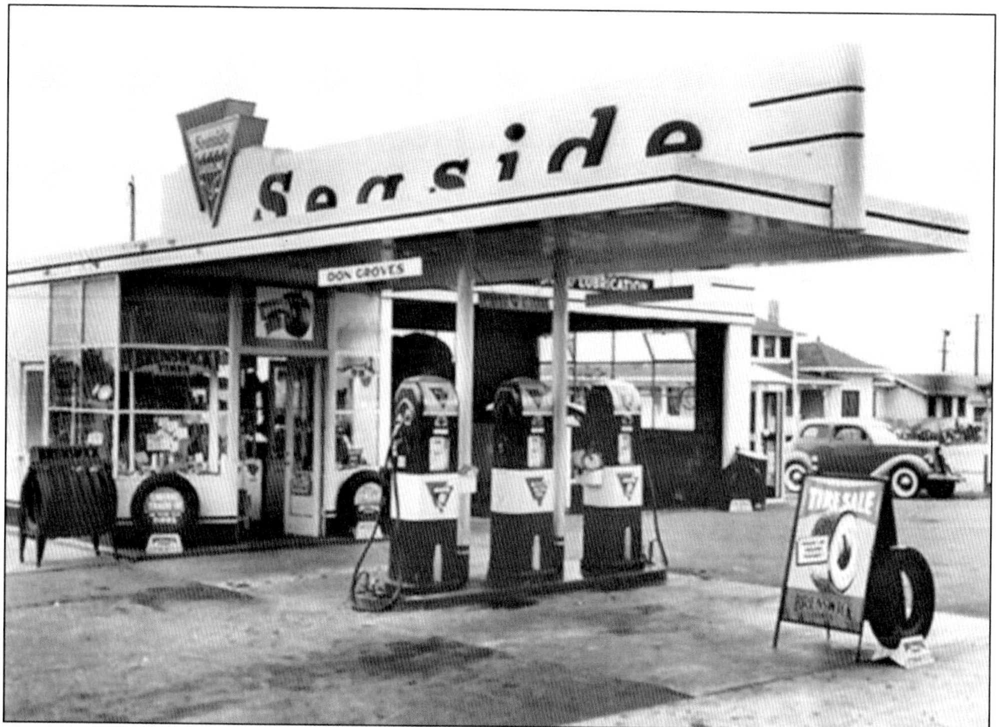

Don Groves' Seaside Station, located on the corner of Maple Avenue and the Coast Highway, served Carpinterians well for decades. It featured not only two-digit gas prices but attendants filling 'er up, inflating tires, checking the fluid levels, and even washing windows, as often as not without even being asked. (Courtesy Carpinteria Valley Museum of History.)

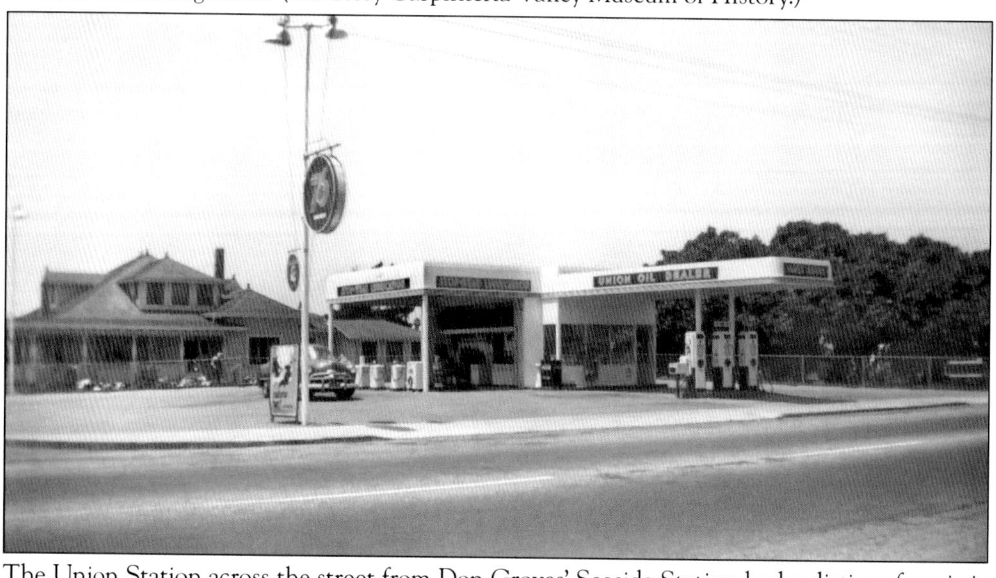

The Union Station across the street from Don Groves' Seaside Station had a distinct futuristic feel. Eddie Macias and Ernie Villapando, who ran this station for years, managed to seamlessly combine the care of their patrons' cars with analytical orations on local football games. This type of relationship was generally the rule, not the exception, when it came to Carpinteria businessmen and their customers. (Courtesy Carpinteria Valley Museum of History.)

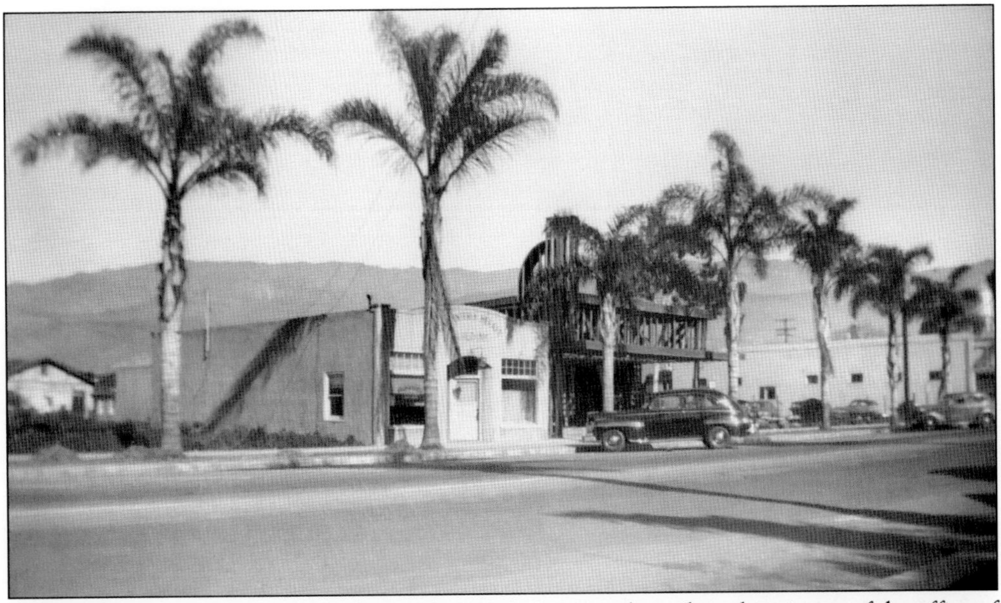

The 800 block of Linden Avenue was just beginning to percolate when this picture of the office of the *Carpinteria Herald*, an early relation of today's *Coastal View News*, and its partially completed neighbor, Vallecito Furniture, was snapped. (Courtesy Carpinteria Valley Museum of History.)

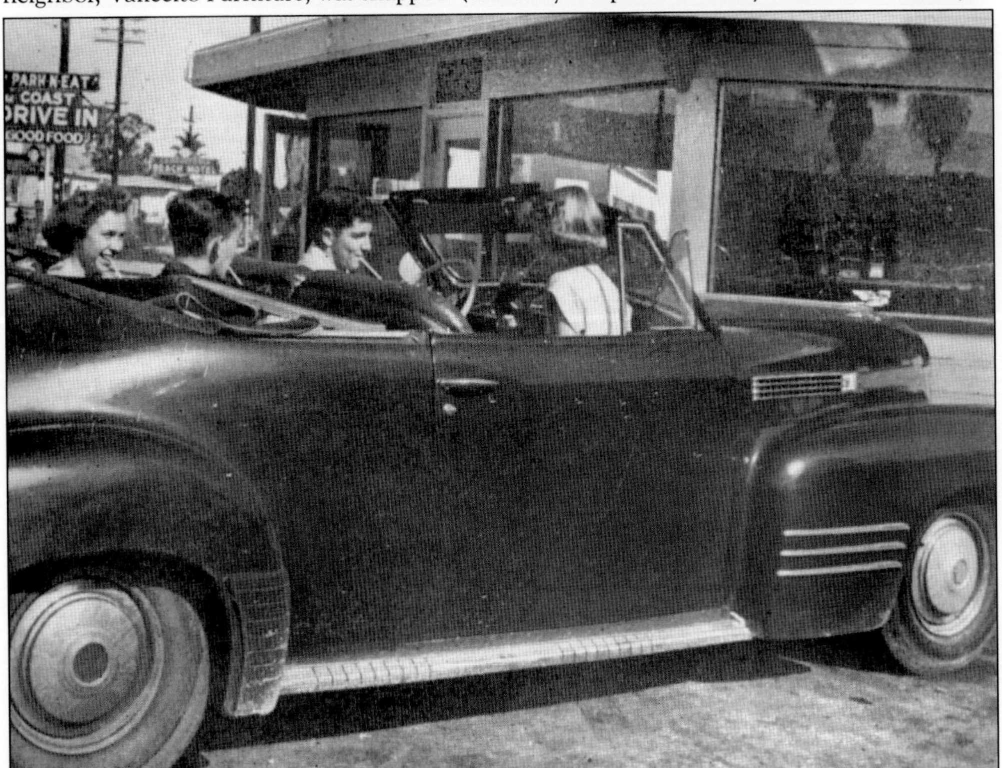

Pictured around 1948, the Coast Drive-In, on the Coast Highway half a block from the high school, was a popular hangout for local teenagers. Fortunately for burger lovers, Foster's Freeze stepped right in when the Coast Drive-In called it a day. (Courtesy Carpinteria High School.)

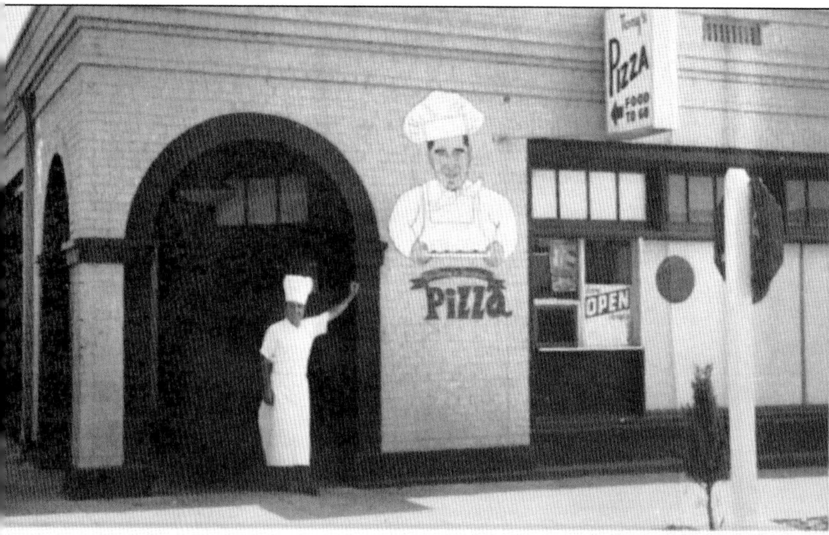

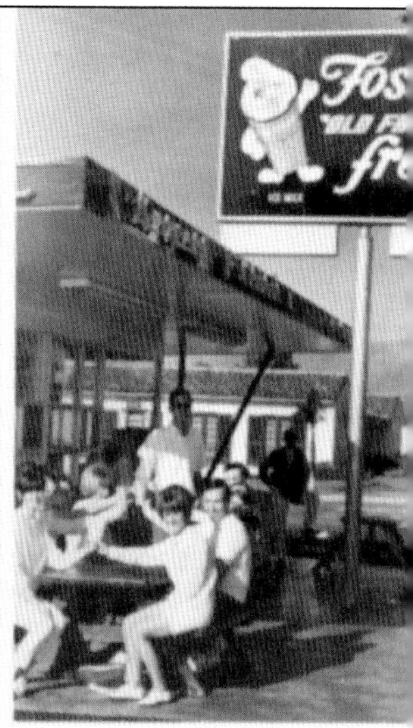
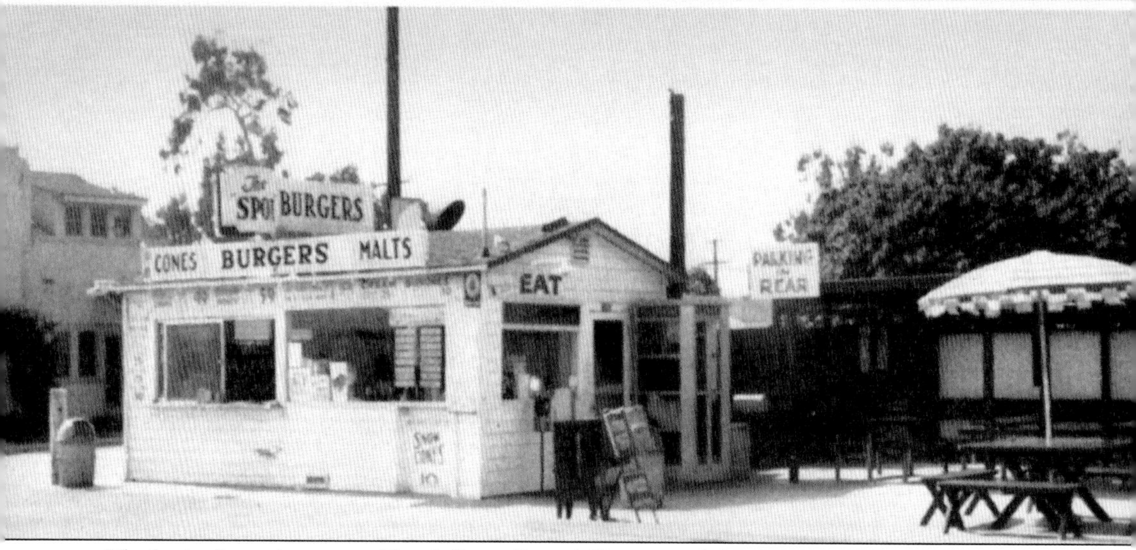

Clockwise from the top are Tony's Pizza, Foster's Freeze, and the Spot around 1960. All three have had long and storied runs in Carpinteria. These culinary legends have epitomized comfort food in the Carpinteria Valley for the better part of half a century. They've been responsible for quelling any number of domestic rebellions over the years. Adolescent mutinies are a specialty—on those nights when it appeared that hormonal teenagers were finally going to gain the upper hand, the mere mention of burgers and fries from Foster's or the Spot, or the materializing of a Tony's pizza, was often enough to stem the tide, thereby returning normalcy to the manor. To Tony's, Foster's, and the Spot—a grateful valley salutes you. (Courtesy Carpinteria High School.)

Three

A Beach for All Reasons

Since 1912, the Carpinteria Chamber of Commerce has trolled for beach-going tourists with the following as bait:

Moderate year round temperatures (60 degrees to 80 degrees)

Ocean temperatures (58 degrees to 72 degrees)

Unrivaled natural wonders

And last, but most certainly not least, the World's Safest Beach.

Over the decades, Carpinteria Beach has hosted beauty pageants, horse races, fashion shows, military installations, shuffleboard seminars, a Spanish language classroom, and a rendezvous for the betrothed—a veritable lazy Susan of activities. The only limit to a Carpinteria beach day is one's imagination. For some, Carpinteria's beaches are a sedative, for others a roller coaster ride, and still for others, anything and everything in between.

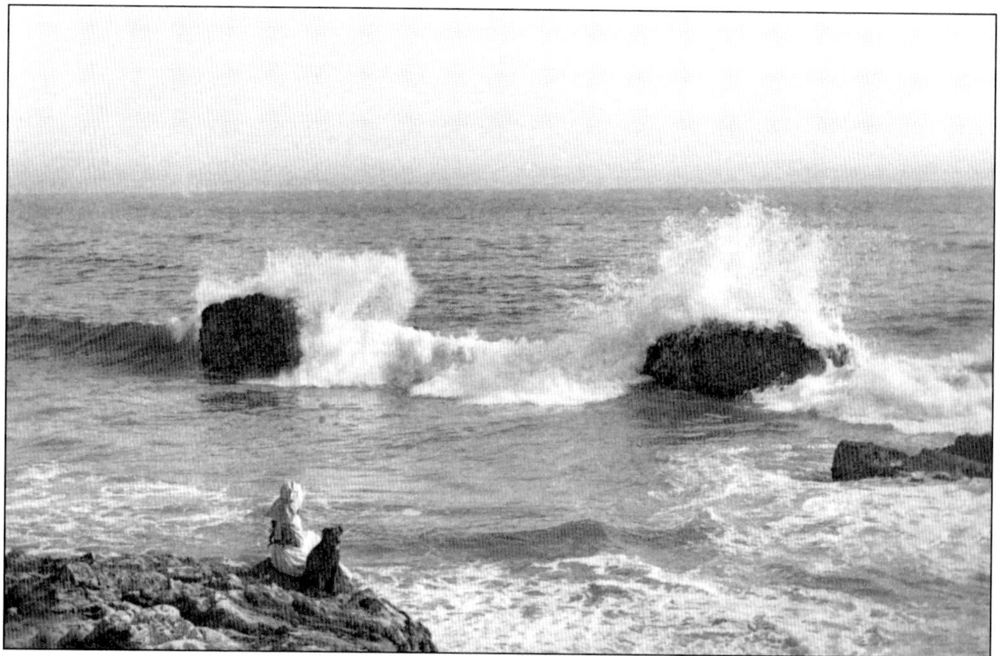

If there's a better place to dust off those cranial cobwebs than at the Jellybowl beach, Carpinterians have yet to discover it. And as every dog lover knows, time spent with a canine compadre increases therapeutic effectiveness exponentially. (Courtesy Carpinteria Valley Museum of History.)

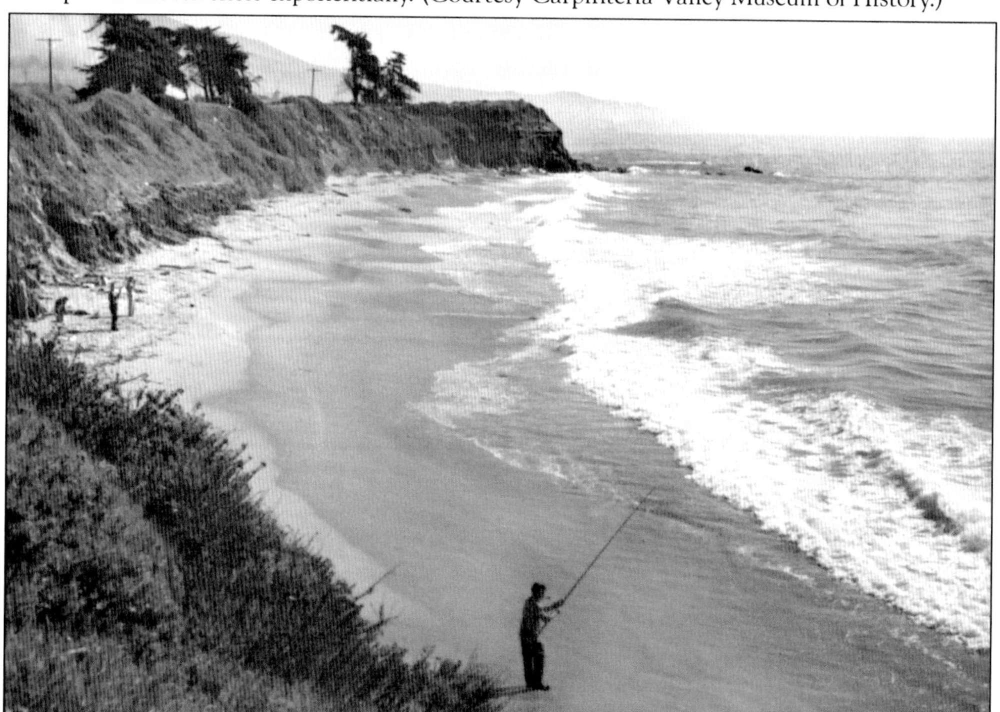

A favorite pastime of significant numbers of Carpinteria beachgoers has always been surf fishing. This angler is trying his luck at Higgins' Cove in 1946. (Courtesy Carpinteria Valley Museum of History.)

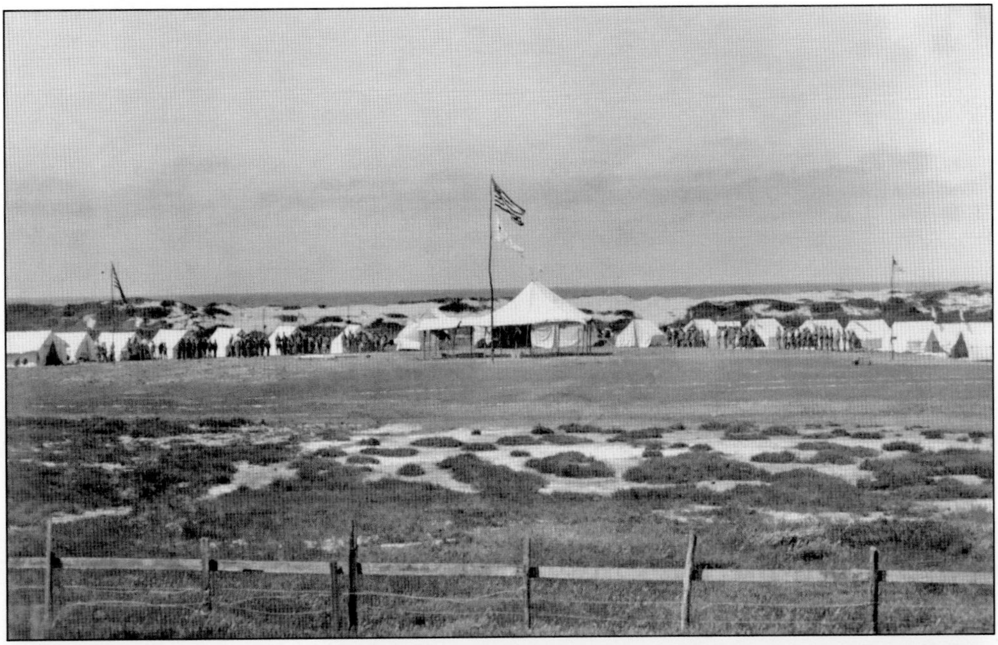

It was safety first on Carpinteria Beach during both world wars. The above photograph is of the Carpinteria constabulary, a military installation that was dug in on Carpinteria Beach in 1917. The picture at right is of an aircraft warning station on the beach during World War II. (Both courtesy Carpinteria Valley Museum of History.)

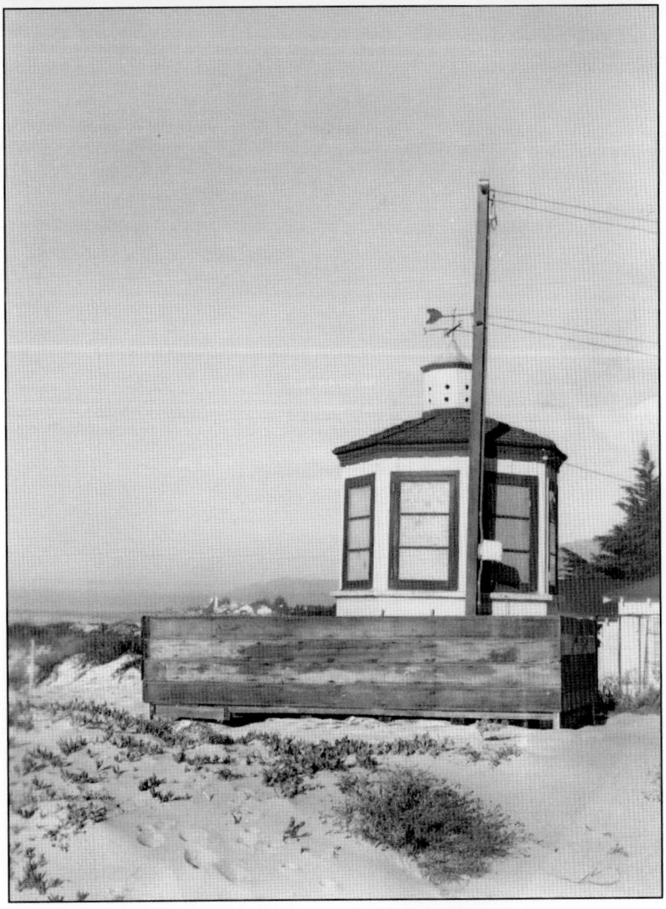

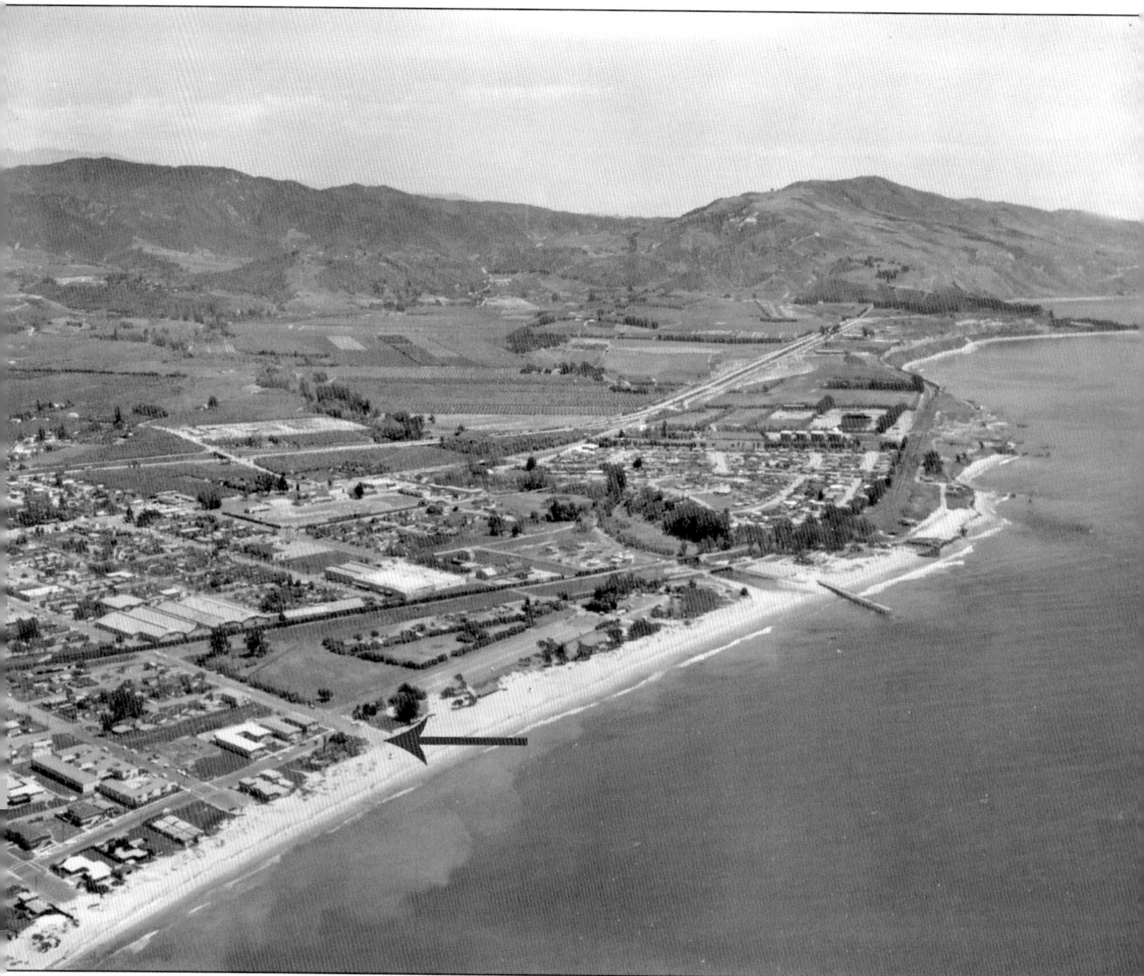

Use the arrow, which is aimed at the beach end of Linden Avenue, as a point of reference for navigating this extraordinary Kodak moment. (Courtesy Carpinteria Valley Museum of History.)

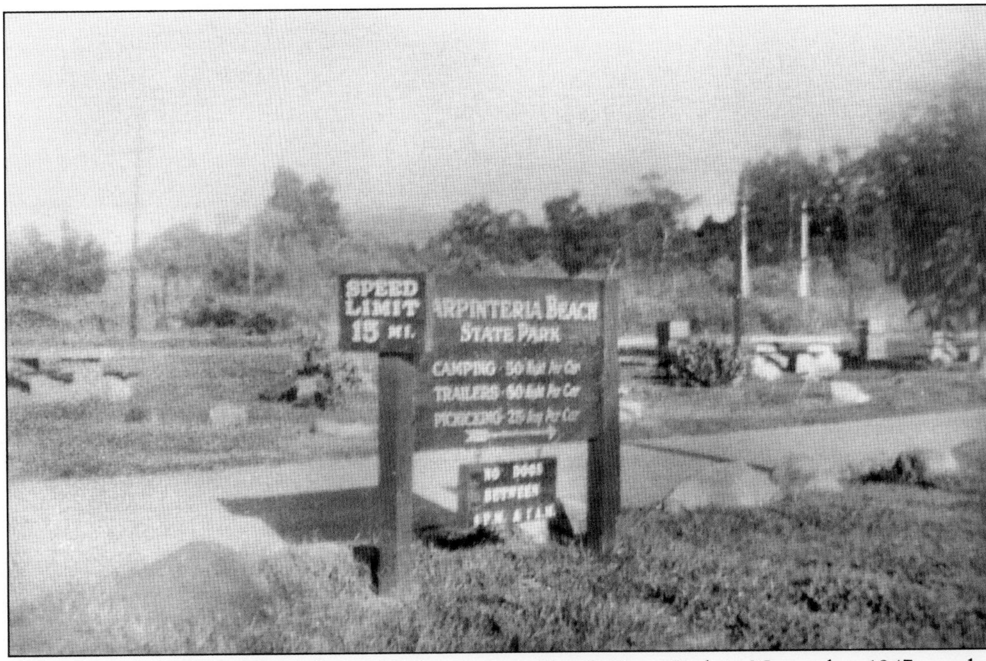

Travelers who had questions about the Carpinteria Beach State Park in November 1947, needed look no further than this sign for answers: 50¢ a night per car, trailers 60¢ a night, picnicking 25¢ per car per day, and no dogs between 8:00 p.m. and 7:00 a.m. (Courtesy Carpinteria Valley Museum of History.)

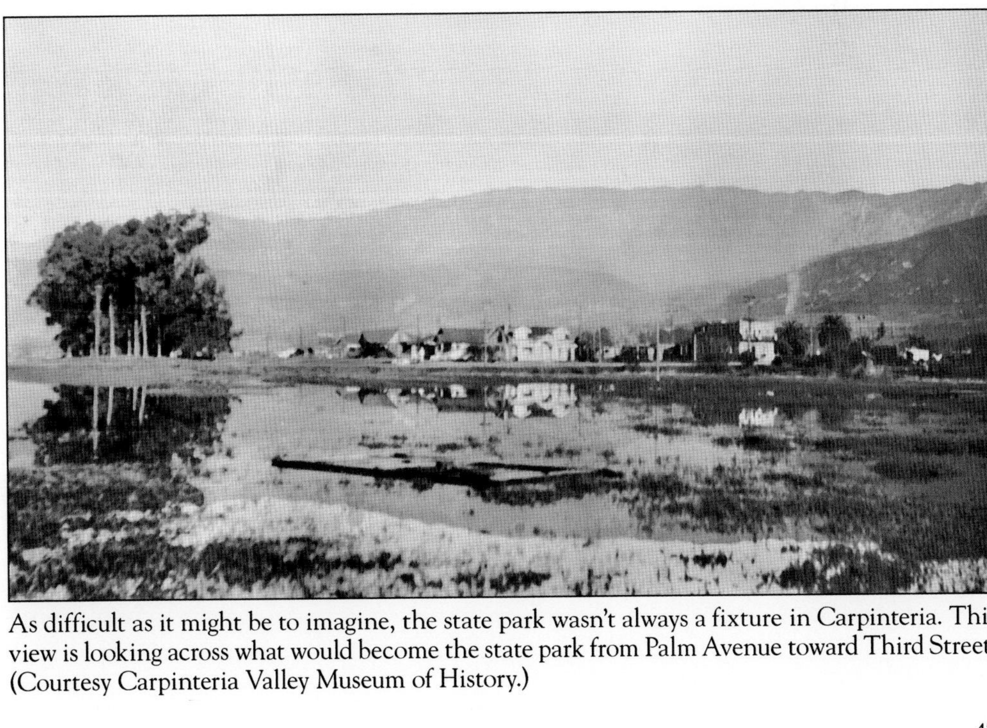

As difficult as it might be to imagine, the state park wasn't always a fixture in Carpinteria. This view is looking across what would become the state park from Palm Avenue toward Third Street. (Courtesy Carpinteria Valley Museum of History.)

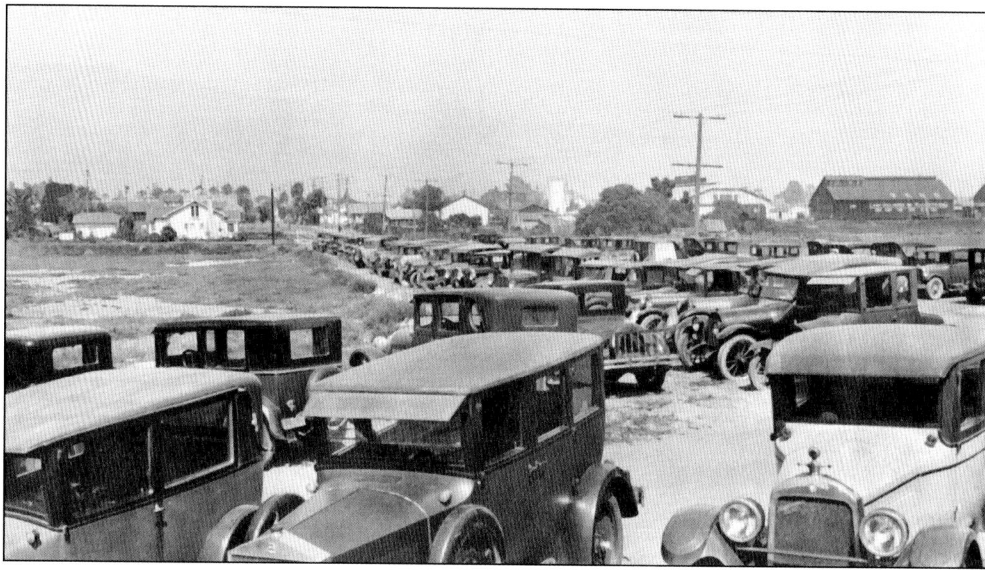

The fact that Carpinteria rapidly became everybody's best-known secret led to Labor Days that found Linden Avenue littered with cars for as far as the eye could see. The view of the Beach Store below features a lone patron, a stand of eucalyptus trees that lined Third Street, and a lot of empty real estate between the foot of Linden Avenue and the Beach Store's nearest neighbors. This shot clearly wasn't taken on a Labor Day. (Both courtesy Carpinteria Valley Museum of History.)

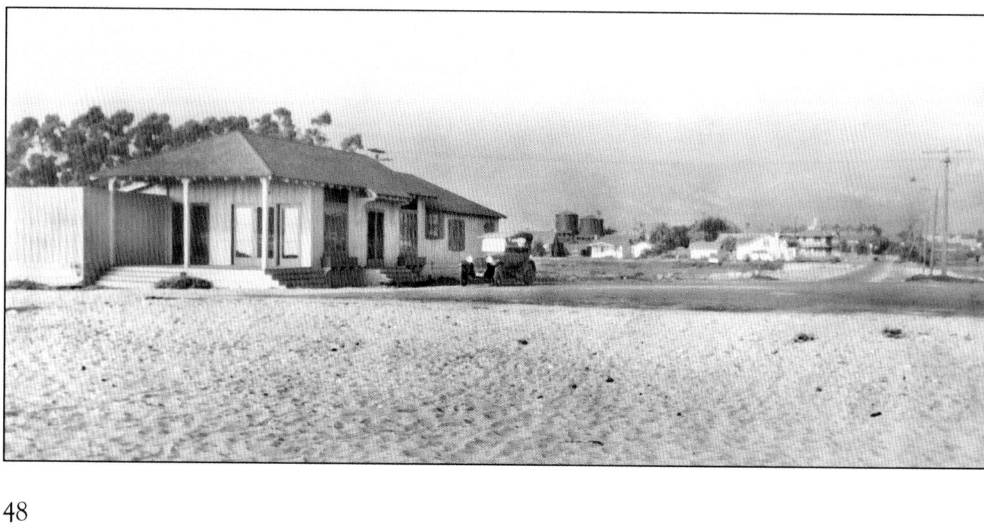

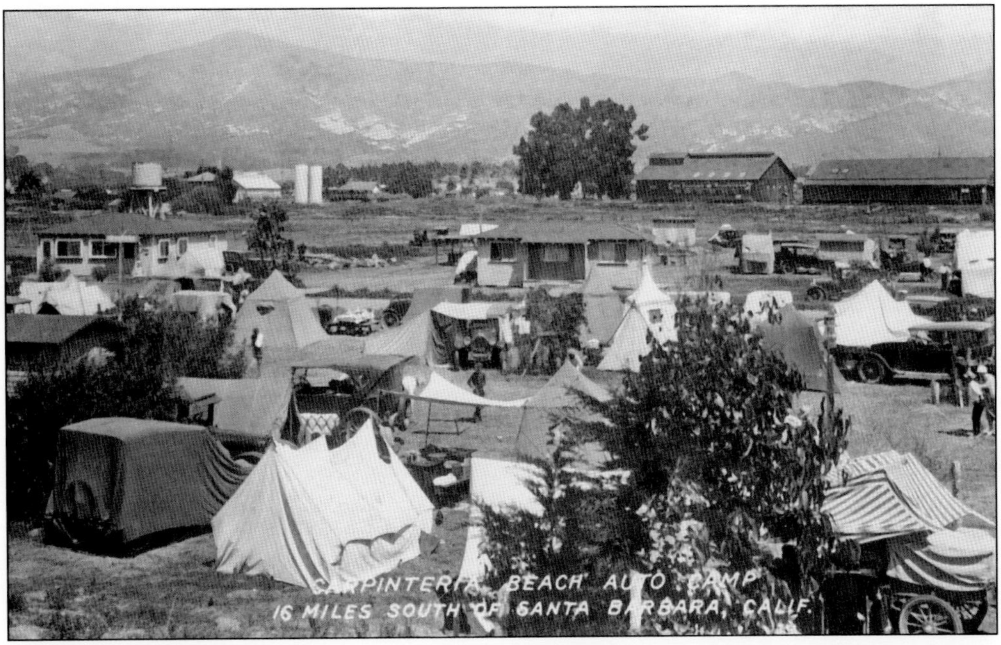

One has to wonder if these folks were camping or homesteading in 1922. The Diamond Walnut Packing House is shown in the background above. The large trees in the rear below were located on Third Street near Elm Avenue. (Both courtesy Carpinteria Valley Museum of History.)

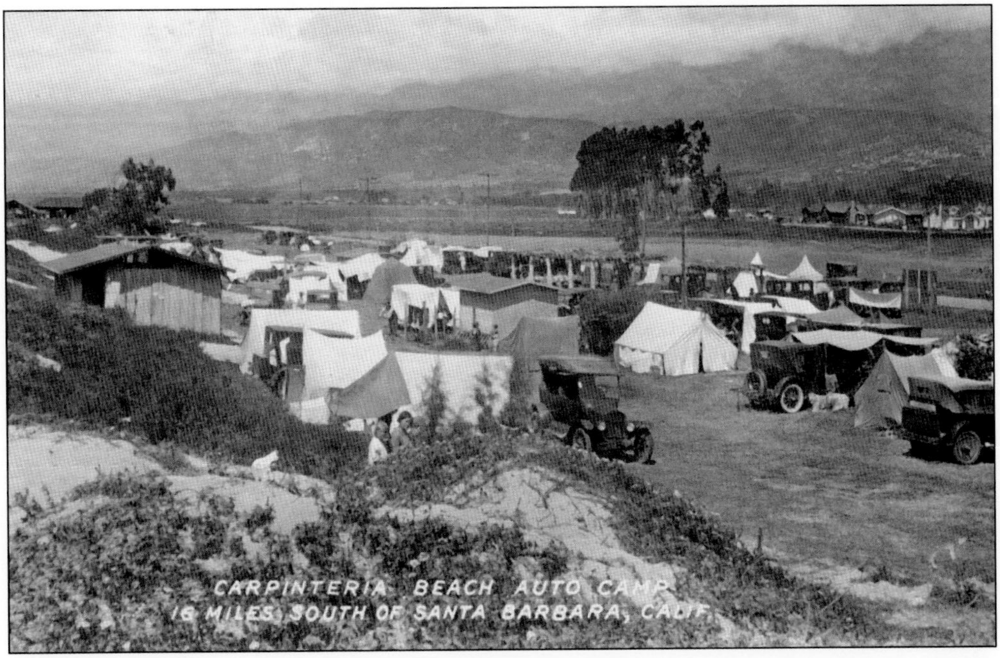

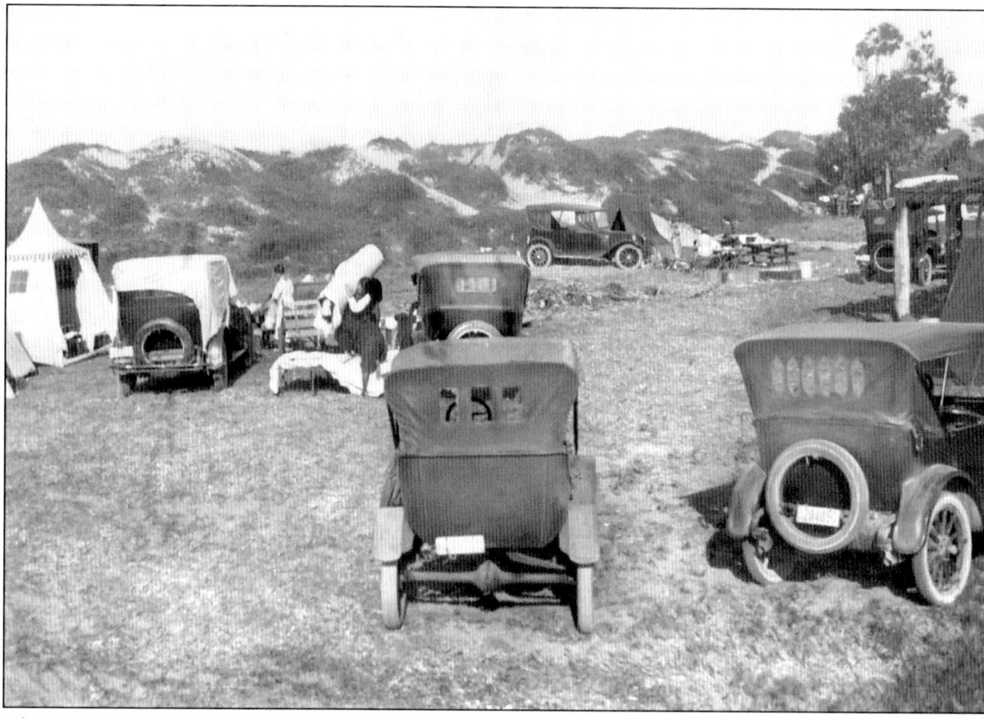

These campers look suspiciously like they might be bivouacking for the long haul in 1924. This picture was snapped at Thomas Fish's Beach Auto Camp in Carpinteria. (Courtesy Carpinteria Valley Museum of History.)

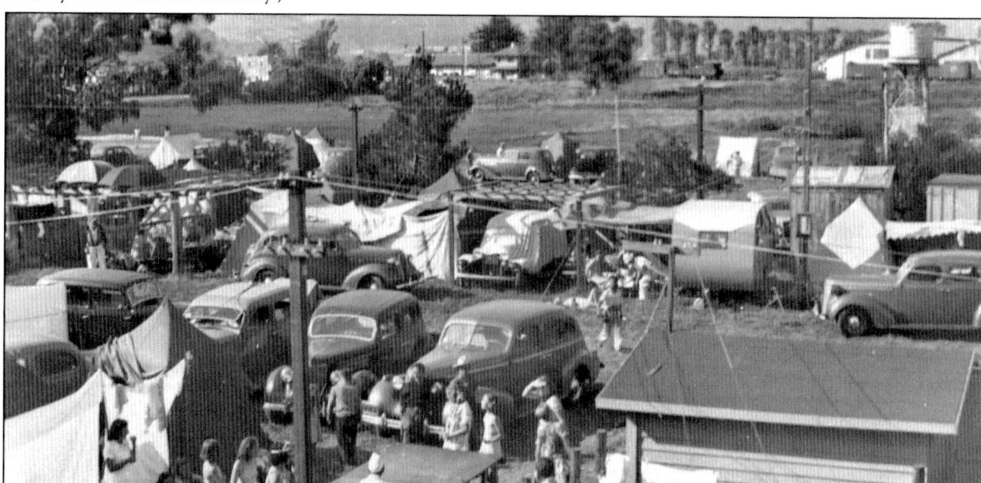

One could easily argue that this 1935 campground scene was where the old line about a picture being worth a thousand words originated. Vacationers who have spent time camping in Carpinteria often rhapsodize about how days spent at the World's Safest Beach are among their most memorable on the planet. To quote the always-erudite Dean Martin, "Memories are Made of This." (Courtesy Carpinteria Valley Museum of History.)

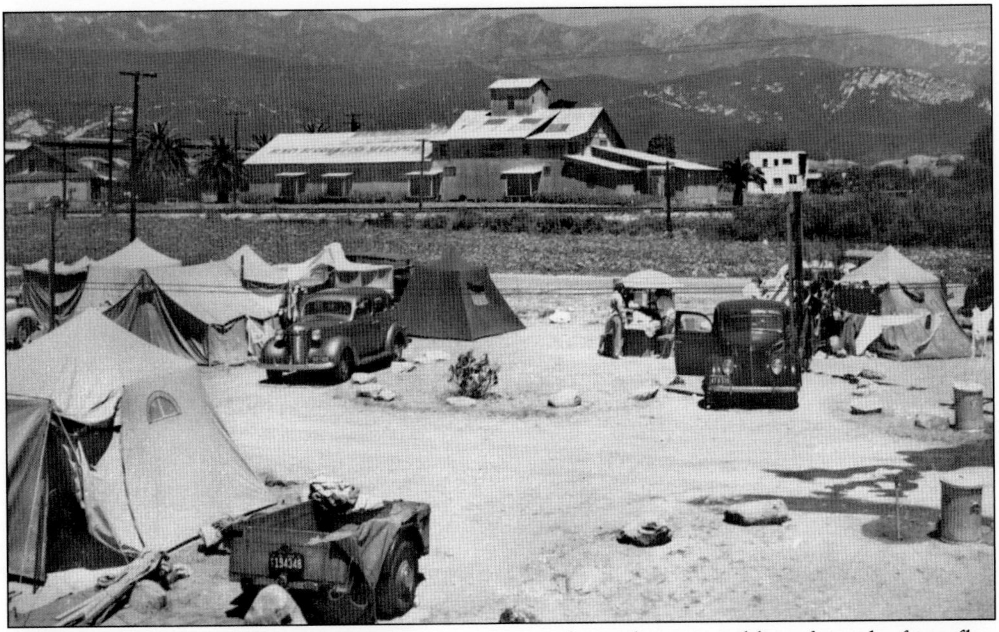

From the mountains to the shore, there were vistas as far as the eye could see from the front flap of these campers' tents in 1941. The auditory highlights provided by freight trains that ran just yards behind these campsites were up close and personal enough to shake tent stakes loose. Fish's Lima Bean Packing House stands in the background next to the railroad tracks, where the Palm Lofts are located today. (Courtesy Carpinteria Valley Museum of History.)

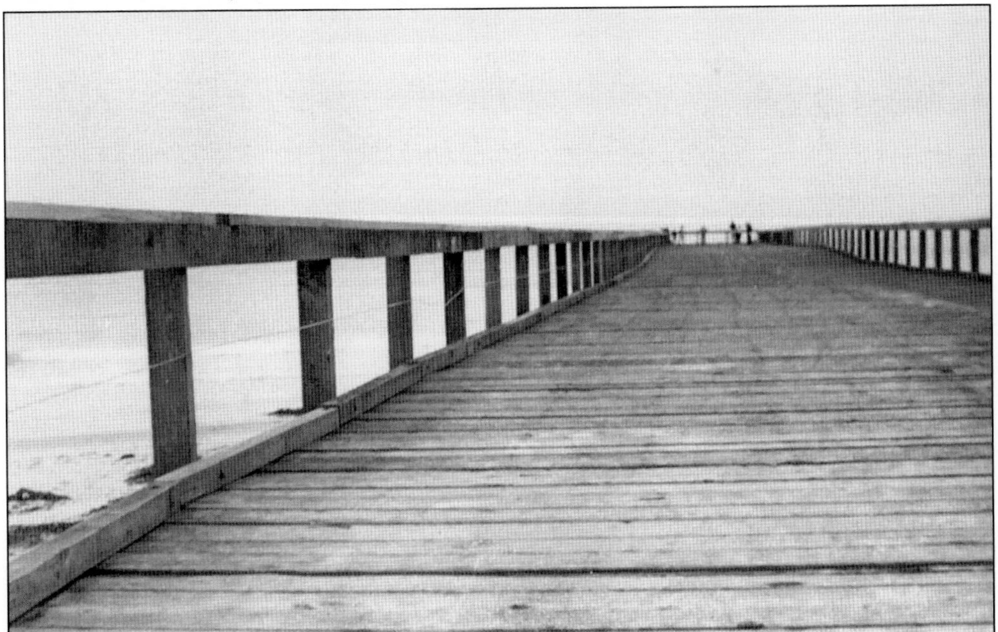

The National Park Service was no stranger to the psychological button-pushing business. Their 1939 print of the Carpinteria pier almost certainly conjured up memories for fishermen, nature lovers, local lotharios, and the occasional misguided youth who suspected that jumping off it would nudge him toward stardom, at least locally. (Courtesy Carpinteria Valley Museum of History.)

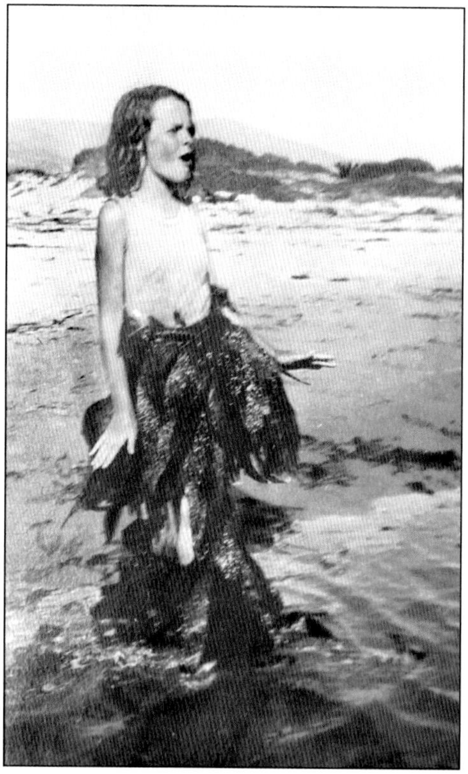

Sartorial splendor unleashed, this young lady has attired herself in a timelessly stylish kelp ensemble around 1935. It was perfect for lazy beach afternoons—water not a problem. (Courtesy Carpinteria Valley Museum of History.)

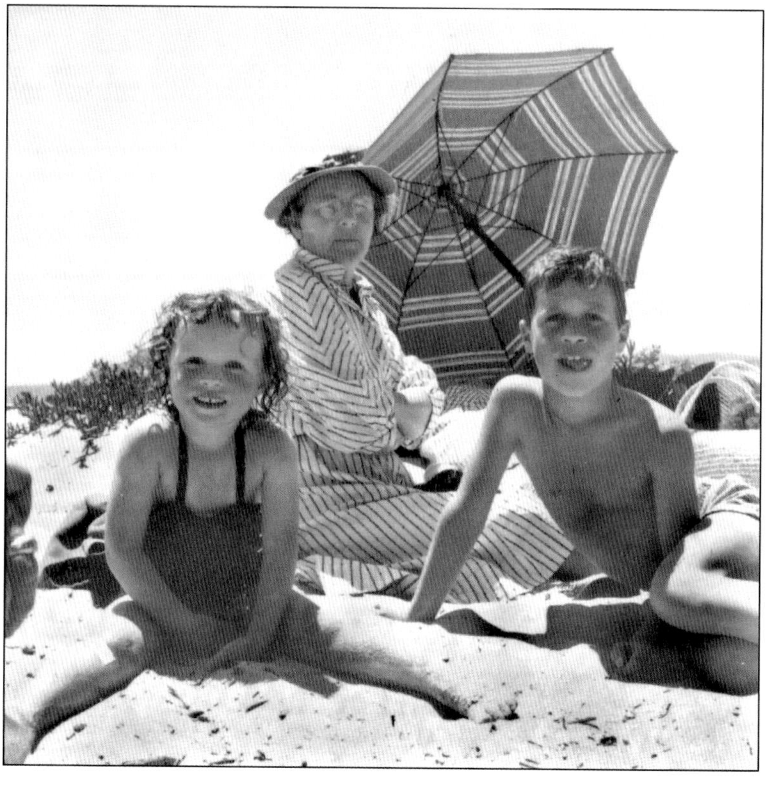

Just because Joe Hendy was working overtime putting the finishing touches on another of his much-loved valley homes in 1925 was no reason Miriam Hendy and the kids, James and little Miriam, couldn't spend the day making like tourists at Carpinteria Beach. (Courtesy Carpinteria Valley Museum of History.)

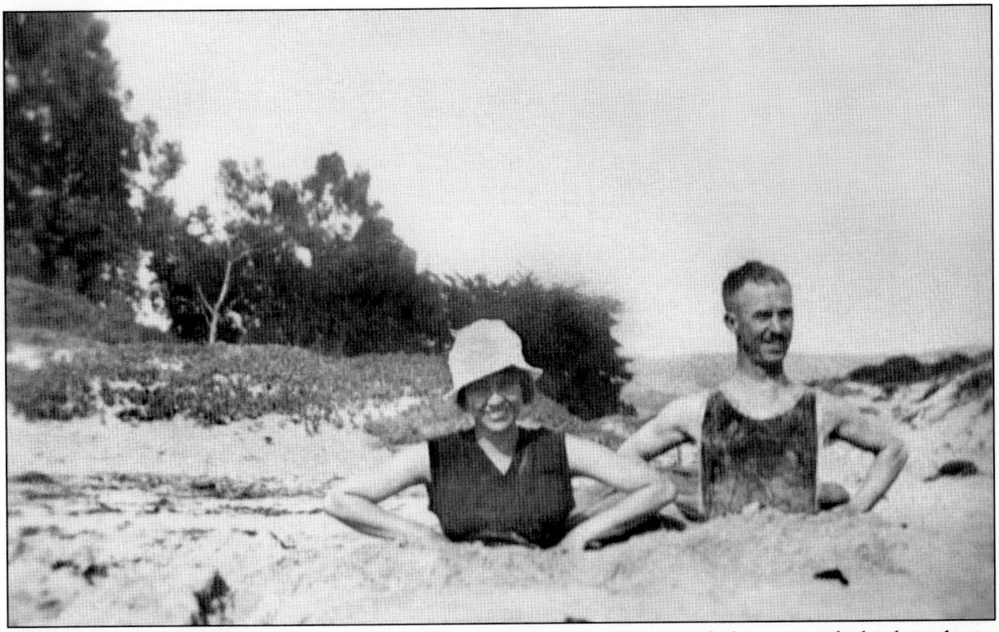

These two merrymakers didn't let formality get between them and their seaside high jinks in 1919. The memo on the reverse of this snapshot reads, "Wig and Dorothea, not even yet fiancés." (Courtesy Carpinteria Valley Museum of History.)

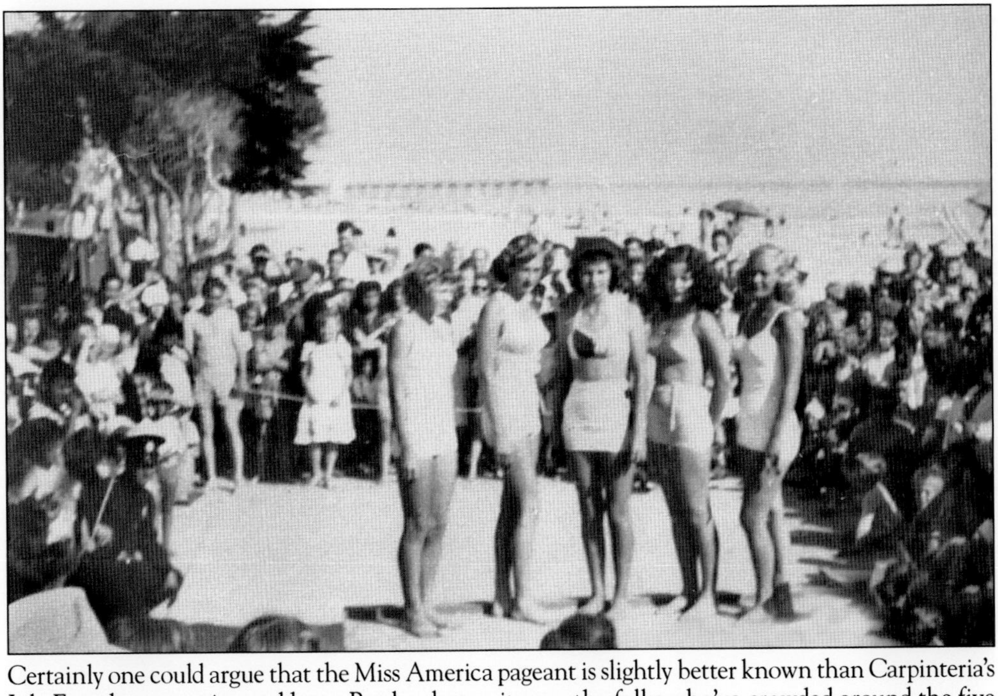

Certainly one could argue that the Miss America pageant is slightly better known than Carpinteria's July Fourth event, pictured here. But be that as it may, the folks who've crowded around the five young finalists in 1949 seem every bit as enthusiastic as the attendees at an Atlantic City event. (Courtesy Carpinteria Valley Museum of History.)

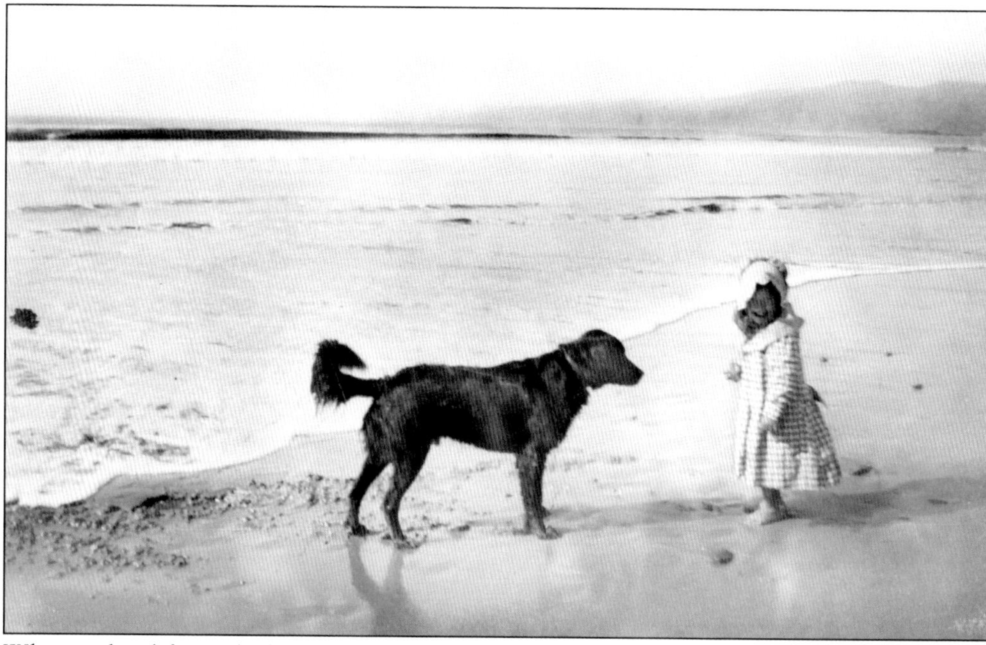

Who needs a lifeguard when man's best friend is on the case? This young lady appears to be looking for some adult muscle to escort her past the resolute family pet. (Courtesy Carpinteria Valley Museum of History.)

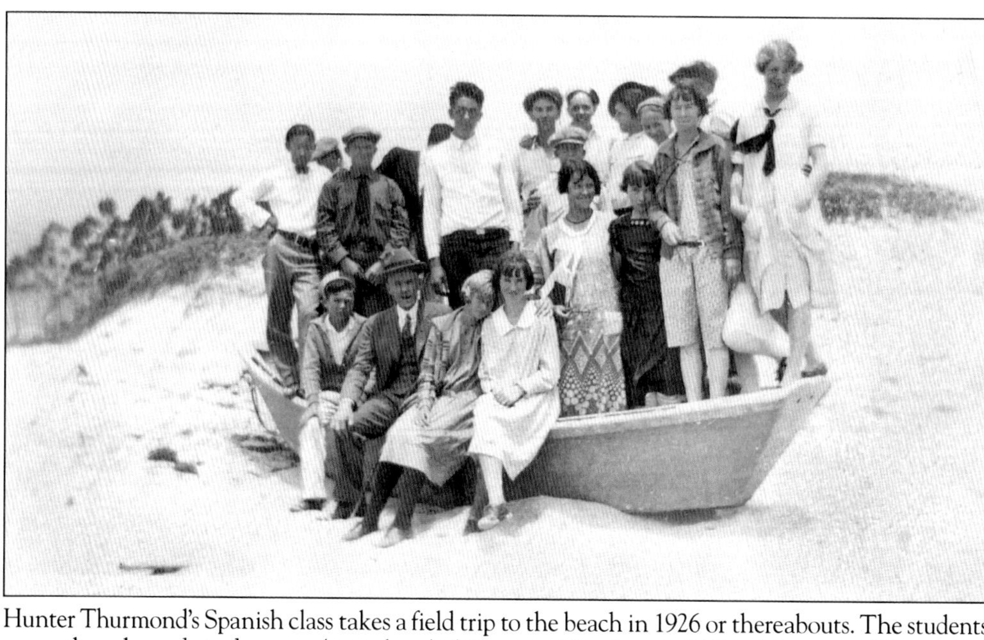

Hunter Thurmond's Spanish class takes a field trip to the beach in 1926 or thereabouts. The students are gathered in a *bote de remos* (a rowboat). (Courtesy Carpinteria Valley Museum of History.)

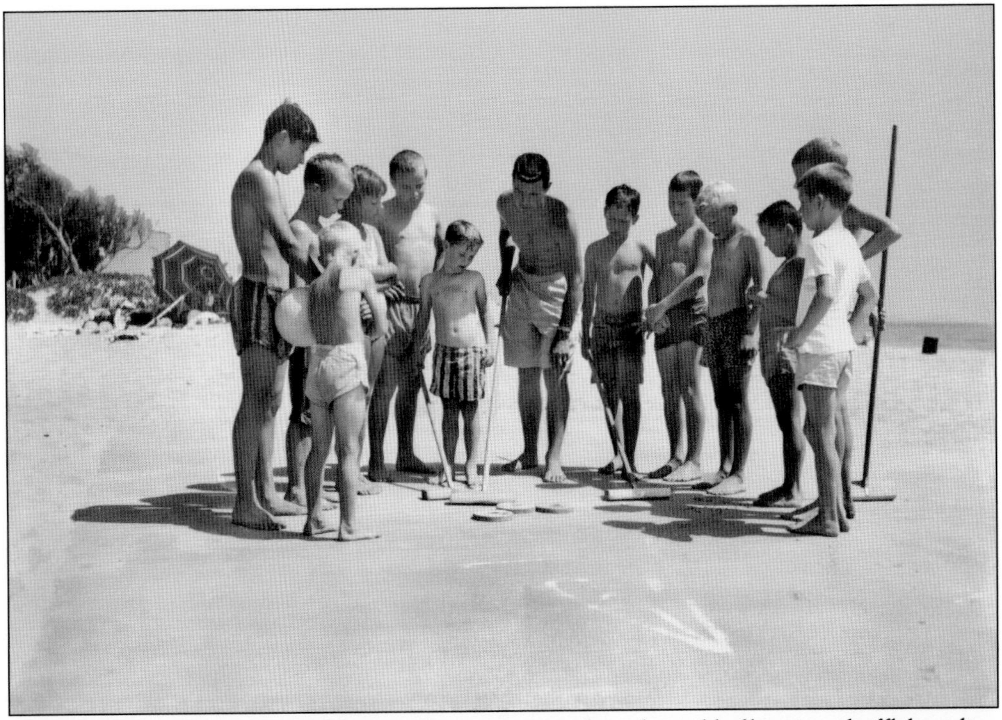

This shuffleboard veteran was educating his protégés in the wily world of big-time shuffleboarding in 1950. (Courtesy Carpinteria Valley Museum of History.)

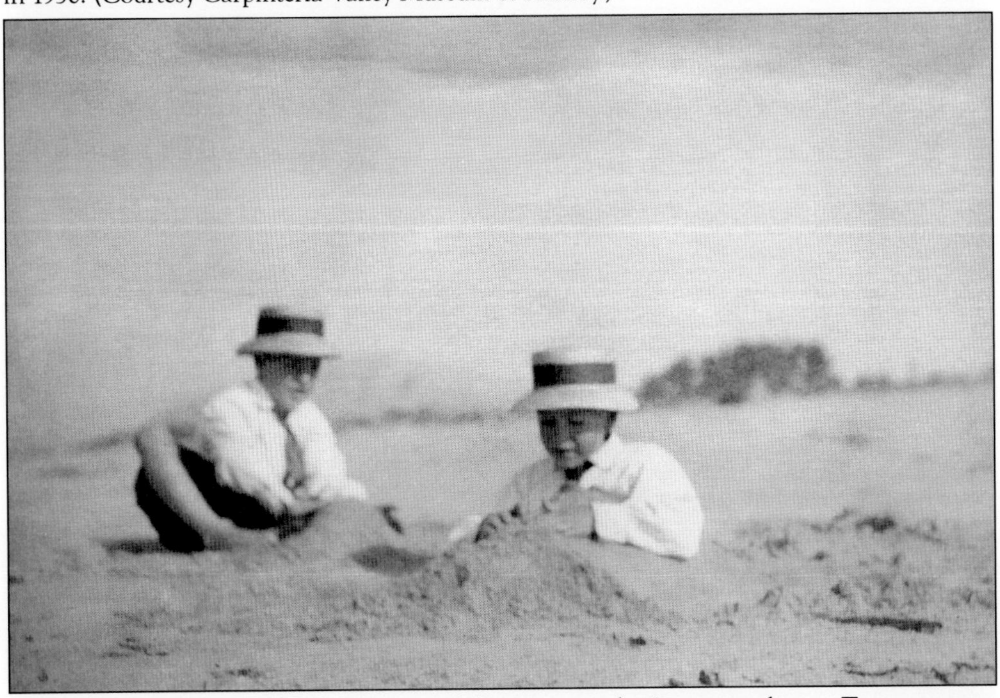

Just because they're up to their necks in sand doesn't mean they're not gentlemen. Two youngsters who appear to be enjoying themselves immensely manage to maintain proper beach decorum, attire-wise, in 1912. (Courtesy Carpinteria Valley Museum of History.)

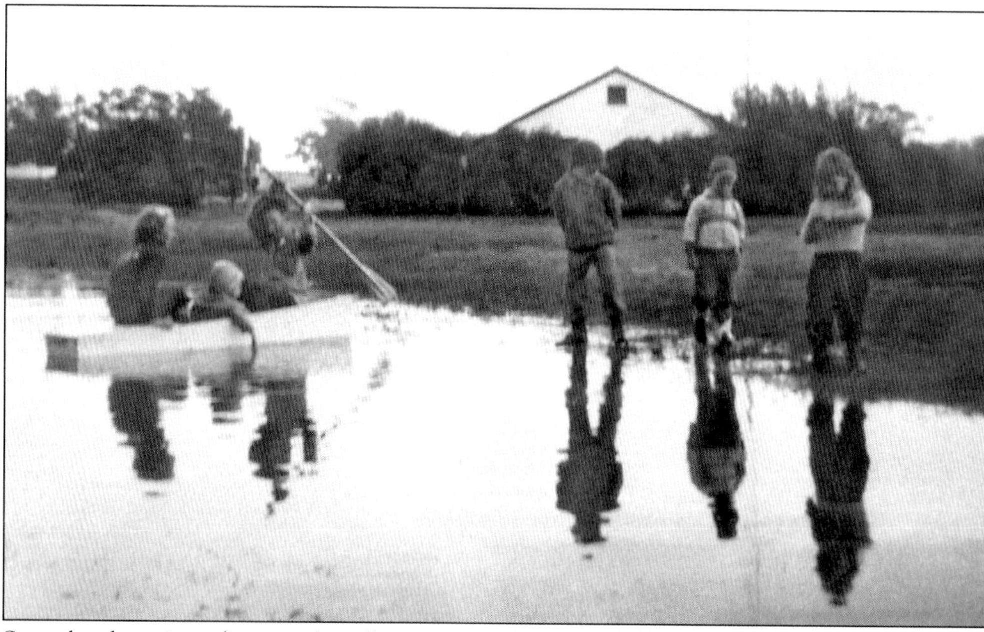

Some local mariners live out their fantasies in a Carpinteria lagoon. Although there is no date accompanying this photograph, it's clearly from an earlier era, as parental health and safety concerns would almost certainly have precluded an adventure of this magnitude in 2009. One has to wonder whether these youngsters or their modern-day counterparts were the bigger winners in the life experience sweepstakes. (Courtesy Carpinteria Valley Museum of History.)

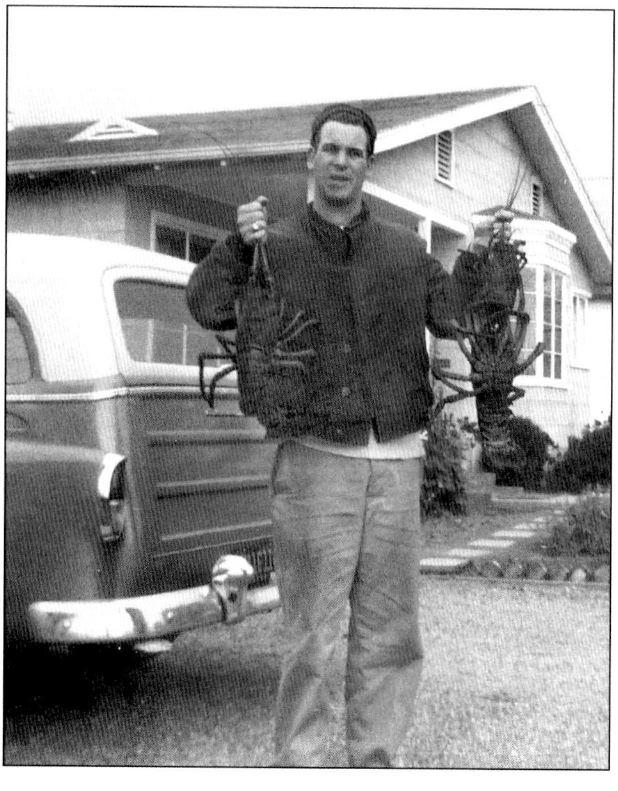

It doesn't take Sherlock Holmes to surmise that this photograph of Bob Latham, lobsters in hand and Chevy wagon cooling its heels to his left, was almost certainly taken in the 1950s. If Carpinterians wanted lobster during this era, they simply checked in with King Neptune at Carpinteria Beach. (Courtesy Vera Bensen.)

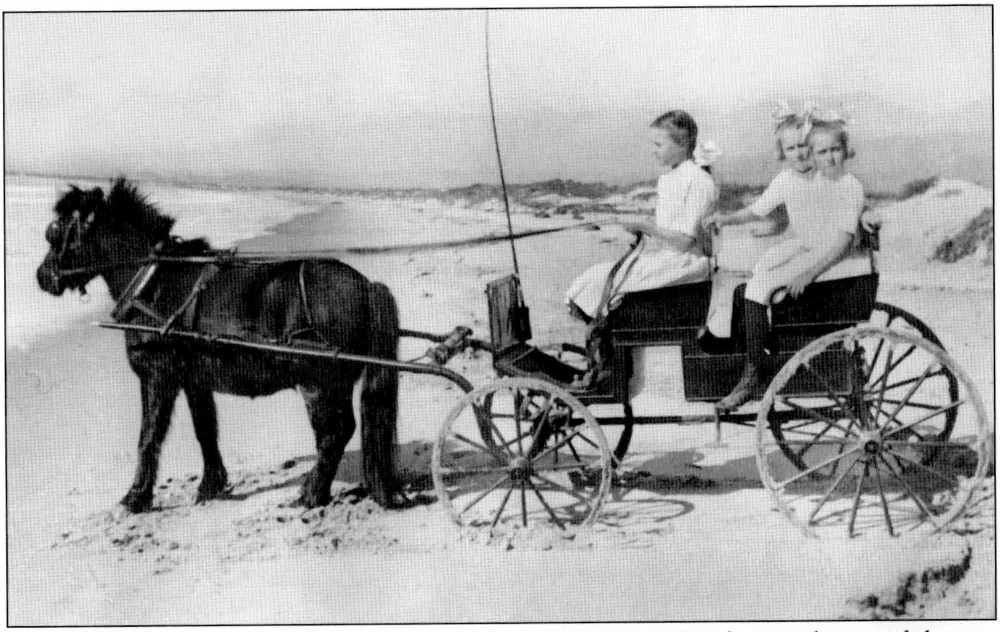

How much better could it possibly get than this—Carpinteria Beach, two close confederates, and a horse and buggy? One has to wonder what motivated Altharetta Franklin, seated in the front, and Geraldine and Josephine Franklin, riding in the rear, to turn around once they took off down the beach in the early 1900s. Dinner perhaps? (Courtesy Carpinteria Valley Museum of History.)

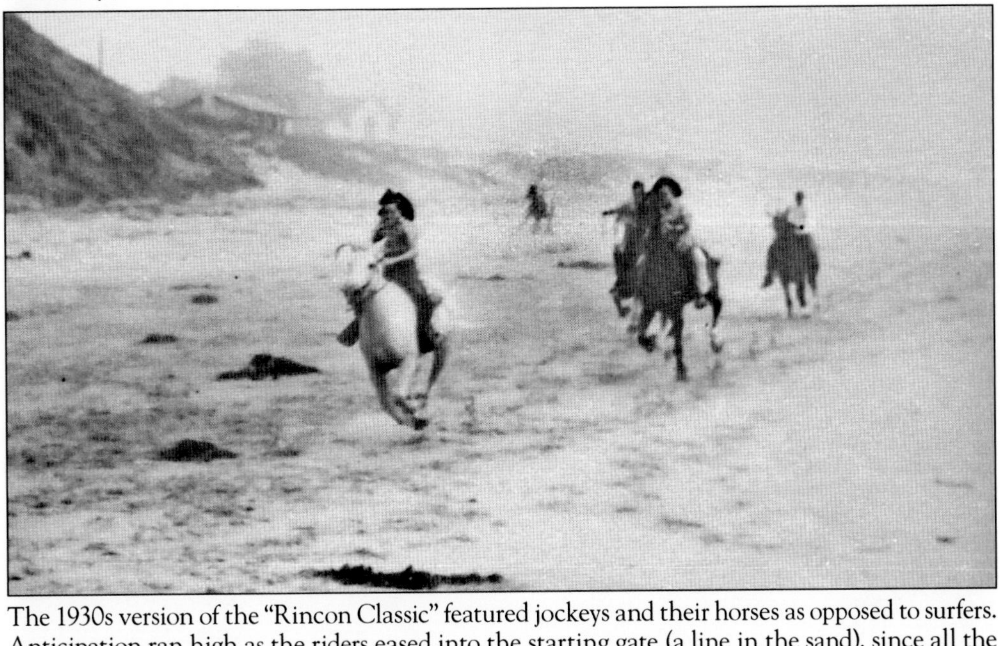

The 1930s version of the "Rincon Classic" featured jockeys and their horses as opposed to surfers. Anticipation ran high as the riders eased into the starting gate (a line in the sand), since all the participants were fully aware of the stakes—bragging rights in Carpinteria and beyond for at least a week. Joan Rock is being pursued by Bonita Baker, Bob Bates, Lawrence Bailard, and an unidentified rider just barely visible in the background. (Courtesy Carpinteria Valley Museum of History.)

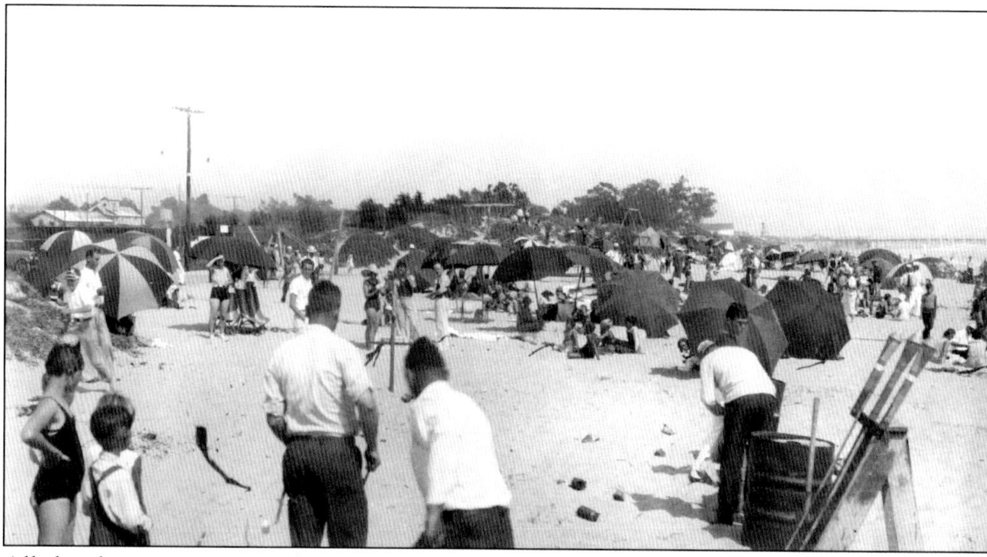

All the elements necessary for a serious July Fourth celebration are present and accounted for in this 1925 image, the major tip-off being the rack of fireworks poised for action. (Courtesy Carpinteria Valley Museum of History.)

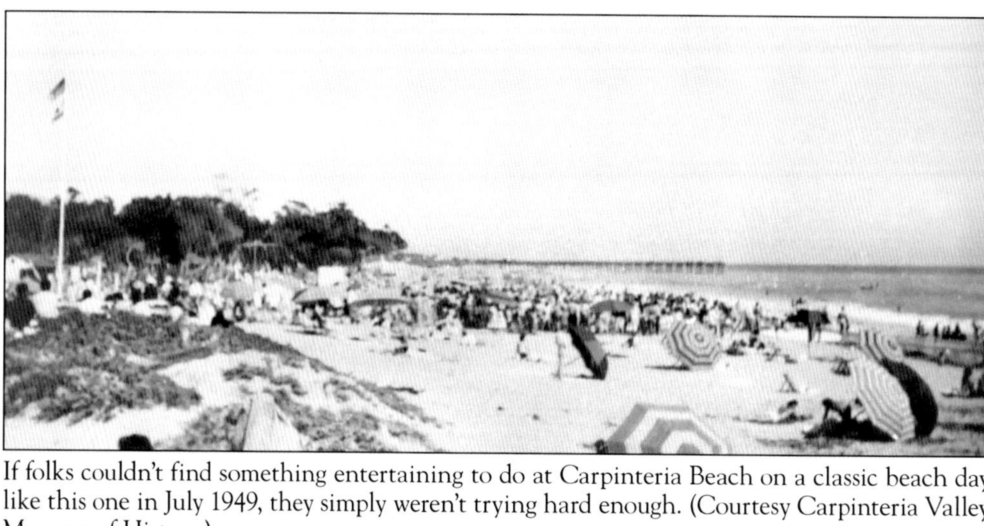

If folks couldn't find something entertaining to do at Carpinteria Beach on a classic beach day like this one in July 1949, they simply weren't trying hard enough. (Courtesy Carpinteria Valley Museum of History.)

Four

Thrills, Spills, and Season's Greetings

The Thunderbowl's story, like a healthy portion of most nostalgic recollections, is an amalgam of reality and legend. Every local who weighs in on the Thunderbowl routinely leads with a pensive gaze, a crooked grin, and the delivery of this line: "I snuck into the Thunderbowl on a weekly basis for years." Each reflection is then embellished with a descriptive listing of highlights that, at least in the view of the Carpinterian doing the telling, borders on the epic, generally rivaling the thrills and spills of the just barely better-known Indianapolis 500.

In some ways, of course, the Thunderbowl was epic. The players included iconic drivers, both male and female: Indianapolis 500 winners Parnelli Jones, Bill Vukovich, and Troy Ruttman (the youngest Indy winner at 21); Indy participant Jack McGraff; Hiela Paulson (the first woman in California to drive a NASCAR stock car); and local legend Spencer Blickenstaff, a studious, dedicated teacher by day who morphed into R. Spencer, a wily, competitive jalopy racer at night. If this isn't tiptoeing along the periphery of epic, one has to wonder what is. How could the Thunderbowl faithful not be captivated by this cast of characters and their daredevil antics?

Meanwhile, at the northwest end of Carpinteria, another kind of magic was materializing. Carpinteria's gigantic roadside Santa and his thematically influenced neighbors on Santa Claus Lane spent more than half a century distributing goodwill and cheer to youngsters of all ages. Santa's efforts led to flattering coverage in three books, two magazine articles, a television spot on Comedy Central, and a short run on an architectural preservation journal's Web site, verifying that the enthusiasm Carpinterians have expressed for their roadside Kris Kringle over the decades is also shared by thousands of Americans nationwide.

The deal that was struck between a Carpinteria juice stand owner and an artistically inclined motorist in 1948 yielded karmic results that far exceeded the $500 that changed hands for the construction of this bearded beacon of merriment.

A racetrack at one end of town and a giant bearded man in red at the other, it could only happen in Carpinteria!

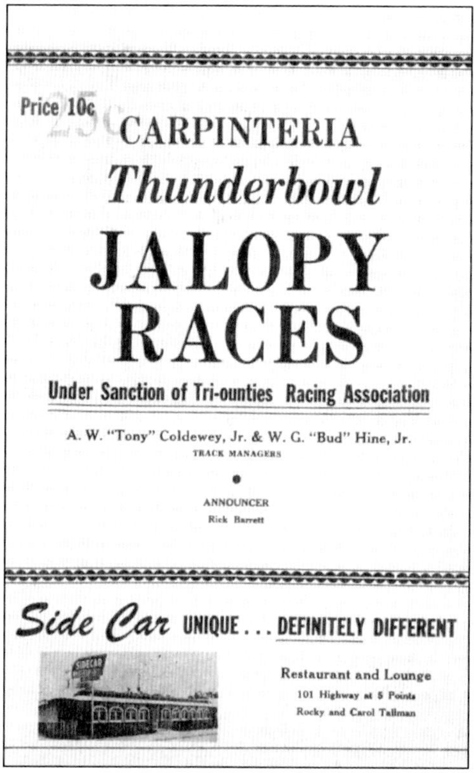

The Thunderbowl Race Track, located at the east end of Carpinteria's stretch of the Coast Highway (today's Carpinteria Avenue), was a home away from home for racing aficionados from the late 1940s right up to the mid-1960s. Midget cars, jalopies, motorcycles, and stock cars were all featured in weekly racing duels. (Courtesy Lee Hammock.)

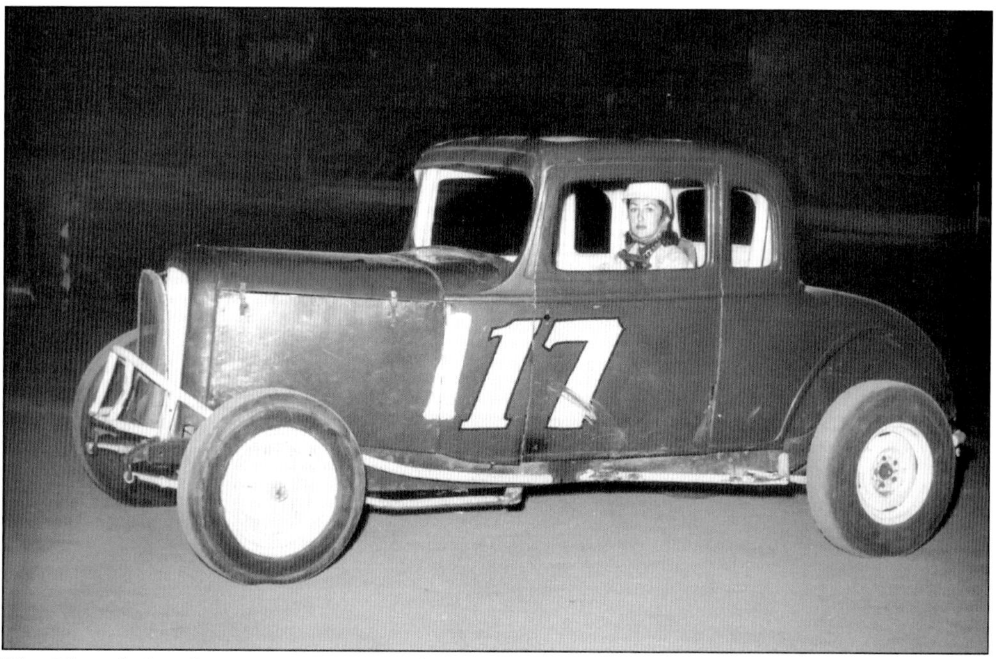

The Thunderbowl's operation was on the cutting edge of equal opportunity employment in 1955, particularly for a sport that was so heavy on testosterone. If you look closely you'll see that there's a young lady—Hiela Paulson, to be more specific—behind the wheel of car 117. (Courtesy Lee Hammock.)

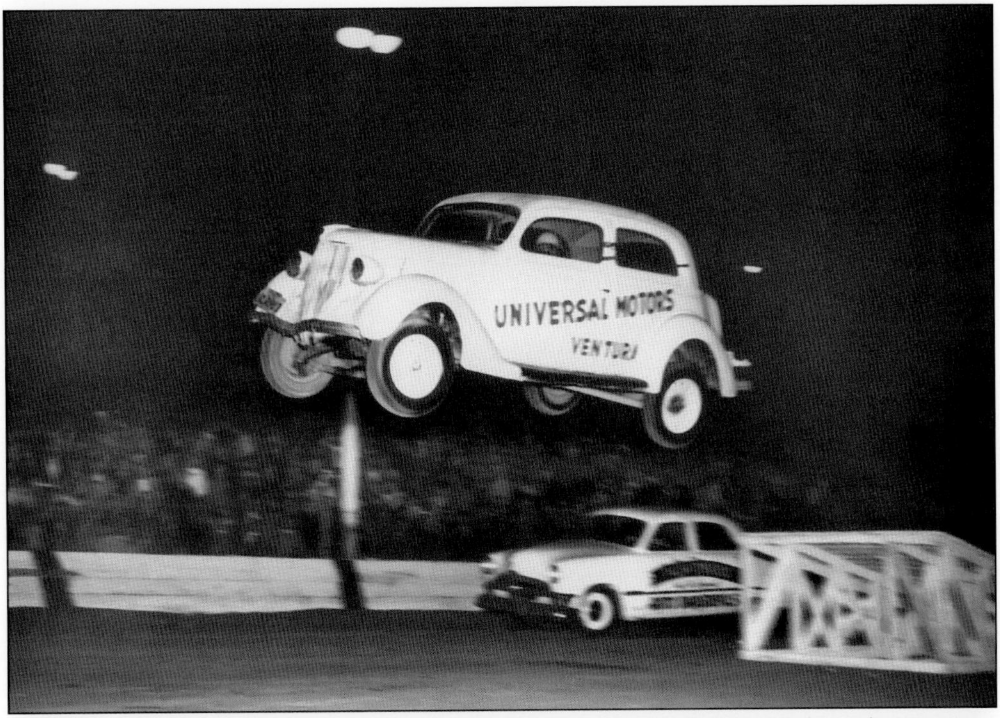

A Universal Motors driver grabs some air in 1951. And you thought Evel Knievel was the originator of all those daredevil stunts of his. (Courtesy Lee Hammock.)

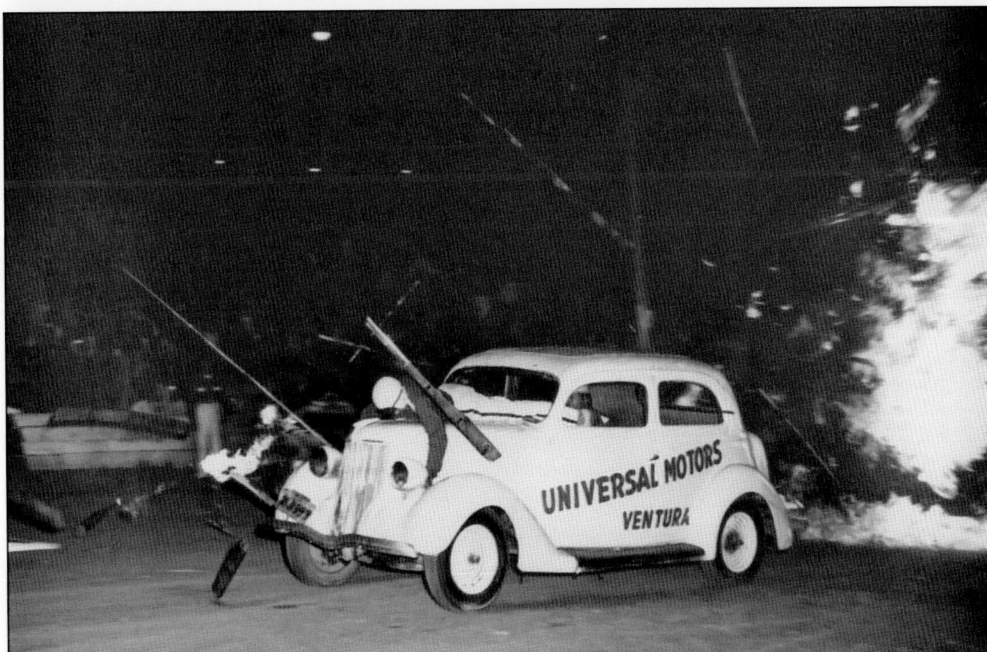

Apparently blasting through a ring of fire had become old news, so the wild man pictured here upped the ante—he rode through the flames lying on the hood of his sedan, with a small assist from a copilot who did the driving. (Courtesy Carpinteria Valley Museum of History.)

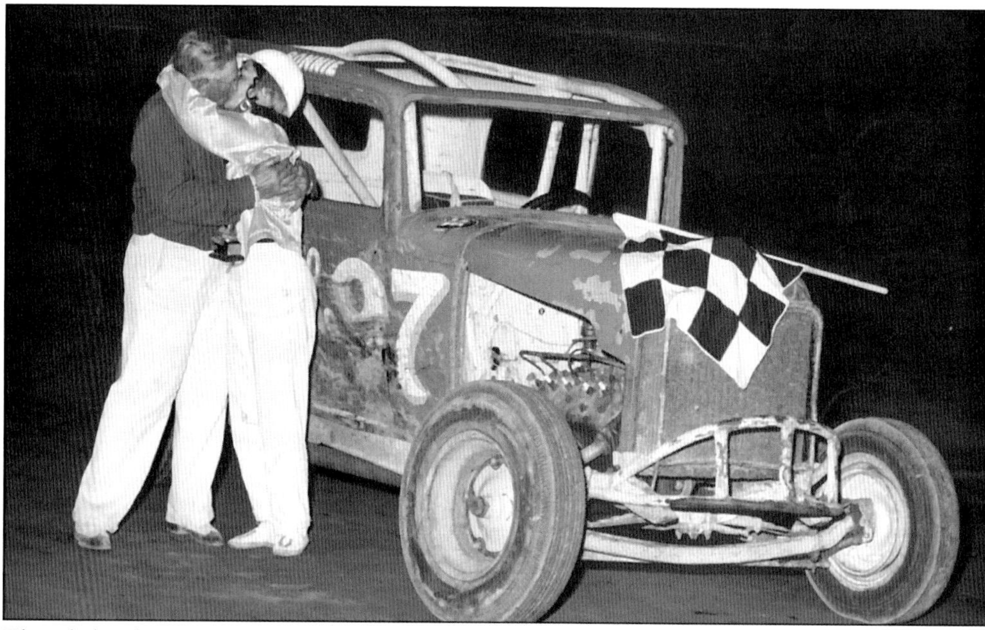

Thunderbowl owner Jim Slaybaugh makes a trophy presentation to a young lady who had just won her heat around 1950 and has the checkered flag on her hood to prove it. A hearty handshake usually sufficed for the men, unless one of the Thunderbowl's trophy girls did the honors, in which case the Slaybaugh technique demonstrated here was generally employed. (Courtesy Lee Hammock.)

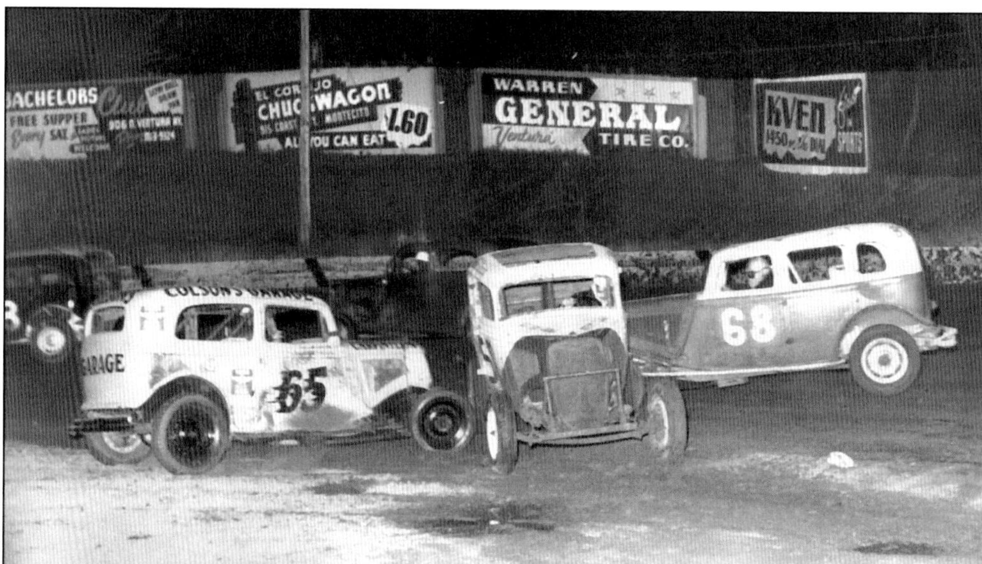

Advertisers lined up to peddle their wares in Thunderbowl programs and on the racetrack's walls. Their enthusiasm for things "Thunderbowlian" made perfect sense when Slaybaugh's participants delivered the level of excitement pictured here in 1950. Number 65 on the left is local favorite Lee Hammock. (Courtesy Carpinteria Valley Museum of History.)

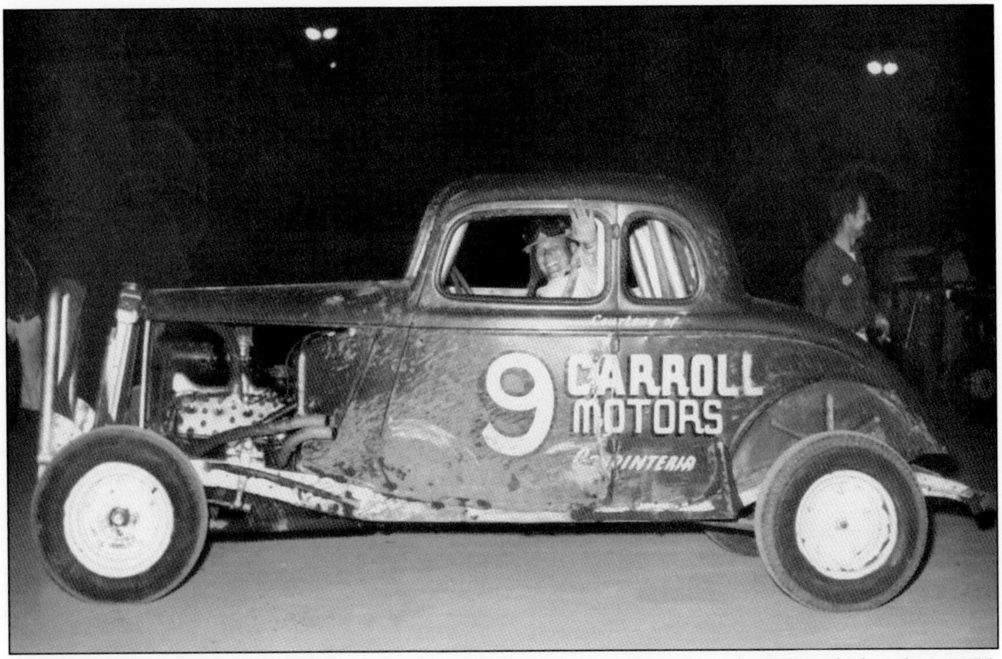

Teacher Spencer Blickenstaff drove under the alias of R. Spencer at the Thunderbowl in 1955. That's "R" grinning from ear to ear as he cruises by in Carroll Motors car No. 9. The magic of the moment appears to have trumped Spencer's concerns about maintaining his clandestine identity. (Courtesy Lee Hammock.)

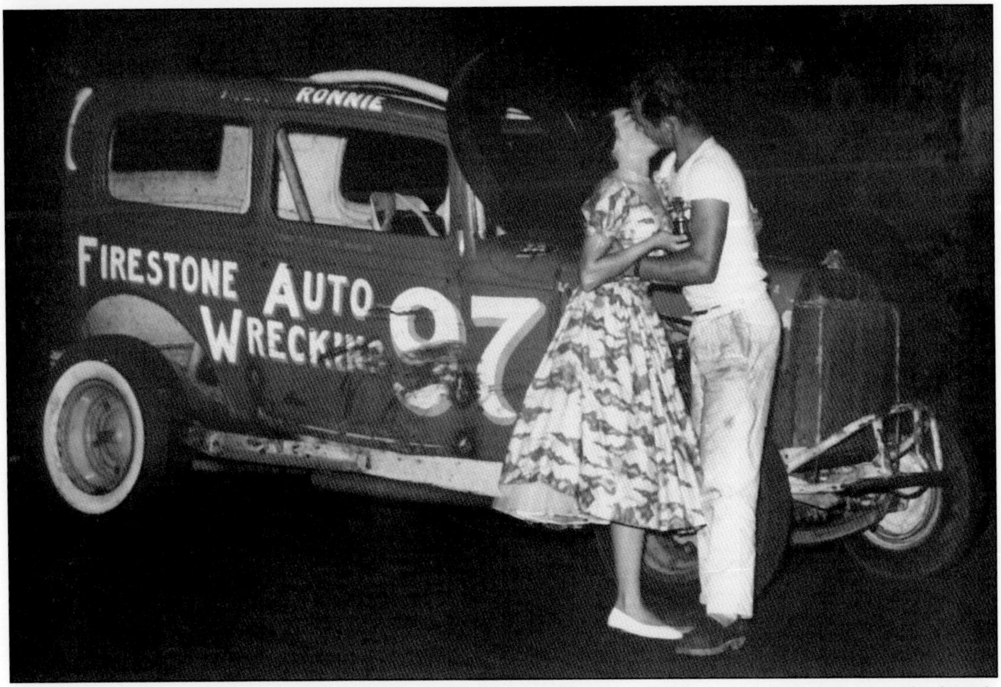

Those who won, as Parnelli Jones made it a habit of doing in 1951, were instantly gratified with a trophy, a brief embrace, and a kiss from the evening's trophy girl. (Courtesy Carpinteria Valley Museum of History.)

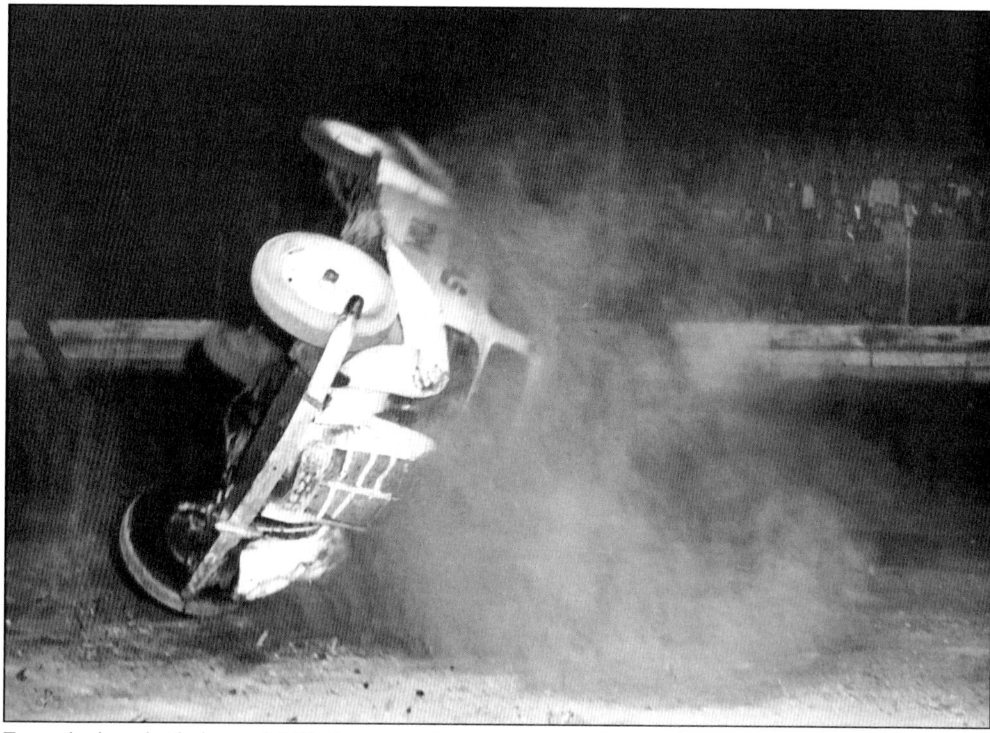

Even the best-laid plans of skilled drivers often go awry, as shown above around 1955. Fortunately, the driver of this rolling jalopy didn't require the services of the gentleman pictured below. (Both courtesy Carpinteria Valley Museum of History.)

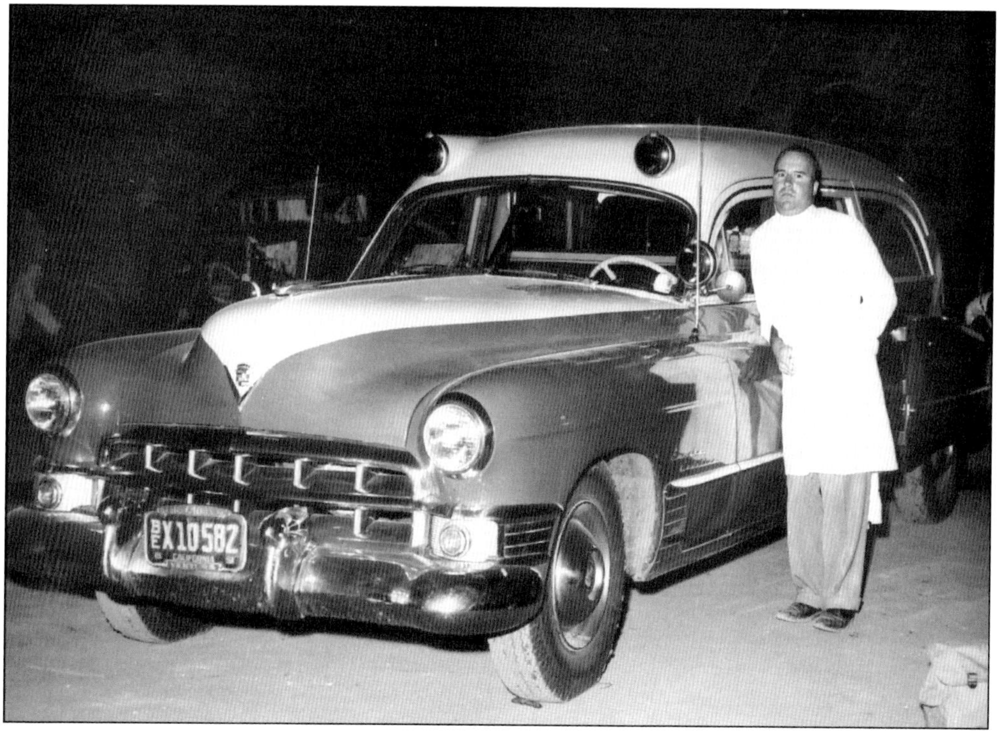

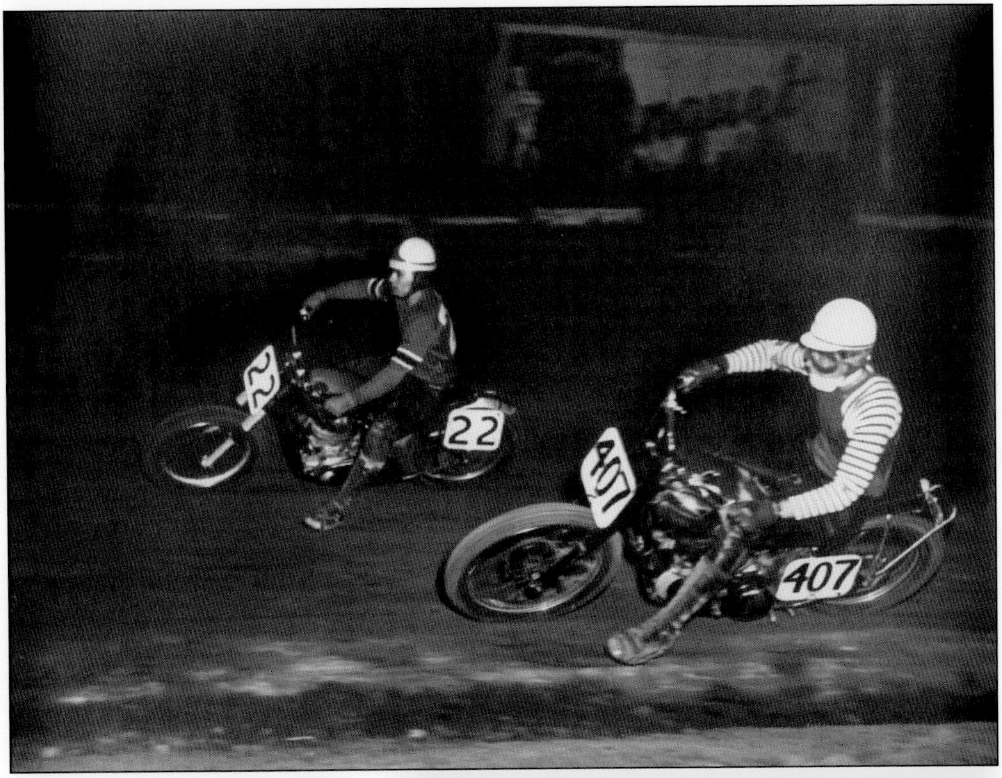

Number 22, Johnny McLaughlin, nosed out Larry Scott, No. 407, in this Thunderbowl duel in 1950, and then, ironically, was handed his trophy by Sandy Scott, who was Larry's wife. (Both courtesy Carpinteria Valley Museum of History.)

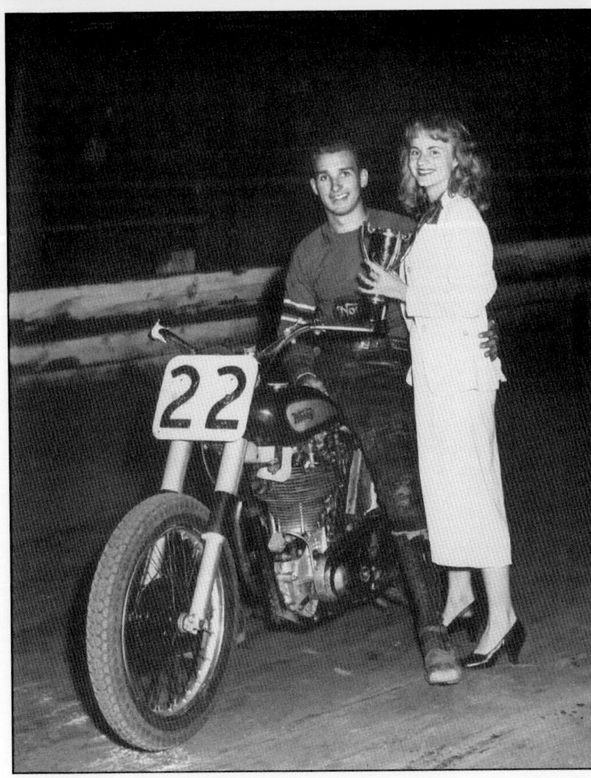

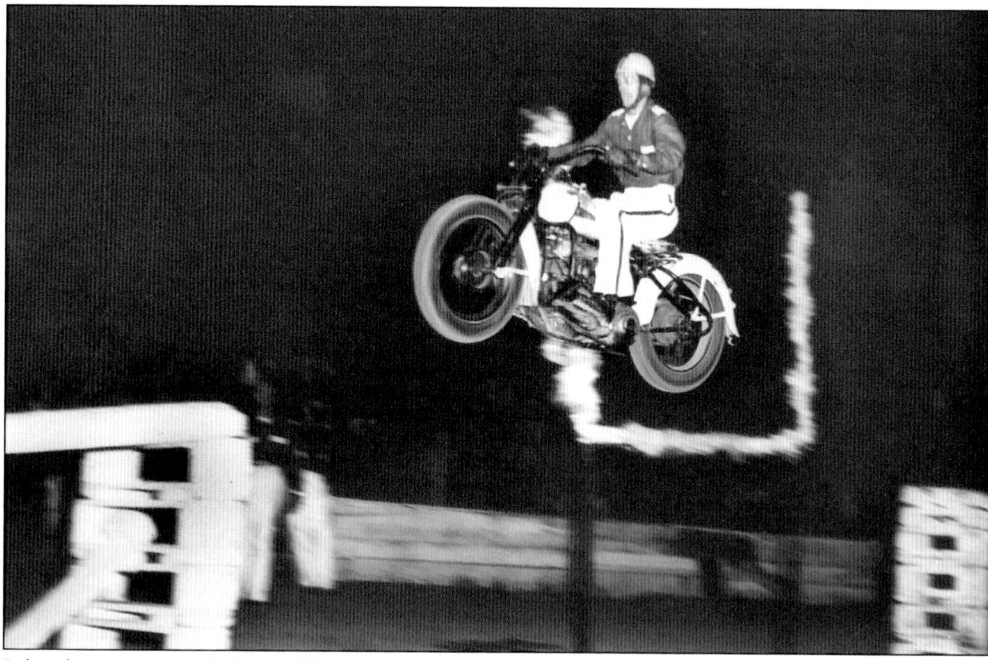

It has been suggested that real bravery is appreciating the danger at hand and pushing on in spite of it. And if that's the case, then this *c.* 1951 motorcycle rider had courage to spare, as he appears to fully comprehend the risks of launching his motorcycle from ramp to ramp through a goalpost of fire. (Courtesy Carpinteria Valley Museum of History.)

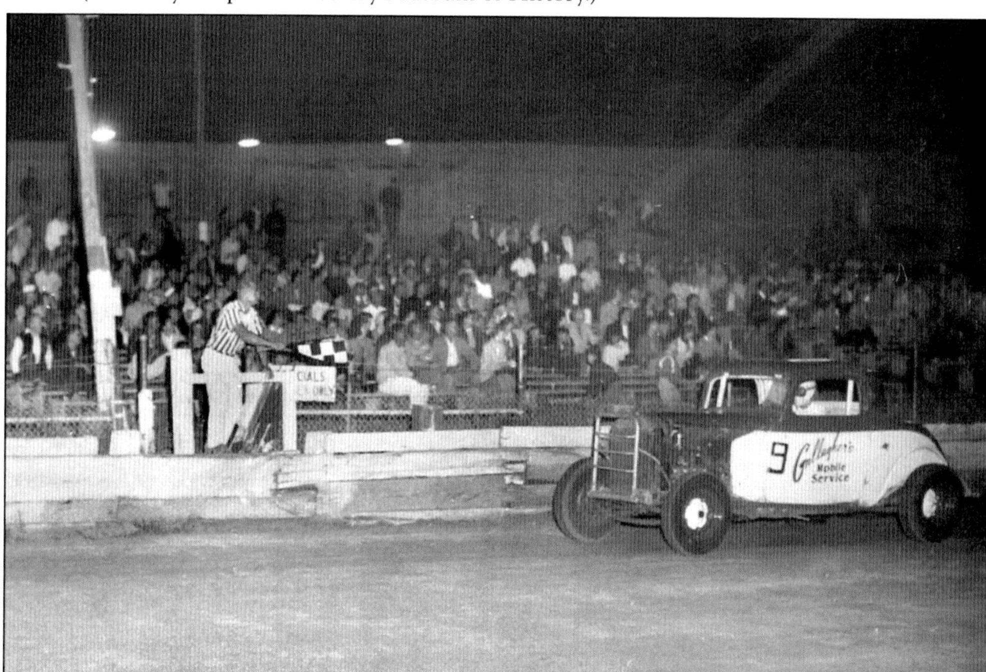

In this *c.* 1950 picture, the checkered flag was being waved for car No. 9, and the crowd went wild. No wonder television hadn't really taken hold—how could it possibly compete with a Thunderbowl date and thrills like this one? (Courtesy Carpinteria Valley Museum of History.)

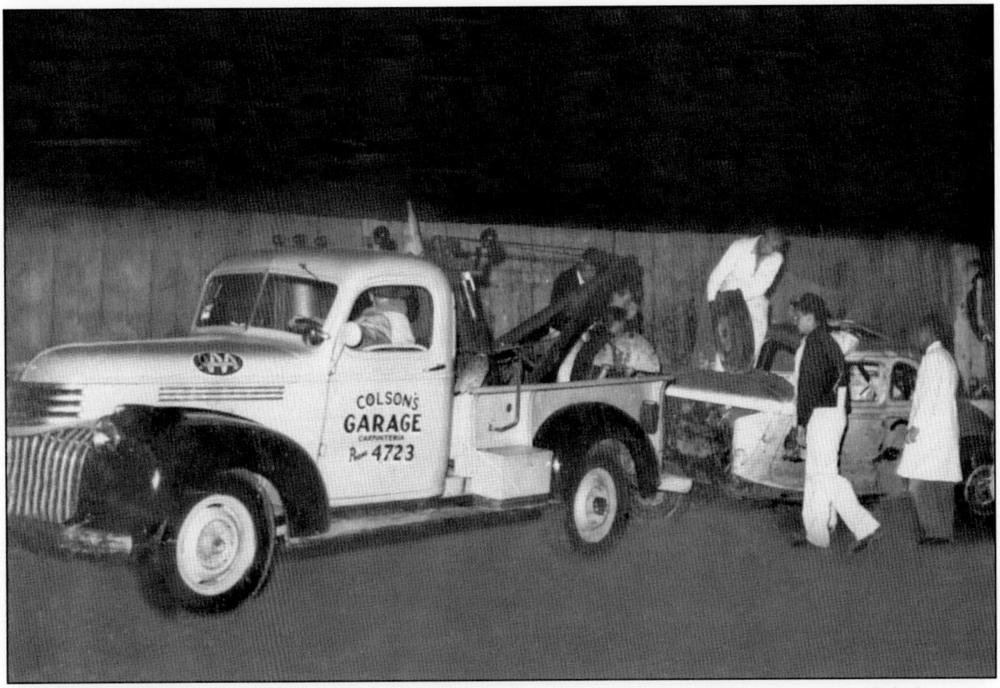

Colson's Garage was a full service Thunderbowl provider in the 1950s. Not only did they tow battered cars off the track, but they sponsored cars that performed on it as well. (Courtesy Carpinteria Valley Museum of History.)

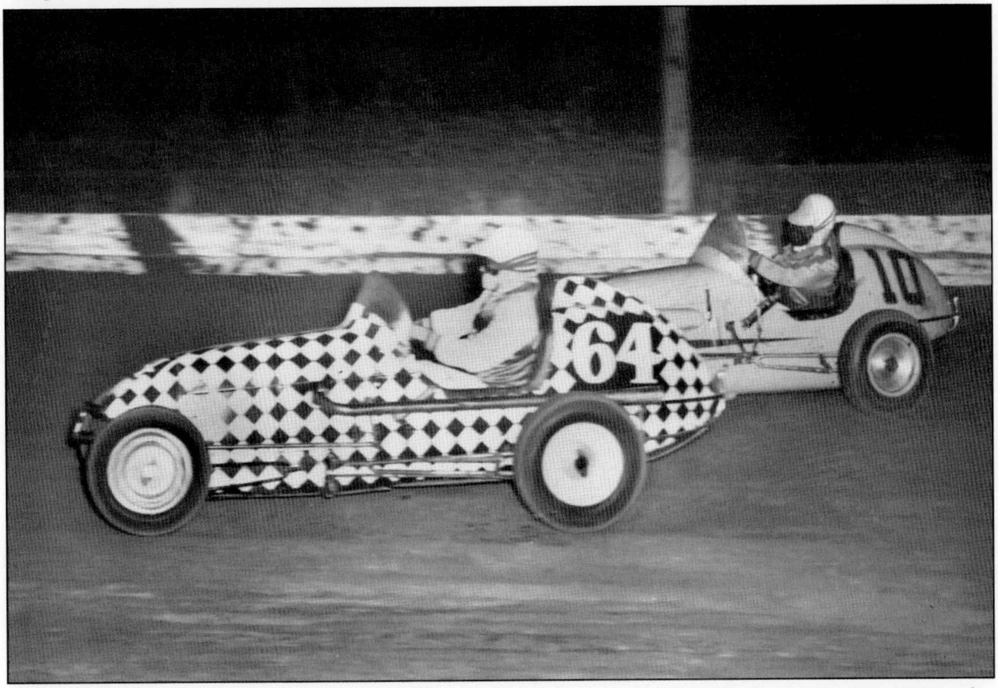

This *c.* 1947 action shot of two midget racers is particularly noteworthy, since No. 64 is the legendary Bill Vukovich, who won the Indianapolis 500 and was later killed in a horrendous crash at Indianapolis as he attempted to win again. (Courtesy Carpinteria Valley Museum of History.)

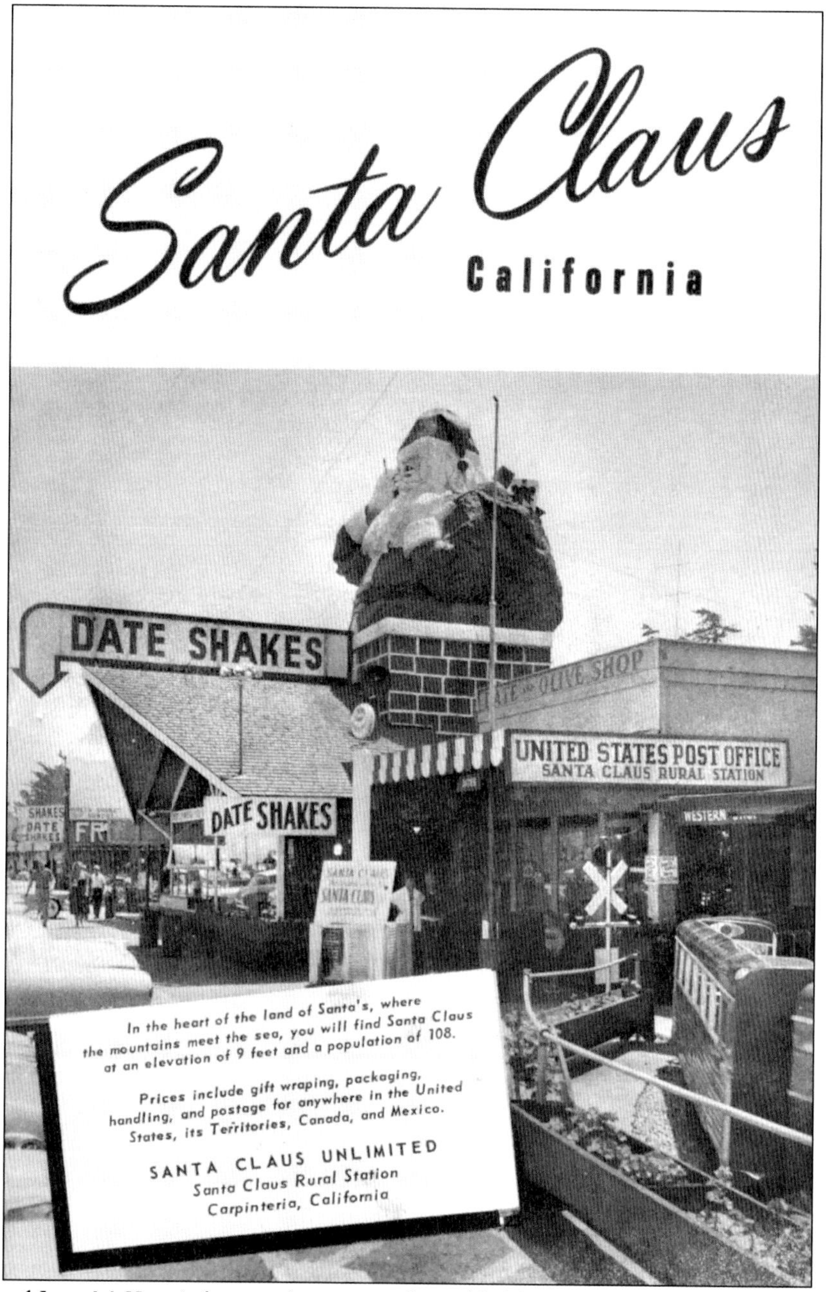

Patrick and June McKeon's five-stool juice stand quickly blossomed into a Santa-driven seaside mall that gained national prominence during its magical run in Carpinteria's northwestern outskirts. During the glory years, Santa was joined on the roofs of his Santa Claus Lane digs by a snowman and a reindeer-driven sleigh. At the height of its popularity, the lane got so "big" that the McKeons began a worldwide mail order business via catalogues like the one pictured here. The text on the catalogue's cover reads, in part, "In the heart of the land of Santa, where the mountains meet the sea, you will find Santa Claus at an elevation of 9 feet with a population of 108. Santa Claus Unlimited—Santa Claus rural station—Carpinteria, CA." (Courtesy Carpinteria Valley Museum of History.)

Being an honorary citizen of Santa Claus, California, was no walk in the park, as attested to in this "Santa Claus Pledge" list. Not surprisingly, the boldfaced bottom line directed all potential card carrying members to "Believe in Santa Claus." (Courtesy Carpinteria Valley Museum of History.)

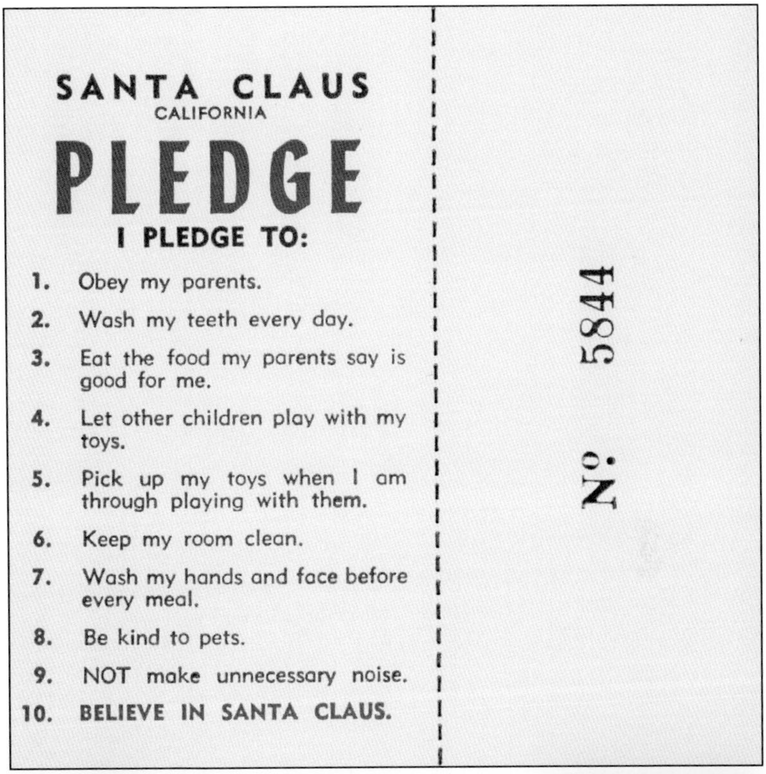

SANTA CLAUS
CALIFORNIA

PLEDGE

I PLEDGE TO:

1. Obey my parents.
2. Wash my teeth every day.
3. Eat the food my parents say is good for me.
4. Let other children play with my toys.
5. Pick up my toys when I am through playing with them.
6. Keep my room clean.
7. Wash my hands and face before every meal.
8. Be kind to pets.
9. NOT make unnecessary noise.
10. **BELIEVE IN SANTA CLAUS.**

Nº 5844

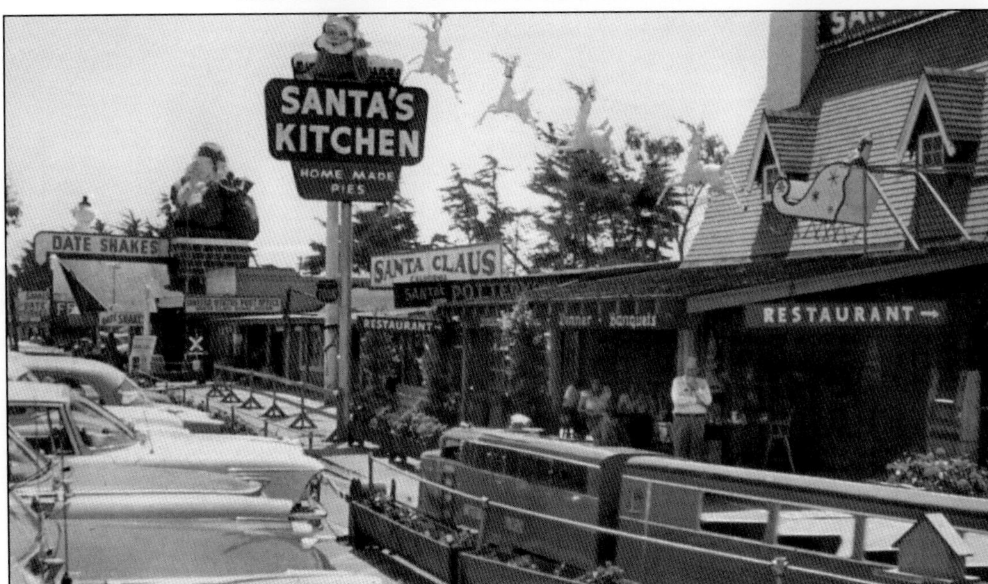

This photograph of Santa Claus Lane was taken in its heyday, the 1950s and 1960s. On the rooftop to the far left is Frosty, who's joined by Santa, his reindeer and sleigh, and a sign for Santa's Kitchen. At bottom right, the lane's train eases into view. Don Ness, an engineer on Santa's railroad, remembers that riders on the train often got more ride than they bargained for, and while this was never an issue for the youngsters, the occasional adult did lobby for early detraining rights. (Courtesy Carpinteria Valley Museum of History.)

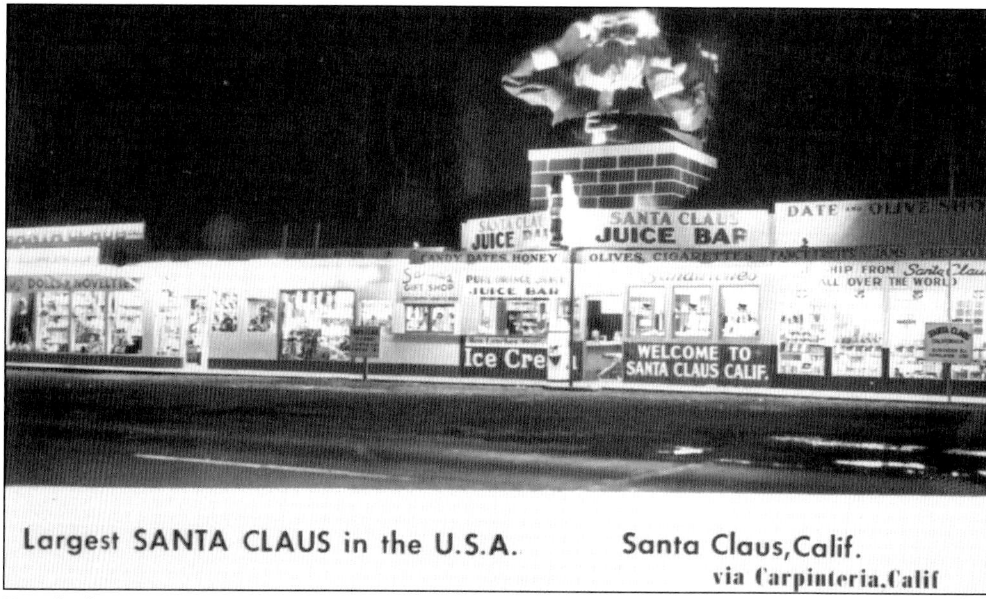

Yes, the largest Santa Claus in the USA did work the night shift. The juice bar immediately under Santa is where the magic all began in 1948. (Courtesy Carpinteria Valley Museum of History.)

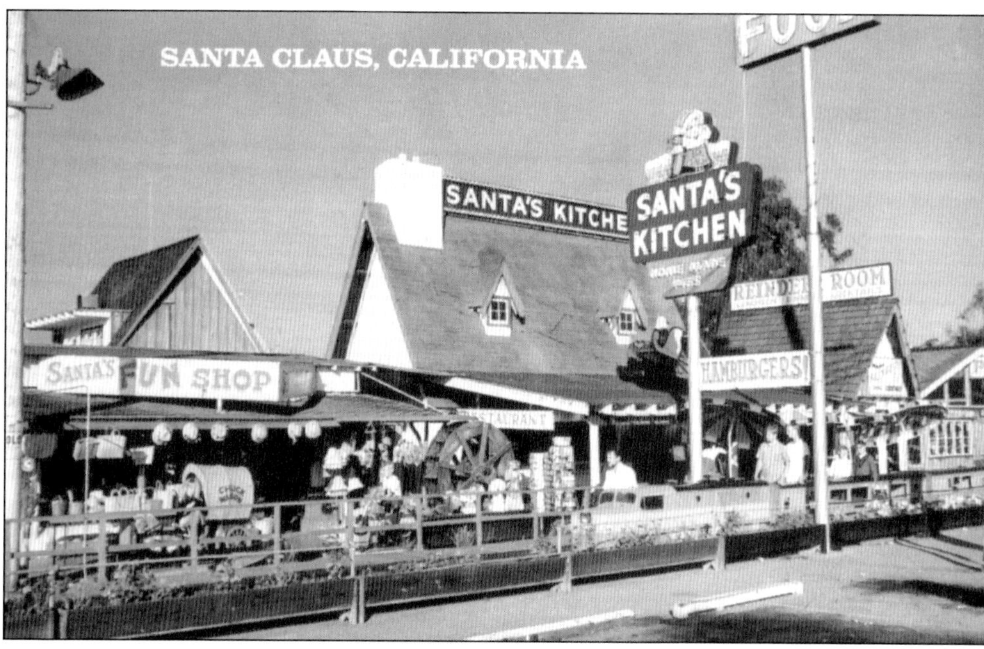

Santa Claus was in good company in Southern California; he shared his first name with Barbara, Maria, Paula, Ana, and Monica. The signage in this postcard of the lane makes it pretty clear that few stones were left unturned in terms of visitor-serving amenities. Where else, for instance, is the date shake considered a staple? (Courtesy Carpinteria Valley Museum of History.)

During the early years, Santa was equipped with a loudspeaker that was employed to lure tourists in off the highway with promises of sugary delights and adventures for the youngsters, thereby making it nearly impossible for dads dedicated to doing another 100 miles before dinner to slip by without causing a juvenile rebellion. (Courtesy Carpinteria Valley Museum of History.)

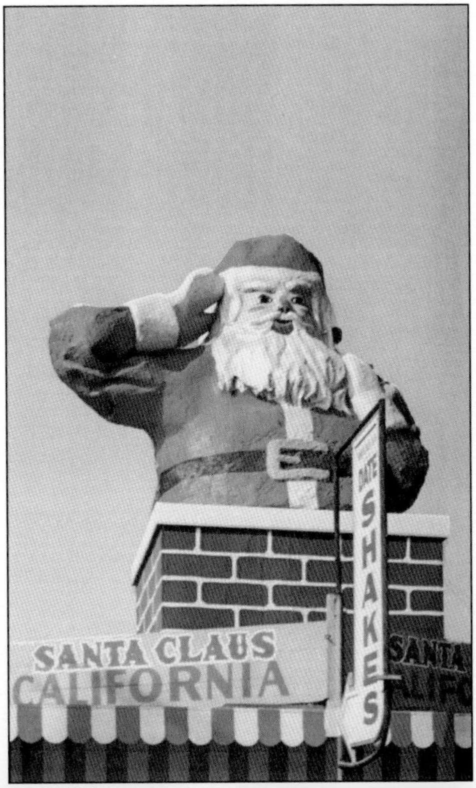

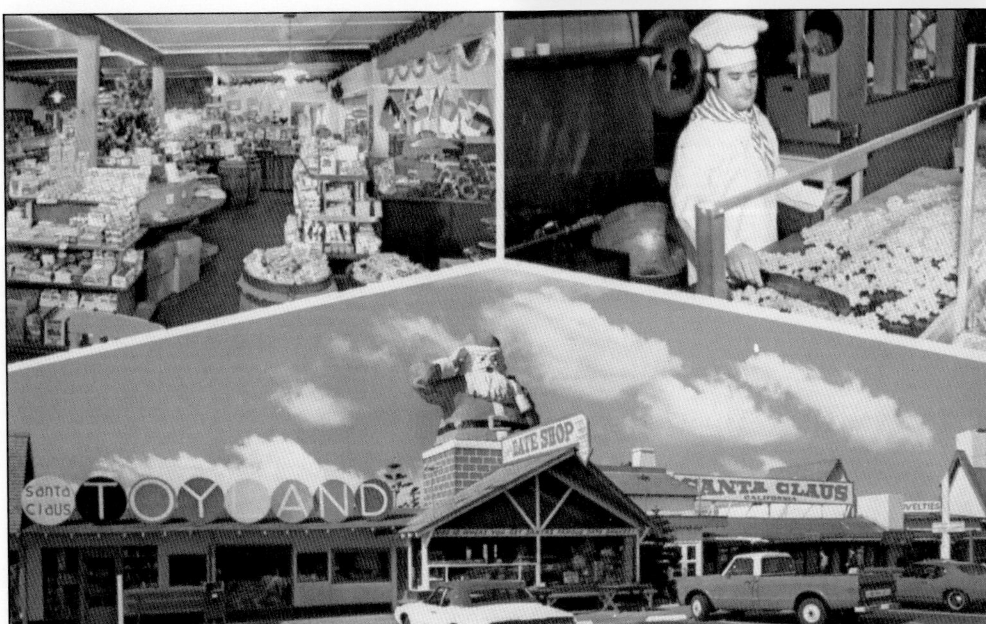

The possibilities for thinning out one's wallet at Santa Claus Lane were nearly inexhaustible. Food, drink, candy, and toys, or a combination of the four, could put a serious crimp in the currency reserves of even the most prosperous visitors to the lane. (Courtesy Carpinteria Valley Museum of History.)

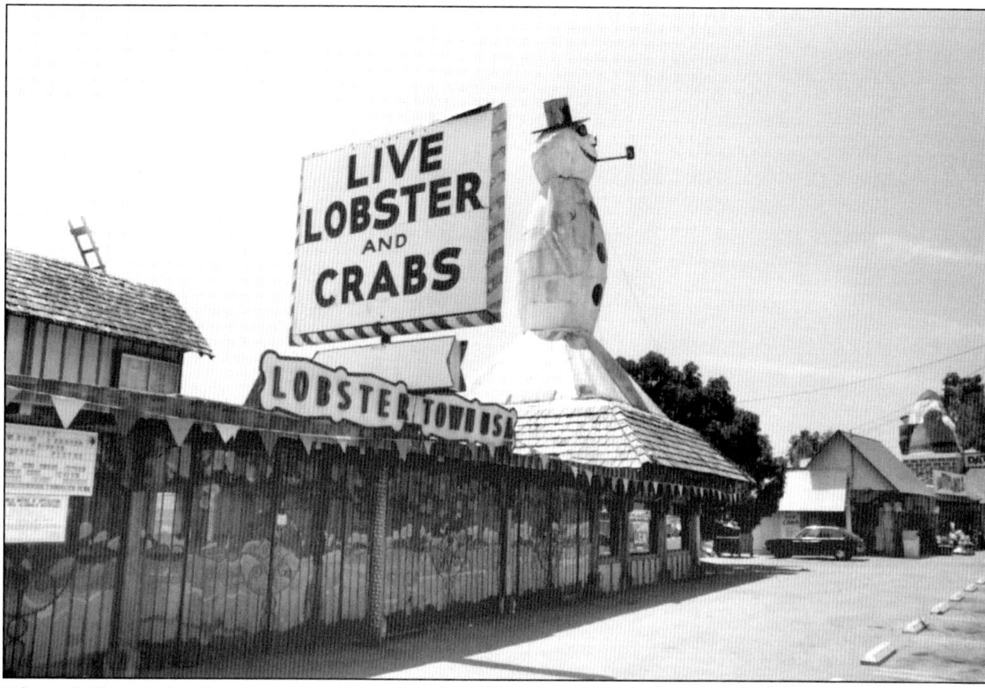

Though Frosty the Snowman's tenure wasn't as lengthy as Santa's, he did add a nice touch during his time in the Southern California sun. (Courtesy Carpinteria Valley Museum of History.)

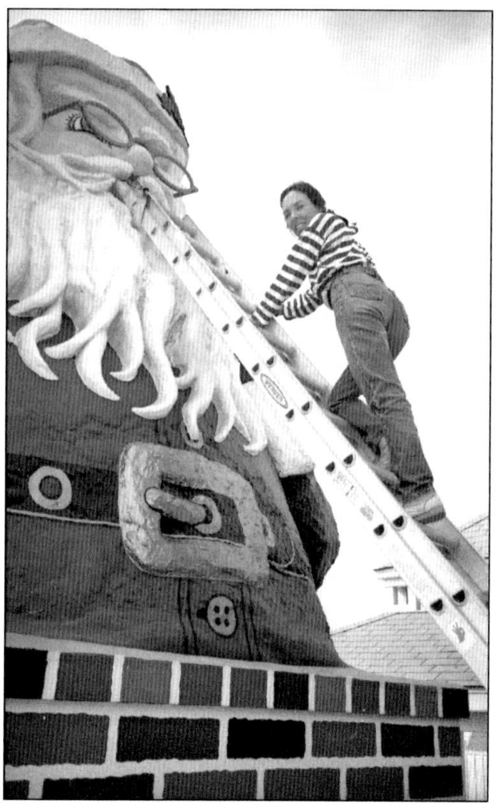

Even Santa required the occasional face-lift. One of his classiest makeovers was done by local artist Lynn Richardson, seen here climbing up to begin a day's work in the 1980s. Santa's specs, as all locals know, are traded for Ray-Ban "Wayfarers" with the onset of daylight-savings. It should be noted that a coalition of Santa's supporters, led by Robert Maxim, worked tirelessly to find a home for Santa Claus when he was muscled off the Lane by a new landlord in 2003. Santa currently can be seen on the mountainside of Highway 101 between Rice Road and Del Norte Avenue in Oxnard where Mike Barber, the president of the Garden Acres Mutual Water Company in Oxnard, has provided a spectacular new venue for Carpinteria's jolly St. Nick. (Courtesy Tom Moore.)

Five

SUMMERLAND

Summerland is located on a 150-acre hillside site overlooking the Pacific Ocean and Channel Islands between Carpinteria and Montecito. The community was founded in 1889 by Henry LaFayette (H. L.) Williams. The property passed through several owners before coming into his hands in 1883, and he would leave his legacy with it. Spiritualism, a religion that believed in contacting the spirits of the deceased through a medium during a séance, was rapidly expanding at the time, and Williams named his town Summerland after a Spiritualist term for the afterlife. He laid out the town in 25-foot-by-60-foot lots, just big enough to pitch a tent. He hoped to develop a place where Spiritualists could hold national conventions and perhaps eventually establish a colony. The name "Summerland" may have had a double meaning to Williams, however. He was a Spiritualist, but first and foremost, he was an entrepreneur. The name was meant to entice people to buy up the parcels of land he was selling.

An indication of Summerland's potential for industry came shortly after its founding, when natural gas was discovered in abundance by the Darling family and other early residents. The natural gas, plus other telltale signs of petroleum, had long drawn interest from speculators. In 1894, a significant discovery was finally made. Smith Cole uncovered a large oil deposit while digging for natural gas, and Williams quickly followed his example, eventually moving his operations offshore. From there, the boom was on, and Summerland's earliest residents, the Spiritualists, who had come seeking a haven of tranquility, largely left. Williams's dream had taken an ironic twist, and he was among the first to cash in.

The oil boom in Summerland gave it a special place in world history. The first offshore oil wells in the Western Hemisphere were dug here. By around 1900, Summerland's population had grown from a few families with unfinished houses and a few dozen in tents to 700 people and a flourishing community with natural gas for lighting and heating, a waterworks facility, lecture halls, a school, a train station, and business establishments. It boasted several newspapers, most prominently the *Summerland Advance Courier*, which called itself the voice of southern Santa Barbara County. More than 100 years later, with a population that has never grown to more than about 1,500 people, Summerland is once again a secluded and tranquil nook overlooking the sea.

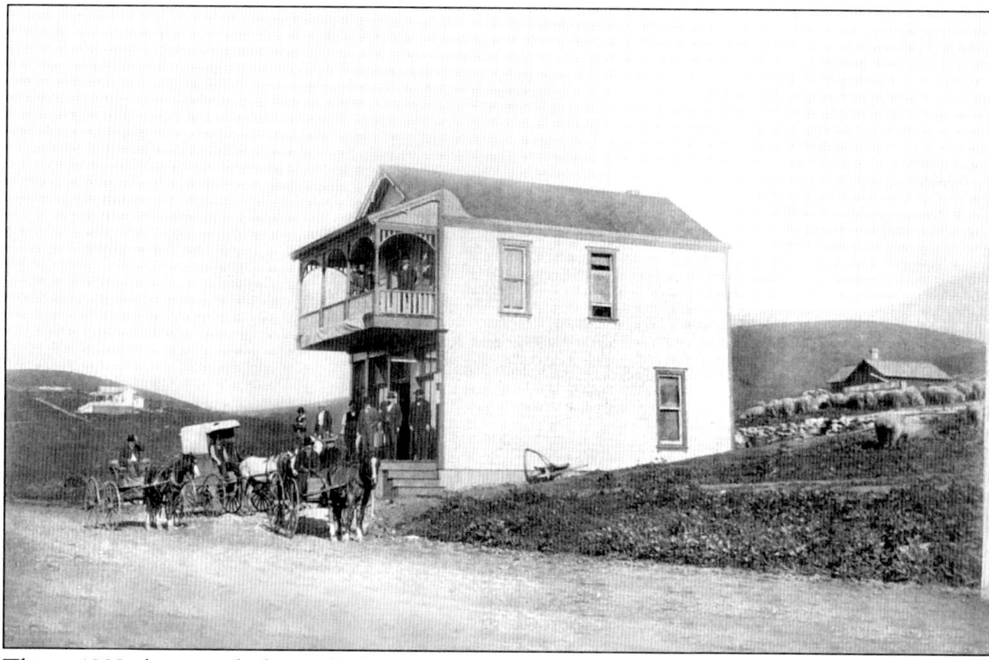

This *c.* 1889 photograph shows the Meginnes residence on the hillside that H. L. Williams would name Summerland on May 12, 1889. The area in and around Summerland was initially called Fenton, perhaps the name of an early settler. It was also called Ortega in reference to the Rancho Ortega, which encompassed the area. (Meginnes family photograph, courtesy Ronald Sheehan.)

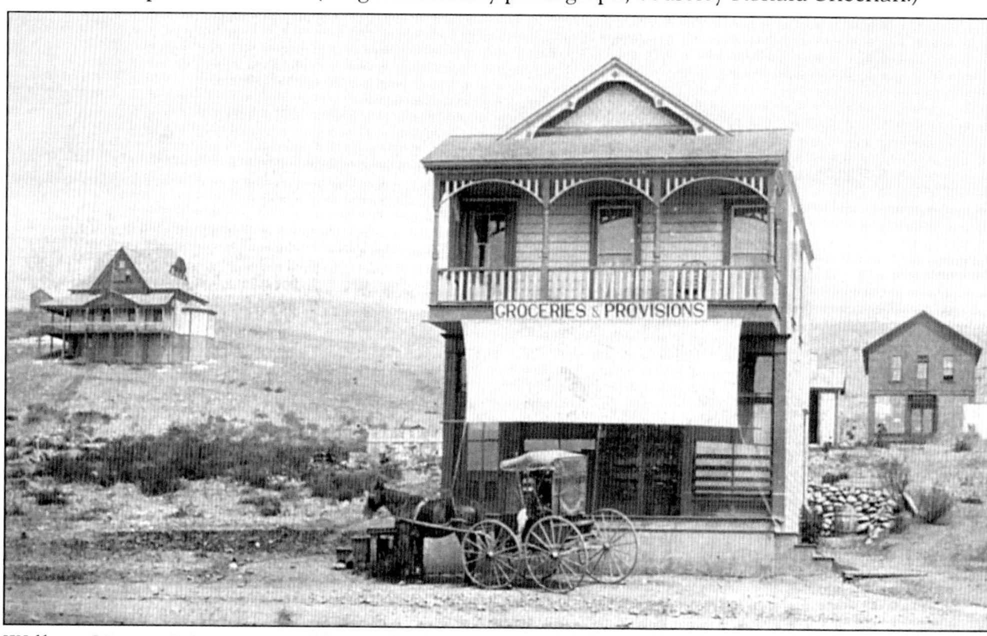

William Harvey Meginnes and his wife, Sarah, opened the first general store on H. L. Williams's Ortega site. Their residence was on the second floor, above the store. Seen here around 1889, it was on Wallace Avenue between Hollister and Colville Streets. The train station depot would be built across the street from it in 1897. Literary Hall can be seen above and to the left. (Meginnes family photograph, courtesy Ronald Sheehan.)

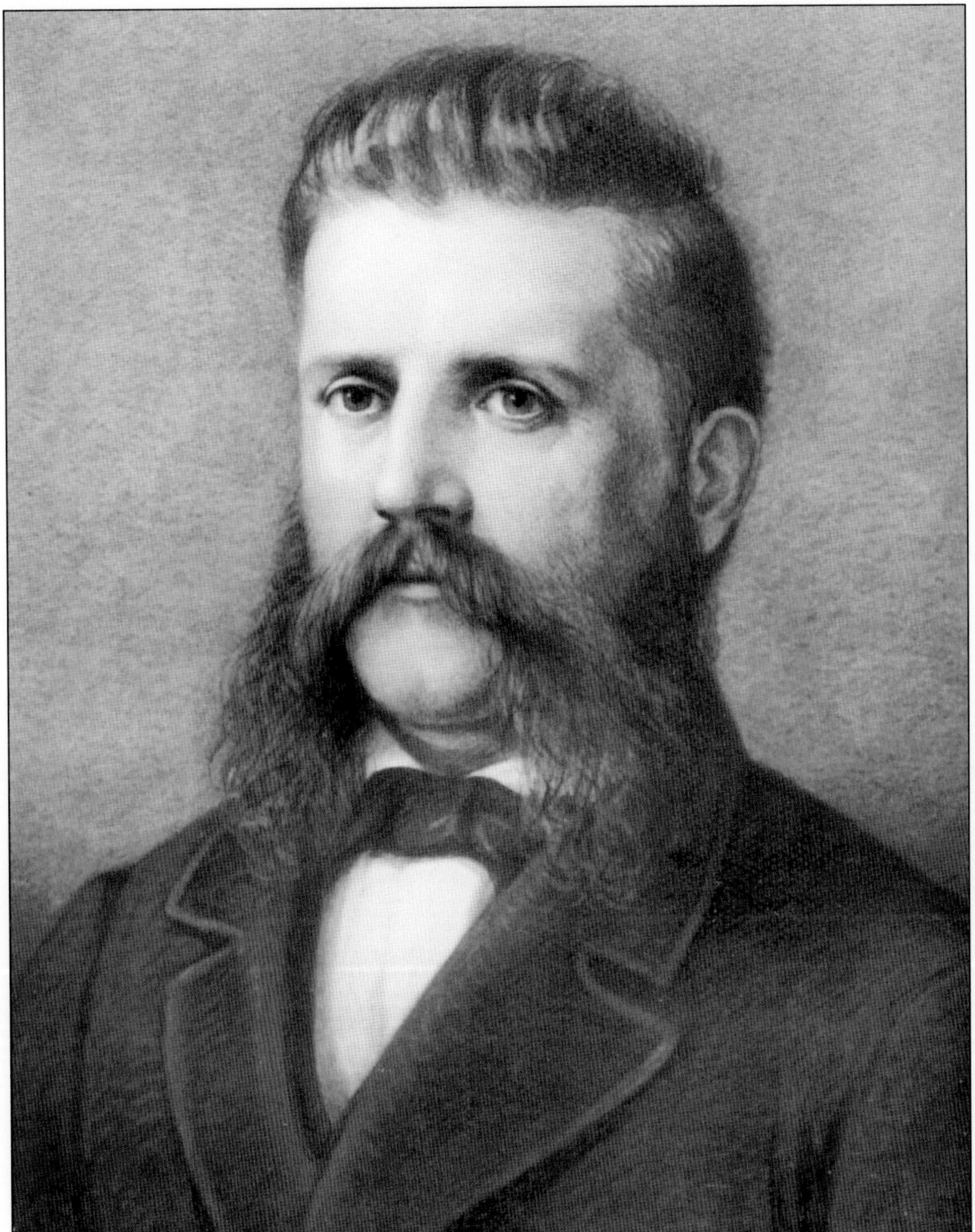

H. L. Williams, pictured around 1860, served as a major in the Union army in the Civil War. After the war and several entrepreneurial ventures, he came to Santa Barbara. In 1883, he purchased the 1,049.88-acre Rancho Ortega, which stretched from Sheffield Drive to Toro Creek. He laid out a roughly 150-acre town on the hillside overlooking the Pacific Ocean and the Channel Islands. Williams named his town Summerland after the term used in Spiritualism as the afterlife or "other side" of life on earth. He advertised worldwide to promote sales of small lots that he had mapped out in his town. The discovery of oil in Summerland, however, changed Williams's perception of Spiritualists. He vowed to get rid of the "cranks" in a letter to his creditors in San Francisco in order to facilitate oil exploration. (Courtesy Rod Lathim, from Spirit of the Big Yellow House.)

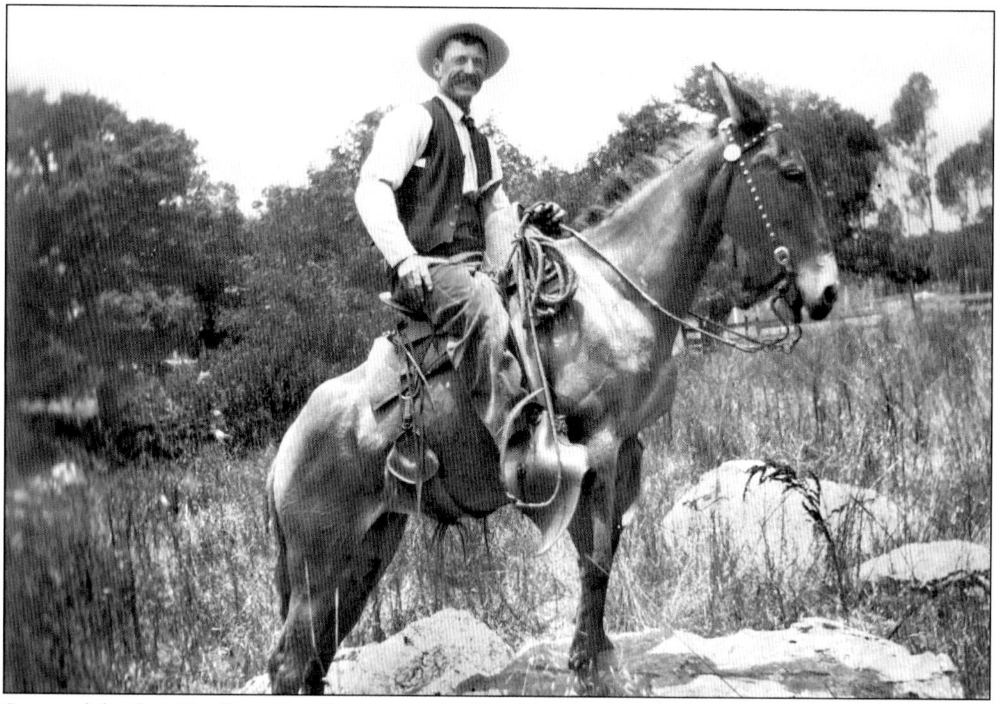

Some of the families from the Carpinteria Valley, like the Smiths and Lamberts, would become synonymous with Summerland's development. In this c. 1900 photograph, Norman Lambert is astride a mule, probably the best means of travel for the hilly landscape of Summerland. Today Summerland's eastern boundary is defined by Lambert Road. (Courtesy Harold and Nancy Smith.)

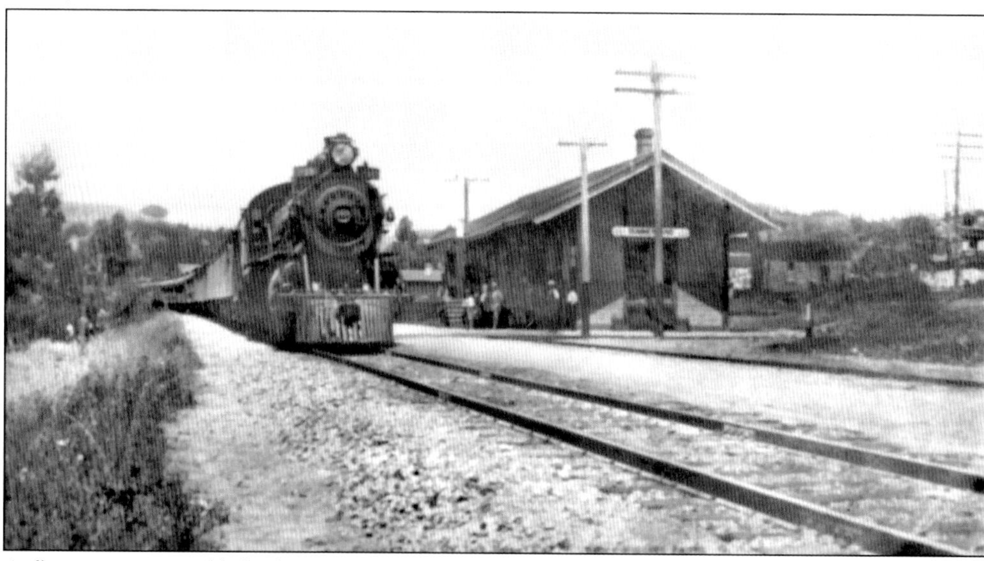

A flag stop was established on the Ortega site in 1887 between the newly established depots in Santa Barbara and Carpinteria. On October 11 that year, the flag stop was officially recognized as a railroad station, one of the few stations so designated prior to the establishment of a township. The train station depot can be seen to the right of this c. 1900 photograph as a train rumbles towards Carpinteria. (Courtesy Carpinteria Valley Museum of History.)

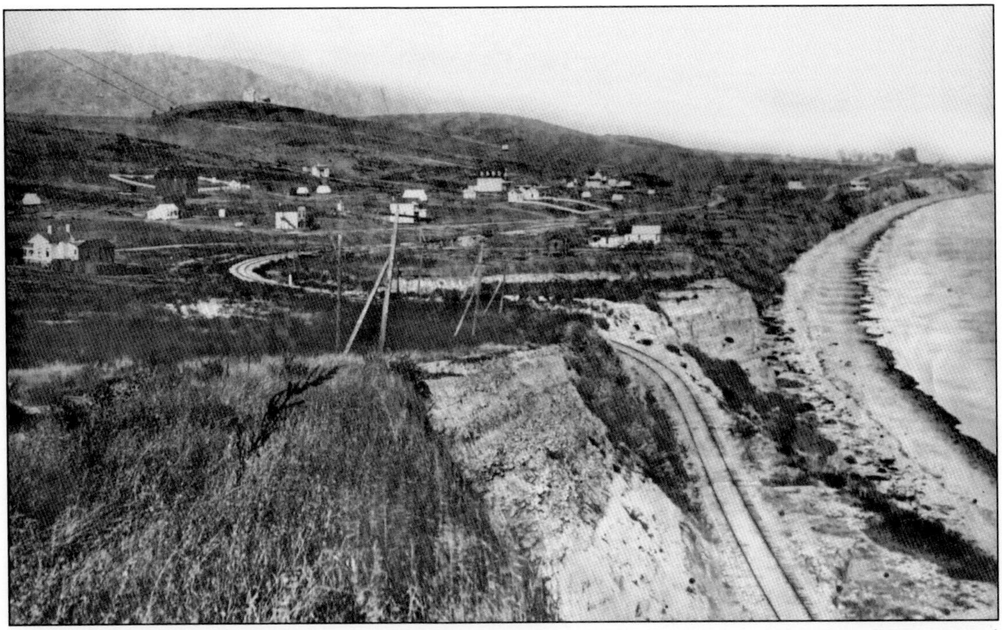

In her memoirs, May Croop Lambert recalled arriving by train in Summerland in 1890 as a girl of 16. She remembered seeing few houses and mostly fields of wild mustard. She described a town of 10 to 12 houses, a train station (probably a platform), a store, a little bakery, a schoolhouse, and a beautiful library on the hill, Literary Hall, which also served as a dance hall. (Courtesy Carpinteria Valley Museum of History.)

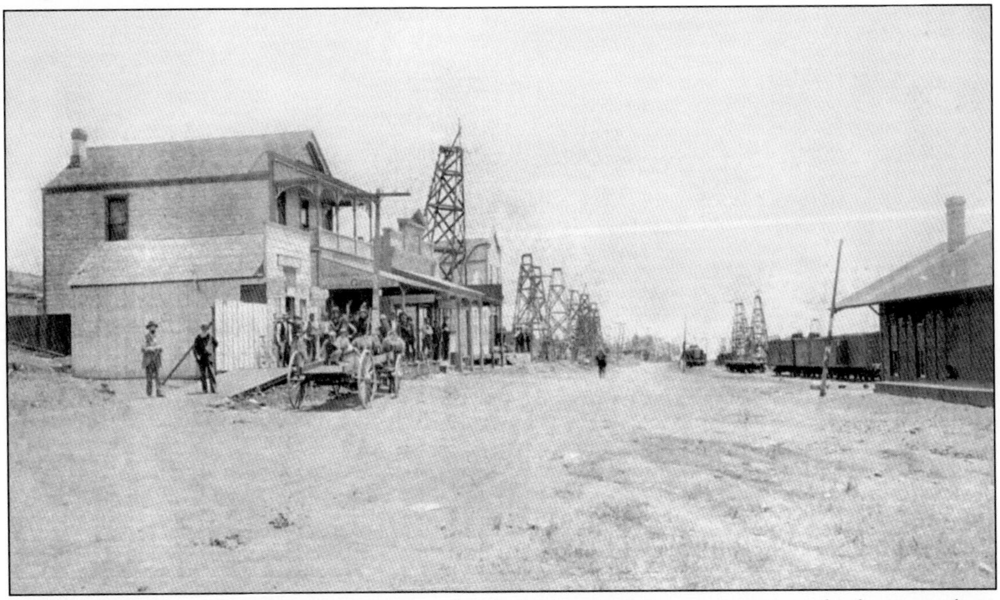

In 1894, Smith Cole is reputed to have dug the first oil well while attempting to dig for natural gas near his home. The result of Cole's discovery is evident in this photograph looking eastward on Wallace Avenue around 1897. The train depot is on the right, the post office and the Meginnes general store on the left, and derricks loom above them. Writes Lambert in her memoirs, "The oil odor was awful, but the money was pouring in." (Meginnes family photograph, courtesy Ronald Sheehan.)

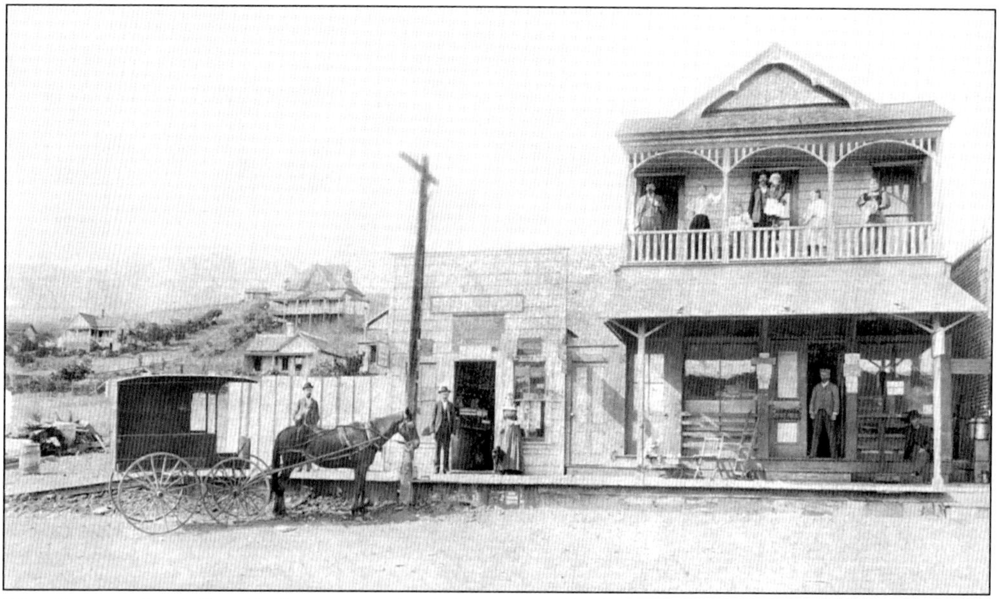

The Summerland Post Office is on the left next to the Meginnes general store in this 1895 photograph. Byron Preston and his wife stand in front of the post office, which also served as the Summerland Drug and Stationery Store, established in 1890. Preston was appointed the Summerland postmaster in 1894. W. H. Meginnes and his wife, Sarah, stand on the balcony with their family. The grocer, Mr. Cook, stands at the entrance of the store. (Meginnes family photograph, courtesy Ronald Sheehan.)

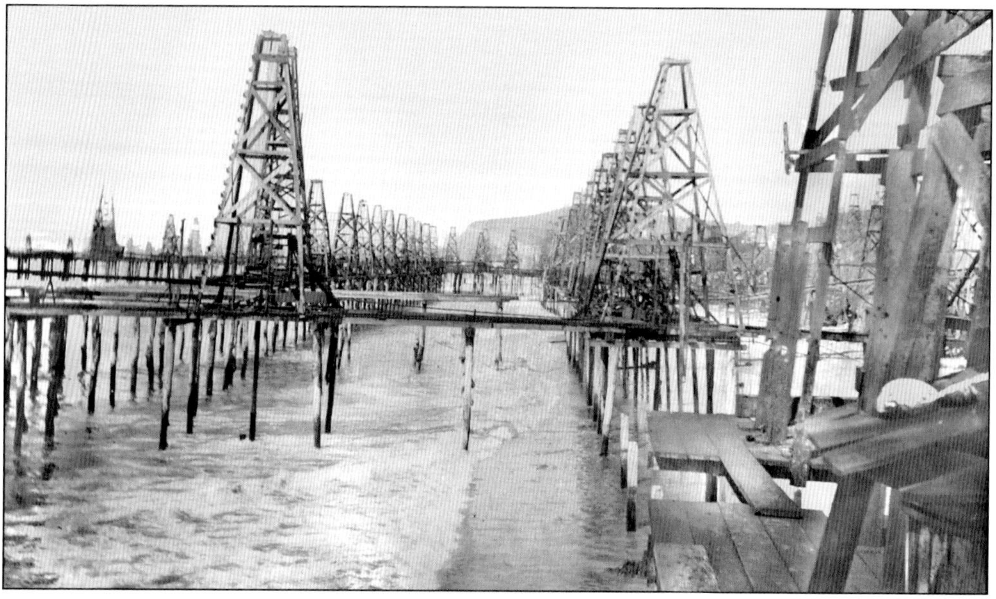

Summerland lore blames Max Fleishmann's Santa Barbara breakwater project for the demise of the Summerland oil industry. The breakwater altered the down-coast sand migration, contributing to the washing out of the offshore oil wells, engine houses, and the wharves and ruining the golden beaches of Summerland by 1932—not that the oil industry had not already diminished the luster of the beaches, as demonstrated by this *c.* 1900 picture. (Courtesy Carpinteria Valley Museum of History.)

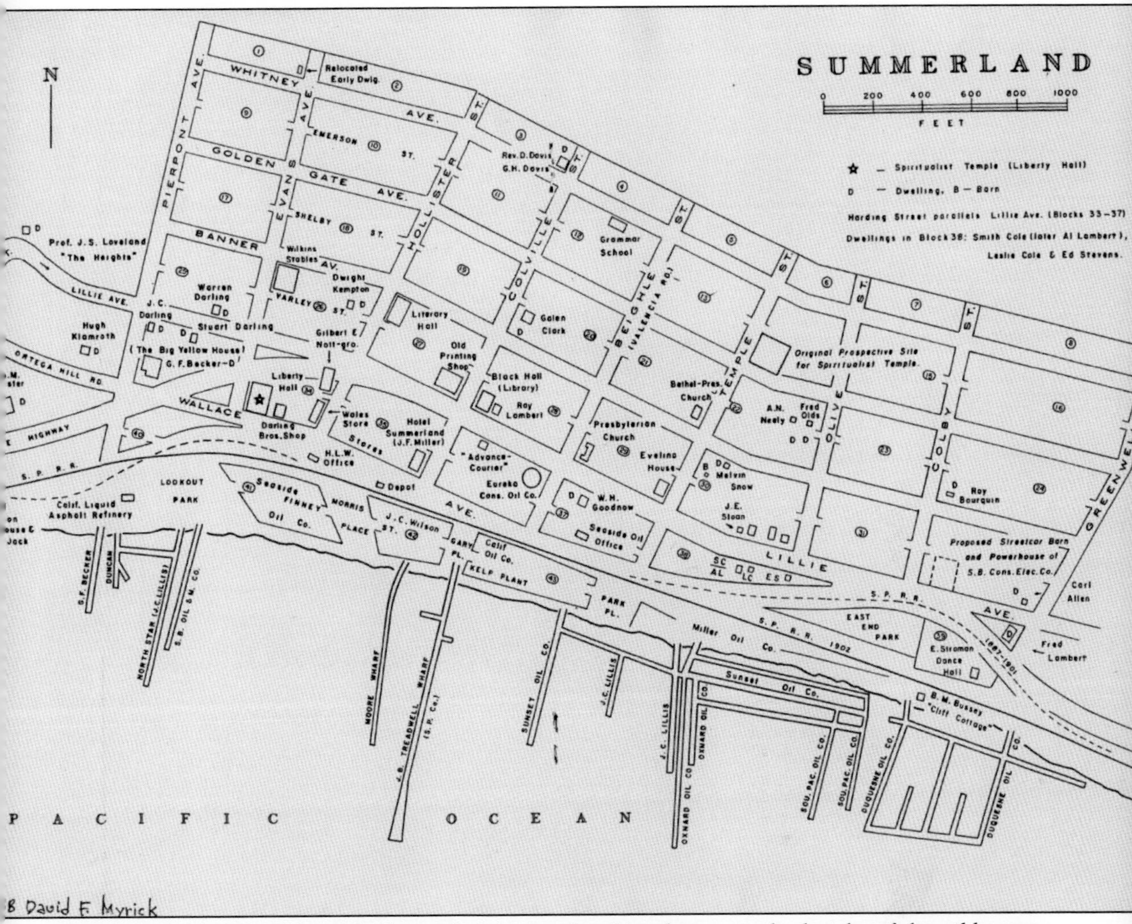

A map drawn by David Myrick shows the Summerland landscape at the height of the oil boom. Except for the removal of the wharves and the 1951 construction of the U.S. 101 freeway, which eliminated Wallace Avenue, the map accurately names and depicts the layout of the town's streets as they look today. Summerland lore has it that J. Paul Getty had an oil concern in Summerland, but that saboteurs from Montecito targeted his wells for mischief. A disgusted Getty is said to have left in a huff. Summerland mythos paints Montecito valley residents as villains during the oil boom period. Montecito residents were said to abhor the smell of oil coming out of Summerland. Montecito was as wealthy then as it is today, and having an odorously vile, blue-collar Summerland as its neighbor may well have been a cause for complaint and a call to vandalistic action. (Courtesy David Myrick.)

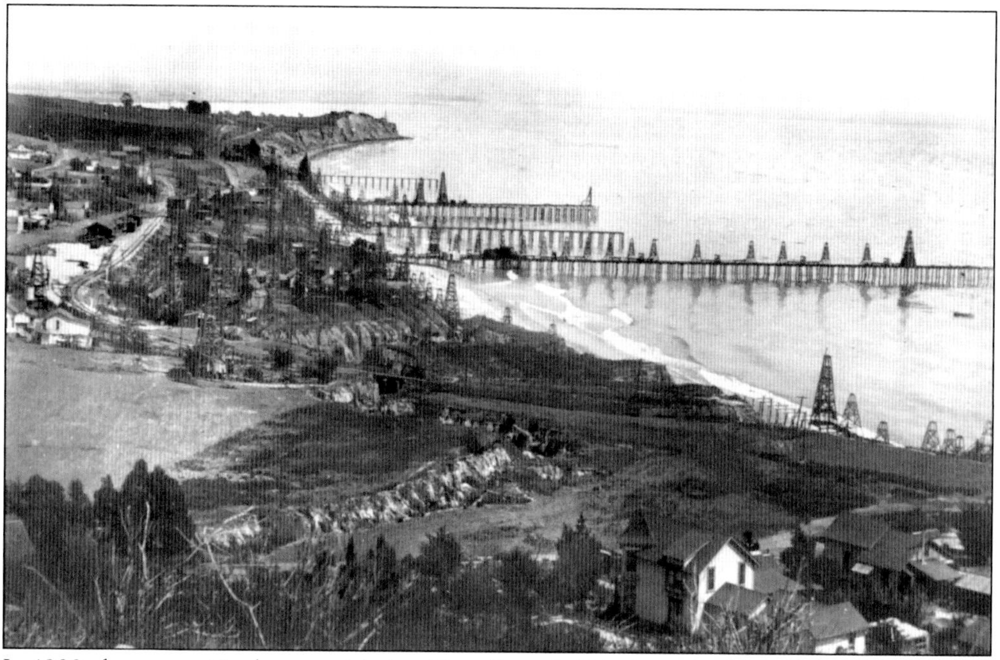

In 1900, there were 11 wharves with 6 to 20 wells each. The longest of the wharves, seen in the center of this picture, was the John B. Treadwell Wharf. It had 18 wells. As the longest wharf, it was also used by ships delivering timber to the Southern Pacific Milling Company, which stood at the entrance of the wharf. (Courtesy Carpinteria Valley Museum of History.)

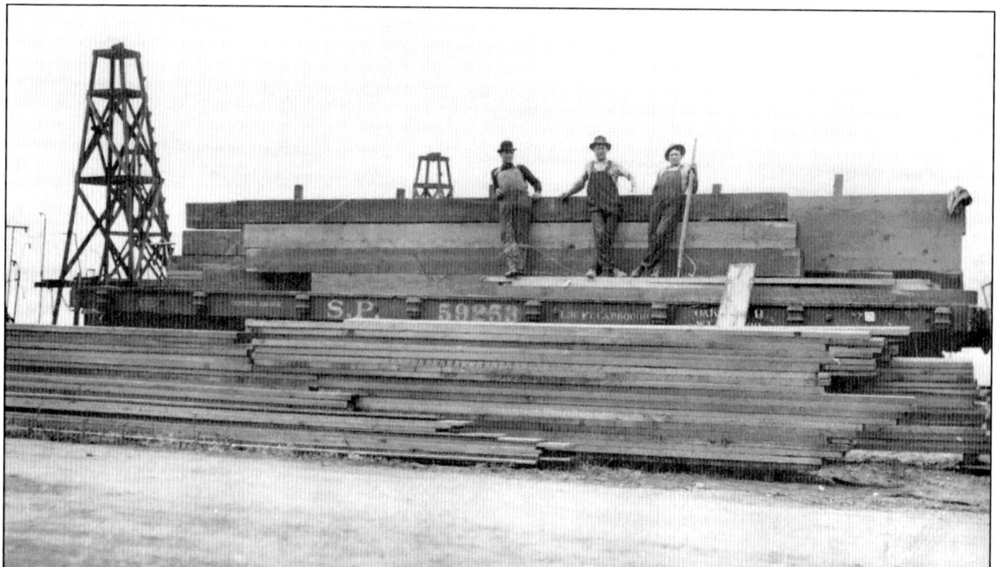

Men of the Southern Pacific Milling Company stand on a timber pile in this *c.* 1900 photograph. Building Summerland required an abundant lumber supply. Entrepreneur that he was, H. L. Williams planted a eucalyptus grove along Lambert Road and Toro Creek to fill the need. The grove later became a monarch butterfly breeding ground recognized the world over. Gas stations hired boys to wash off smashed butterflies from the windshields of cars during the migrating season. (Courtesy Carpinteria Valley Museum of History.)

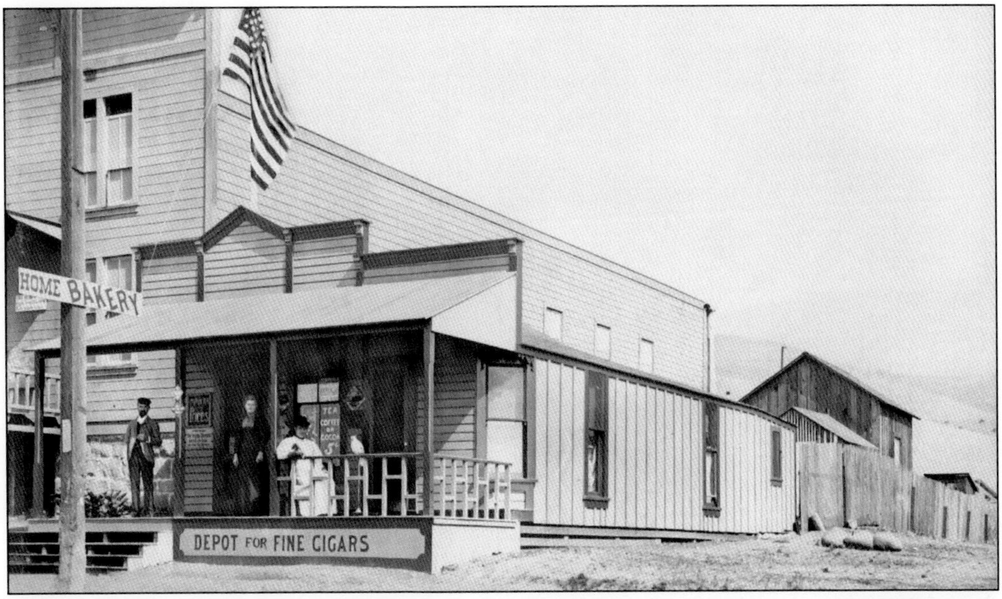

With the oil boom, business opportunities abounded. Blacksmiths, carpenters, tank builders, drug stores, hotels, laundry houses, real estate offices, barbershops, postal service, hardware stores, dance halls, and many saloons took up residence in Summerland. There were five newspapers! The town flourished. Pictured here around 1892 is the Hancock General Store on Wallace Avenue between Evans Avenue and Hollister Street. Liberty Hall, the Spiritualist temple, is to the left of the store. (Courtesy Carpinteria Valley Museum of History.)

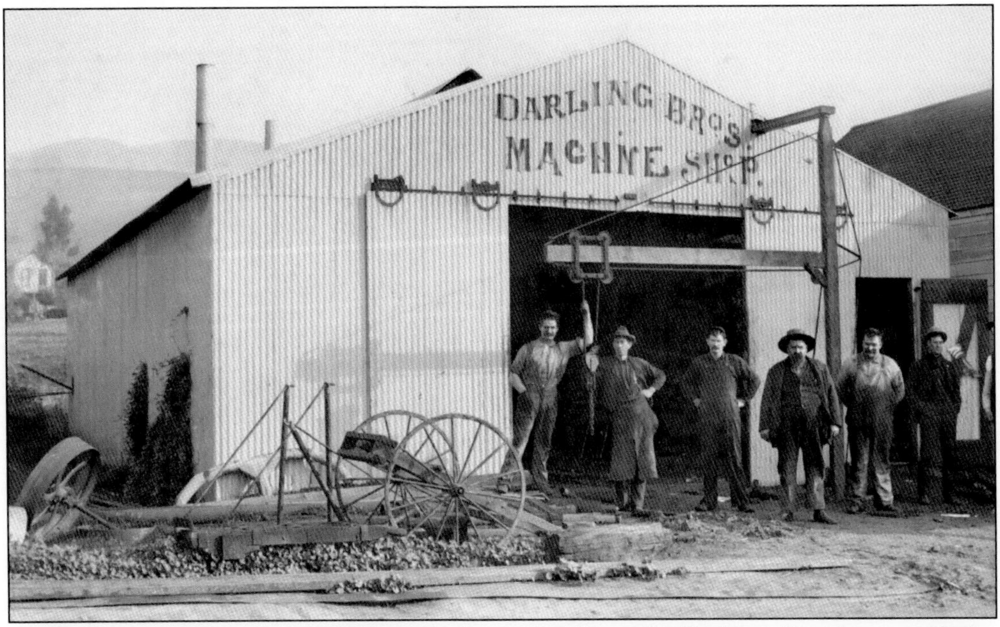

One of Summerland's original and most enduring families is the Darlings. Standing outside the Darling Brothers Machine Shop around 1900 are, from left to right, Wayne Darling, Will McIntyre, Jerome Potter, Warren Darling, Stewart Darling, and an unidentified man. The picture here is of their first business structure. It was on Wallace Avenue, the main business thoroughfare of Summerland's early days. (Courtesy Carpinteria Valley Museum of History.)

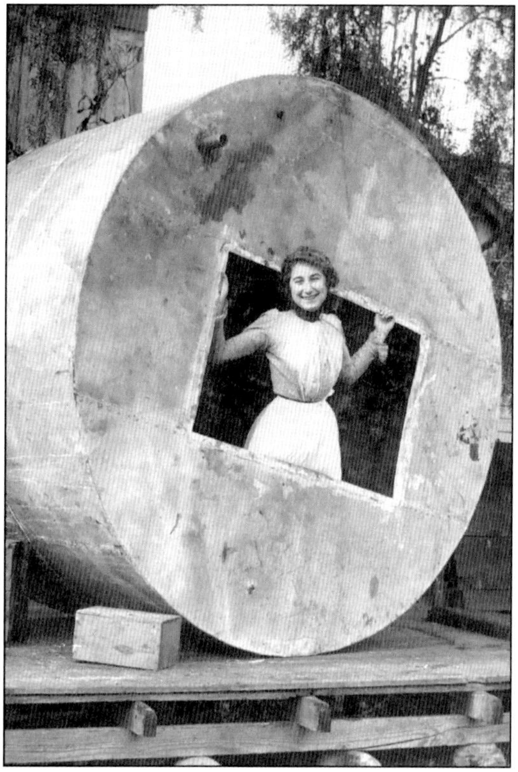

Gertrude White smiles at the camera while standing inside one of Thomas Halley's tanks around 1905. Halley, a tinsmith, made galvanized water storage tanks at his shop on Lillie Avenue between Colville and Beighle Streets (now Valencia Road). Homes had two tanks, one for rainwater and the other for water from the town system that tapped into Toro Creek. The lack of a fresh water source limited Summerland's development for most of the 20th century. (Courtesy Carpinteria Valley Museum of History.)

Galen Clark, the first state-appointed guardian of California's Yosemite Park and Maricopa Grove, purchased a group of lots from H. L. Williams to build a home in Summerland. It is a Summerland landmark today and was used as the logo for Summerland's centennial celebration in 1989. It is still standing at 2355 Shelby Street. Clark can be seen on the left side of the balcony looking out towards the Pacific Ocean in this c. 1900 photograph. (Courtesy Carpinteria Valley Museum of History.)

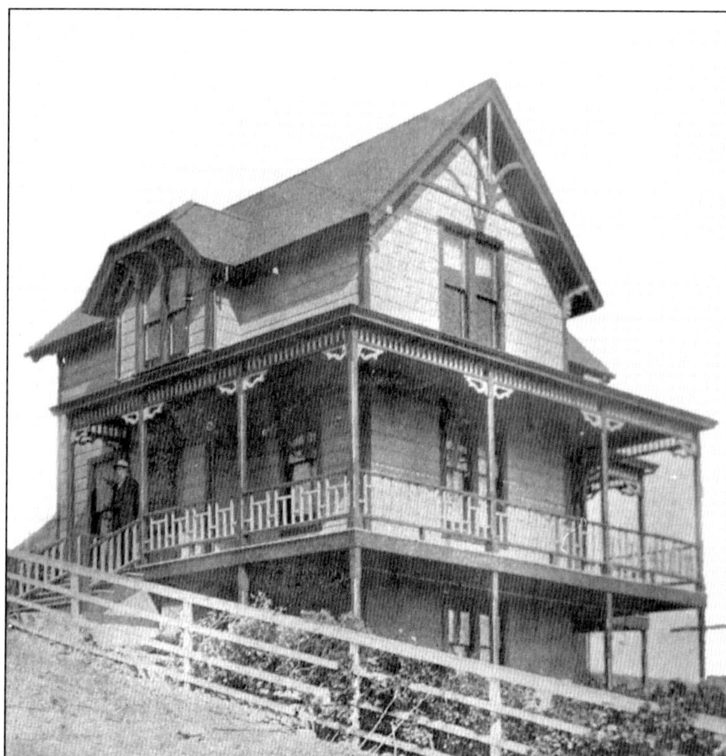

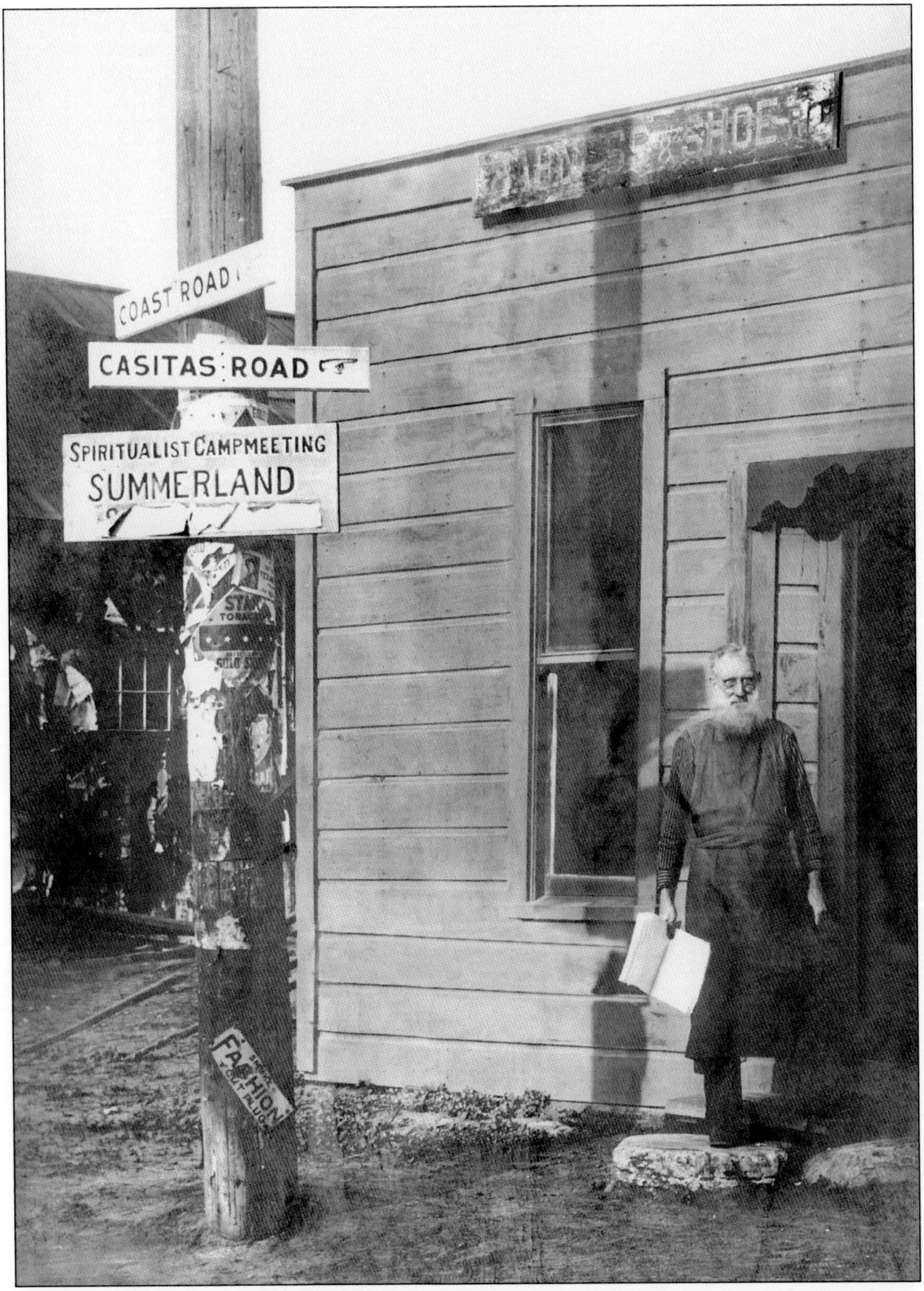

Southwick's Harness and Shoe blacksmith shop demonstrates Summerland's ties to the Carpinteria Valley in this c. 1900 photograph. The shop stood in Carpinteria along the Coast Highway, near what today is Carpinteria Avenue. On the pole next to the apron-clad craftsman are signs pointing travelers in two directions. An advertising sign says that one can attend a Spiritualist camp meeting in Summerland. (Courtesy Carpinteria Valley Museum of History.)

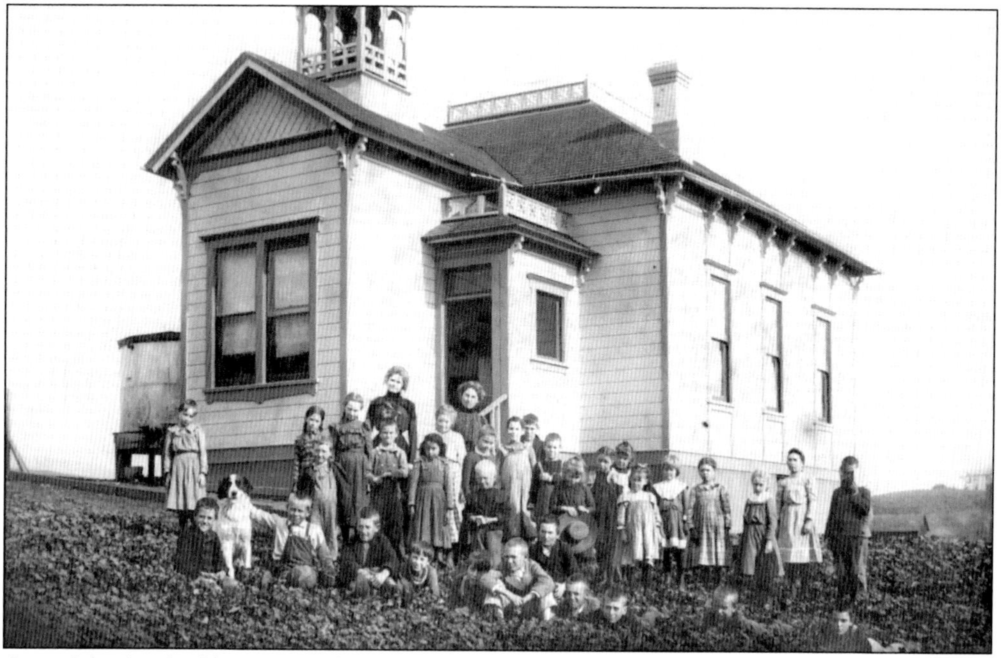

One of the first buildings erected in Summerland was the school at the top of Whitney Avenue, as seen in this *c.* 1895 photograph. With the oil boom, the school went from a dozen students to about 80. In 1919, a new school was built on the western corner of Valencia Road and Lillie Avenue for younger children. The steep walk up Whitney Avenue was reserved for the older children. (Courtesy Carpinteria Valley Museum of History.)

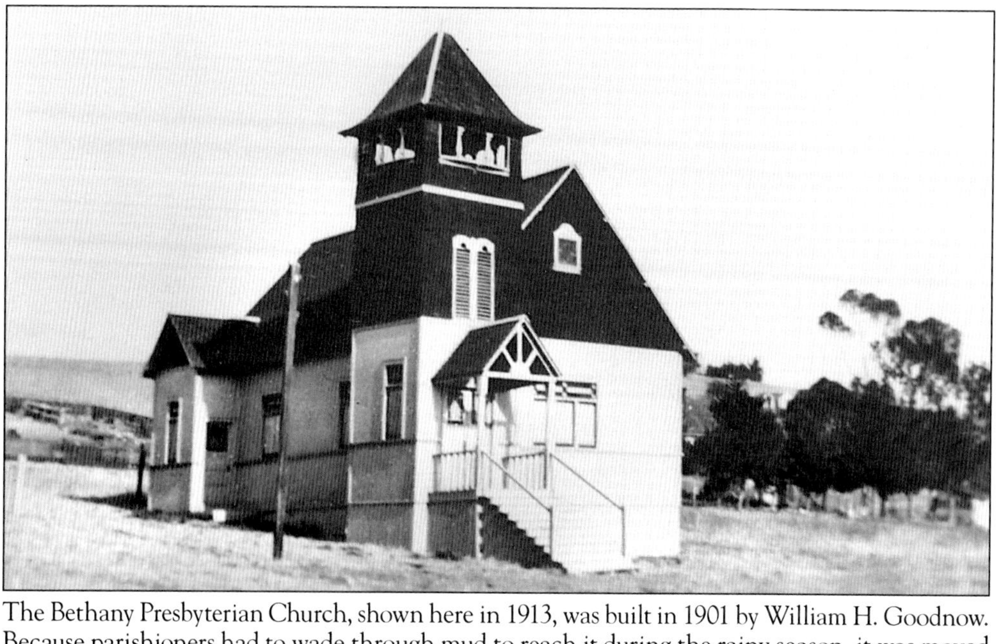

The Bethany Presbyterian Church, shown here in 1913, was built in 1901 by William H. Goodnow. Because parishioners had to wade through mud to reach it during the rainy season, it was moved in 1910 from its original site on Banner Avenue to its present location on the corner of Valencia Road and Lillie Avenue. Lillie Avenue was said to be a better site because it was paved. (Courtesy Carpinteria Valley Museum of History.)

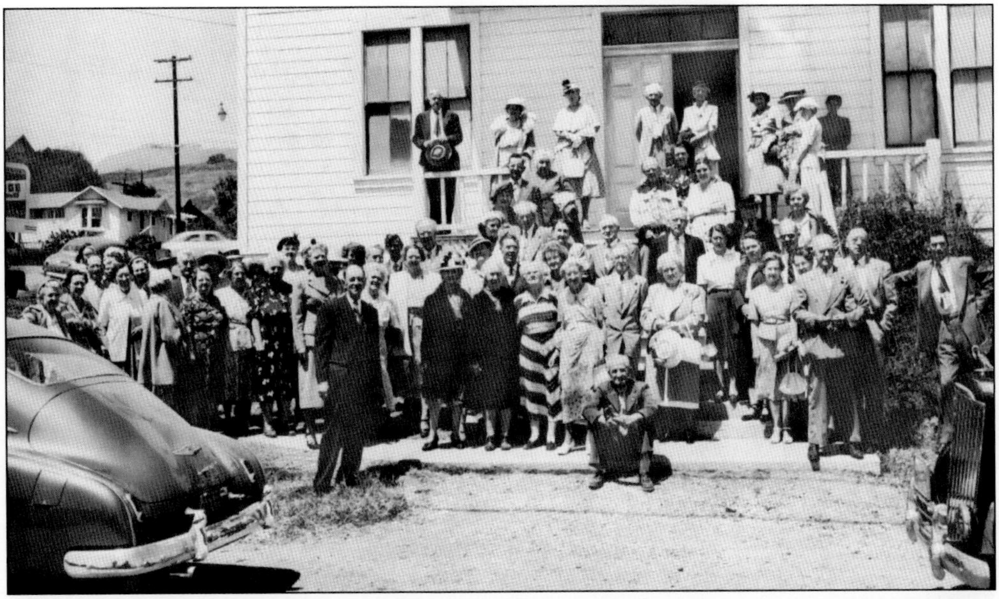

The center of Spiritualist activity in Summerland was Liberty Hall. It was located on Wallace Avenue between Evans Avenue and Hollister Street. It was demolished in 1951 to make way for the U.S. 101 freeway. The gathering in this *c.* 1951 photograph of Liberty Hall shows an elderly congregation, perhaps the remnants of the Summerland Spiritualist era. The congregation joined with Santa Barbara Spiritualists after the demolition of the temple. The church remains active to this day. (Courtesy Carpinteria Valley Museum of History.)

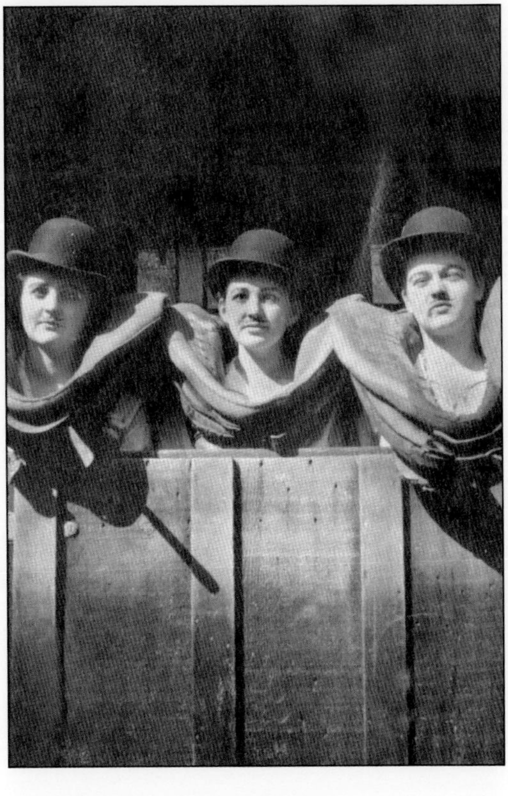

Summerland retained its frontier look well into the days of moviemaking. The Flying A Stock Company, which had established a movie studio in Santa Barbara in 1913, used Summerland as a favorite locale to film westerns. The actors on the left are looking out of a barn in or around Summerland. They appear to be in a western comedy, as evidenced by penciled moustaches, bowler hats, and horse collars around their necks. (Courtesy Harold and Nancy Smith.)

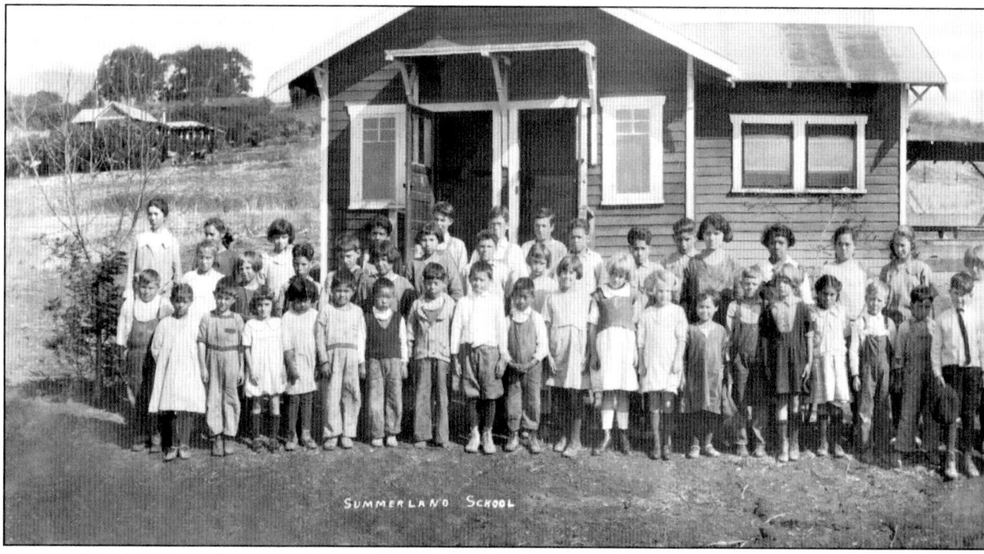

During World War I, Summerland attracted multiethnic workers and their families, as this c. 1920 class photograph of the Summerland School on Lillie Avenue and Valencia Road attests. At that time, California law prohibited several minority groups from using public schools. Summerland was a blue-collar community that presented equal opportunity for anyone willing to work hard. The evidence from this photograph is that the children were afforded the same opportunity. (Courtesy Carpinteria Valley Museum of History.)

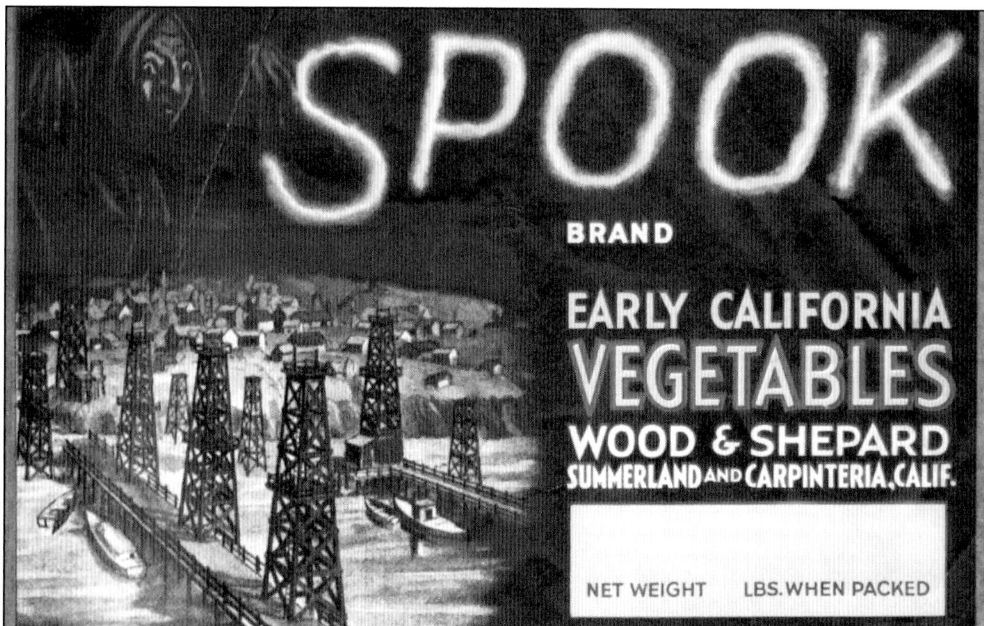

Summerland was dubbed "Spookville" as a result of its initial status as a Spiritualist meeting place and the séances that were held in Liberty Hall. This c. 1920 Spook Brand vegetable label illustrates Summerland's early history succinctly with a Spiritualist medium at the top left, the Summerland hillside illuminated by natural gas in the background, the wooden piers in shallow ocean water, and the majestic, offshore oil derricks in the foreground. (Courtesy Jim Campos and Richard Partida.)

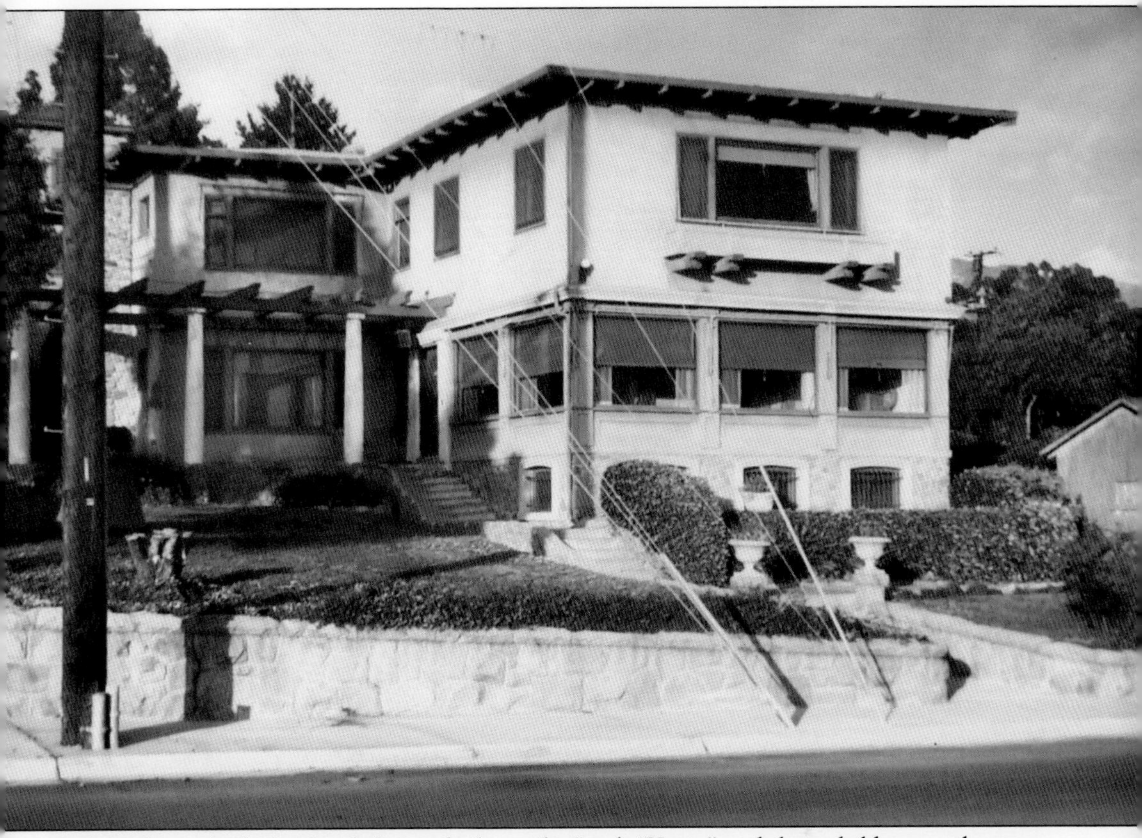

H. L. Williams built the family home for his wife, Sarah "Katie," and their children on the west side of Ortega Hill. He also built a house just east of Ortega Hill that was to become one of the landmarks in Summerland, the Big Yellow House, shown in the photograph. The structure was originally a single story built in 1884, and H. L. rented it to his associate, Albert Norton. After Williams's death in 1899, resulting from the effects of a fall into one of his wells, Agnus, his second wife, took up residence in the house. She and her new husband, George Becker, remodeled the house in 1912. While Agnus was married to Williams, she became interested in Spiritualism. She held séances in her new two-story home, which is said to be inhabited by otherworldly spirits to this day. For his part, Becker bought out Williams's children's interest in the oil companies and took over field operations. In 1924, according to a report Becker wrote, he owned around 75 percent of the oil interests in Summerland and about a third of the town. (Courtesy Carpinteria Valley Museum of History.)

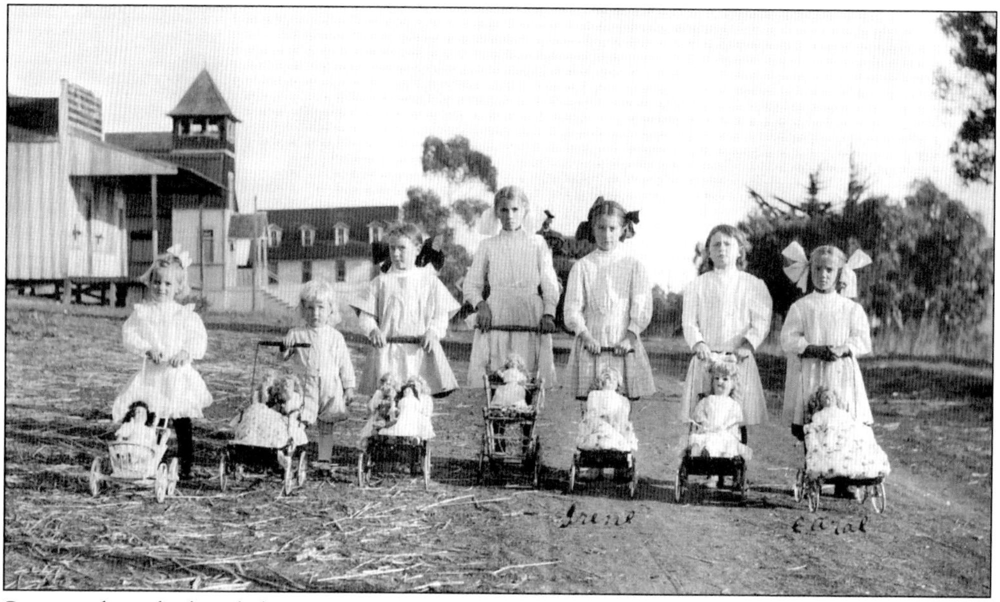

Seven girls with their baby carriages and porcelain dolls stand in the middle of Lillie Avenue around 1912. In the background are the Bethany Presbyterian Church and the Evelina House. The Foster-Cole dollhouse, where the girls may have obtained the dolls and carriages for the photograph, was on the corner of Valencia Road and Varley Street, across from the church. The dollhouse was removed in 1928 so that a new school could be built. Summerland students are served at this site to this day. (Courtesy Claire Roberts.)

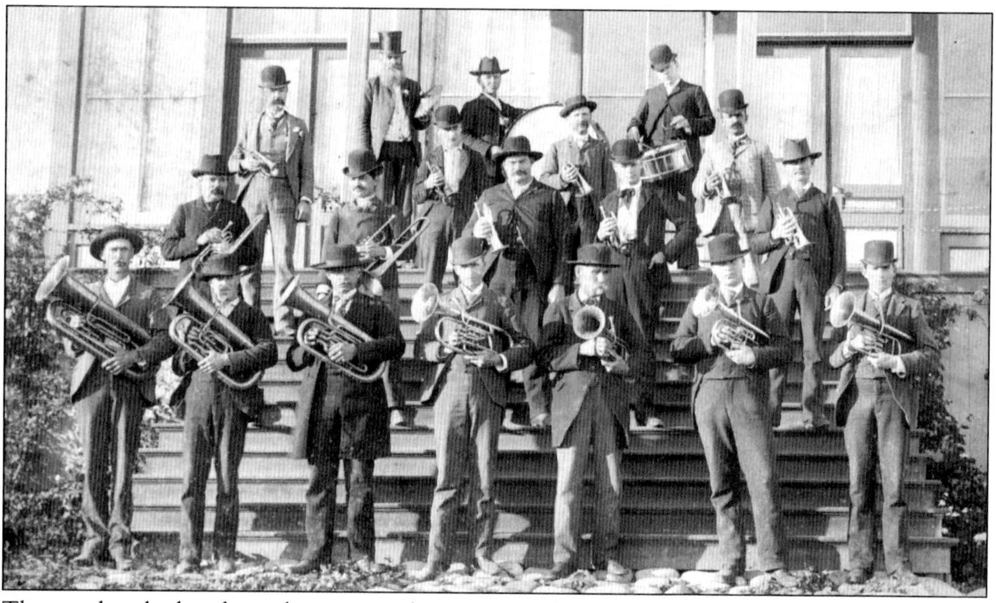

The two hotels that figured prominently in Summerland's early history were the Miller Hotel and Boarding House (Hotel Summerland) near the train depot on Wallace Avenue, built in 1898, and the larger 20-room Evelina House (often spelled "Evalina") on Summerland's other main road, Lillie Avenue, built perhaps as early as 1888 on the Ortega site. The Summerland brass and percussion band poses for this *c.* 1900 picture in front of the Evelina House. (Courtesy Carpinteria Valley Museum of History.)

May Croop Lambert and her family arrived by train in Summerland a year after its founding. To celebrate her 100th birthday in 1974, the County of Santa Barbara proclaimed her the First Lady of Summerland. In her memoirs, she tells this early Summerland story: "My brothers and other children used to go out after supper, and play baseball along what is now Lillie Avenue. When it began to get dark, they would drive short pieces of pipe into the ground about five or six inches, and would light them, and there would be a gas flame at least a foot high from the top of the pipe." (Courtesy Carpinteria Valley Museum of History.)

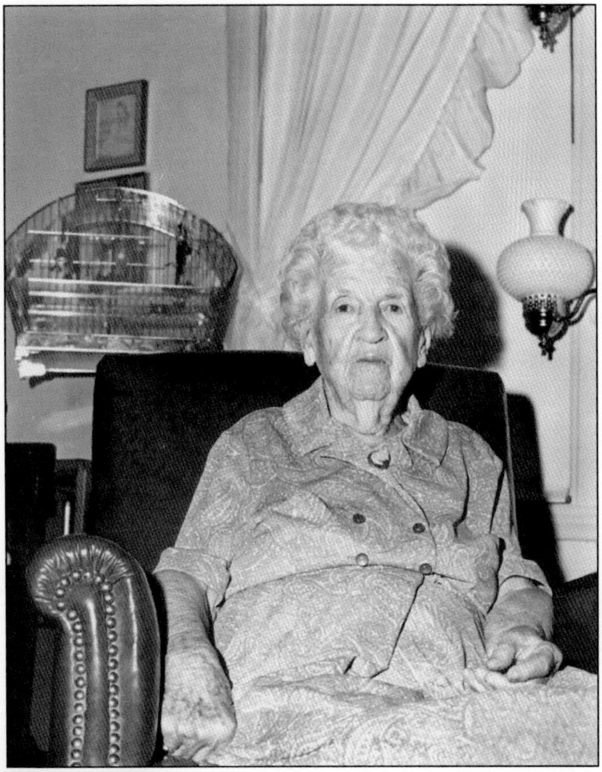

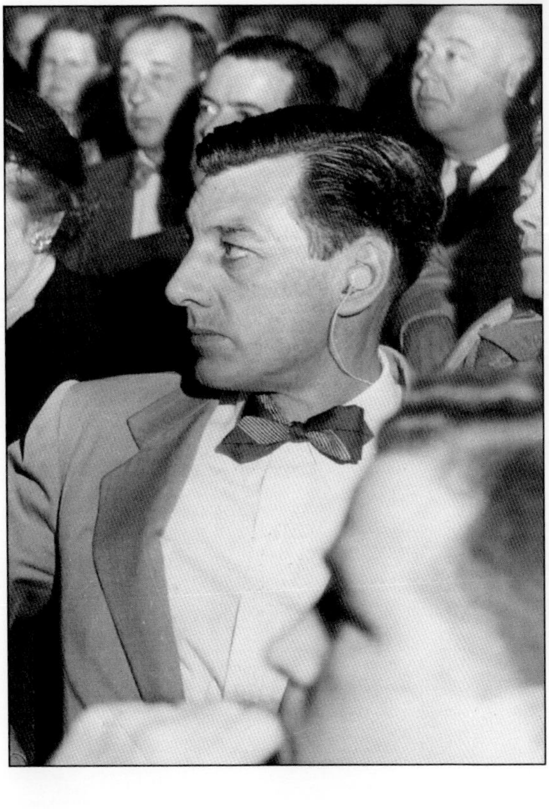

After the oil industry died in the 1930s, Summerland settled into a sleepy existence and was dubbed "Slumberville." In 1955, however, the community awoke under the leadership of Milton Duncan, pictured in the center. He formed the Summerland Citizens Association and did battle with Montecito residents at the Santa Barbara County Planning Commission to build a factory at the top of Ortega Hill. The association won, and Josten's, a jewelry manufacturing company, provided jobs and an improved business climate in Summerland. (Courtesy the Duncan family.)

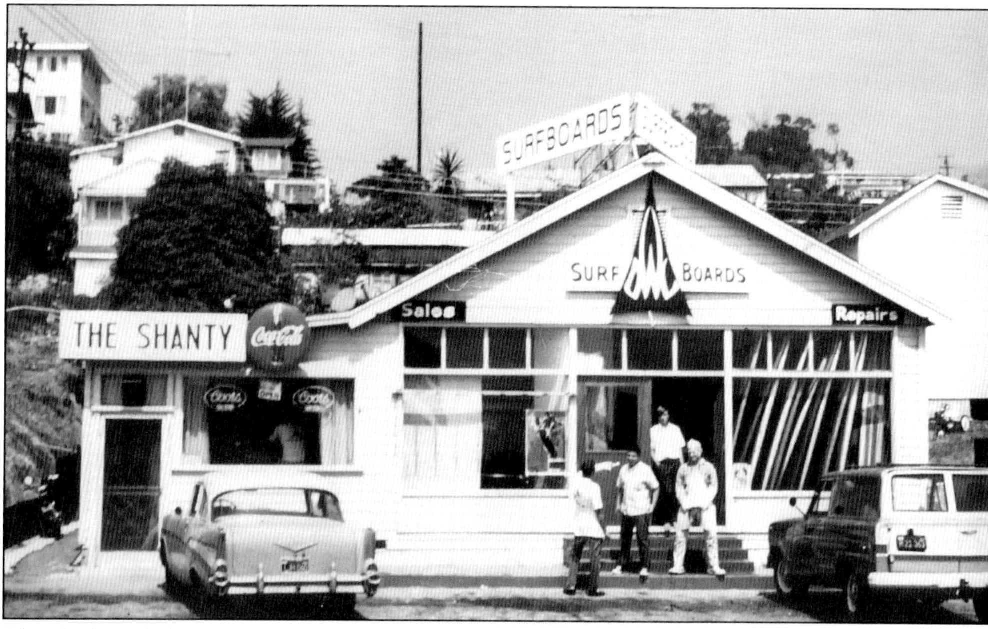

The Owl Surf Shop on Lillie Avenue was owned by Jeff White from 1962 to 1966. During this time, Summerland attracted a young crowd of new residents because of its inexpensive land values. Some were surfers drawn to the beaches of Summerland and Serena, and others were free-spirited hippies who sometimes lived 20 people to a household in what the locals called party houses. The Shanty burger joint is also pictured here. (Courtesy Jeff White.)

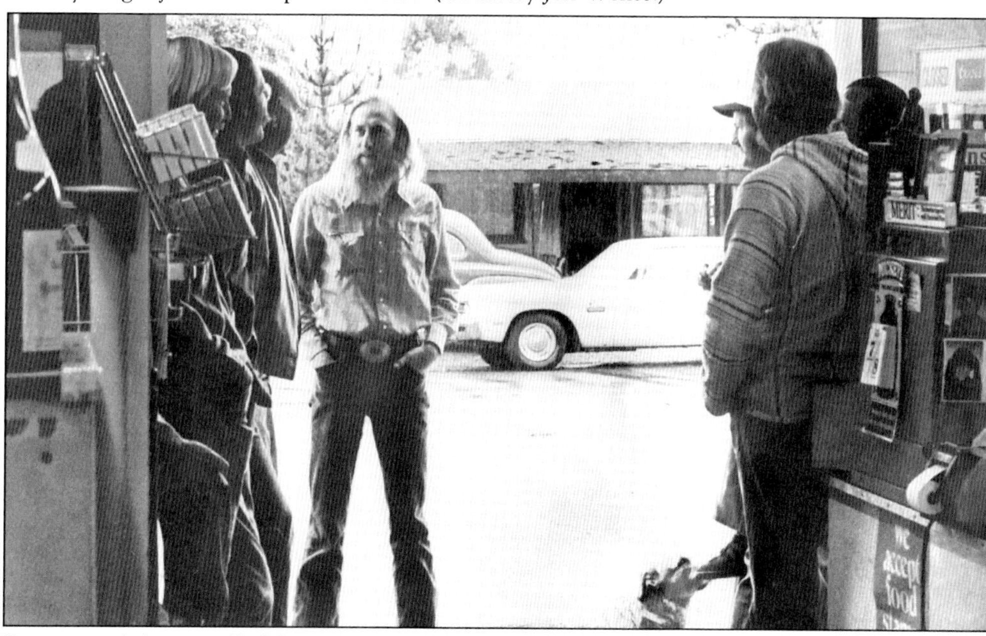

Denizens of the so-called Banner Manor on 2382 Banner Avenue, one of many Summerland party houses of the late 1960s and 1970s, flank Jack Barnard inside Lucky's Market (Summerland Market) looking out towards Lillie Avenue around 1970. From left to right are Billy Larisick, Bob Massey, "Doc," Mr. Barnard, Bob Norris, and Richard Peterson. The dog, Serano, lazes on the step outside of the store. (Courtesy Jack Barnard.)

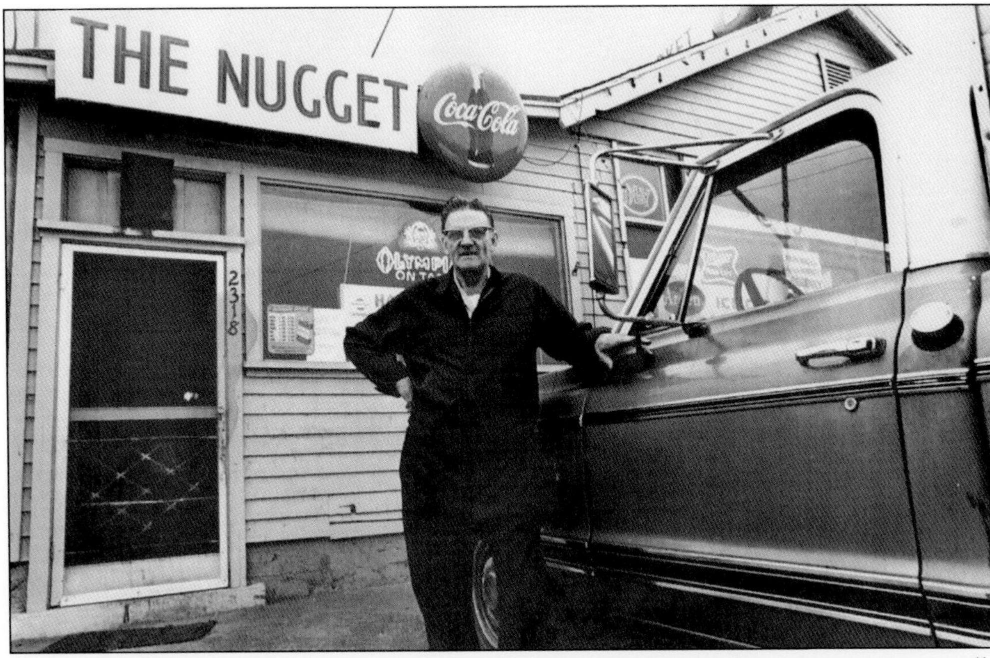

Roland Trombley, the first proprietor of the Nugget restaurant along Lillie Avenue, poses proudly in front of his establishment around 1970. A favorite hangout for the locals, word-of-mouth advertising brought new customers from outside Summerland to the narrow rectangular restaurant that featured a bar and a sitting area behind it. (Courtesy the Nugget.)

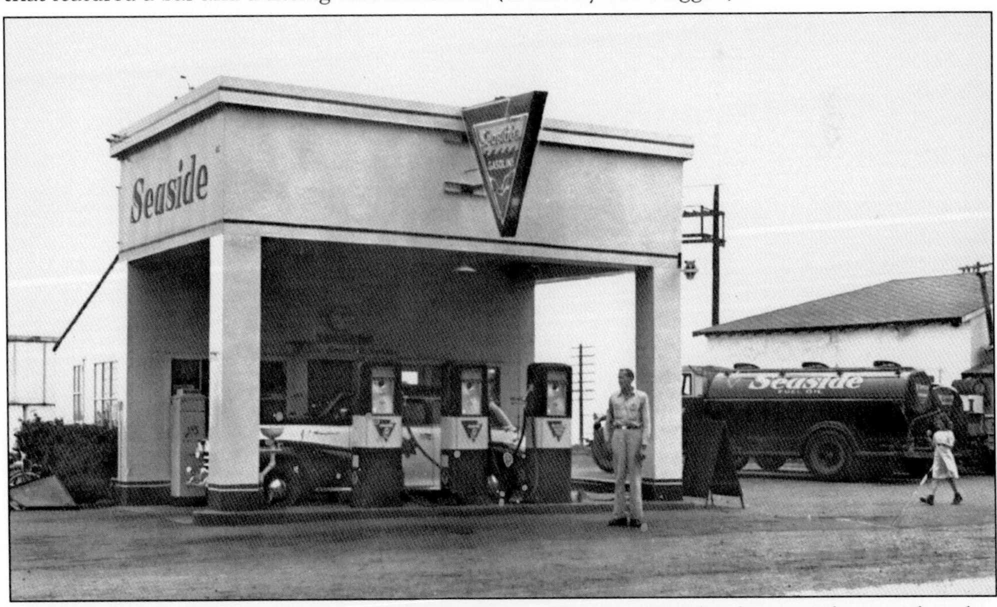

The Seaside Oil Company was established in Summerland in 1898 by three residents with stakes of $5 worth of stock shares each and two businessmen from outside the area with close to $100,000 in shares each. Presumably the Summerland residents supplied the know-how and the outsiders the capital. Summerland housed the company's main office for many years, plus an oil refinery. Walt Zisman's Seaside station is pictured on Lillie Avenue. Walt is standing in front of the station around 1950. (Courtesy Carpinteria Valley Museum of History.)

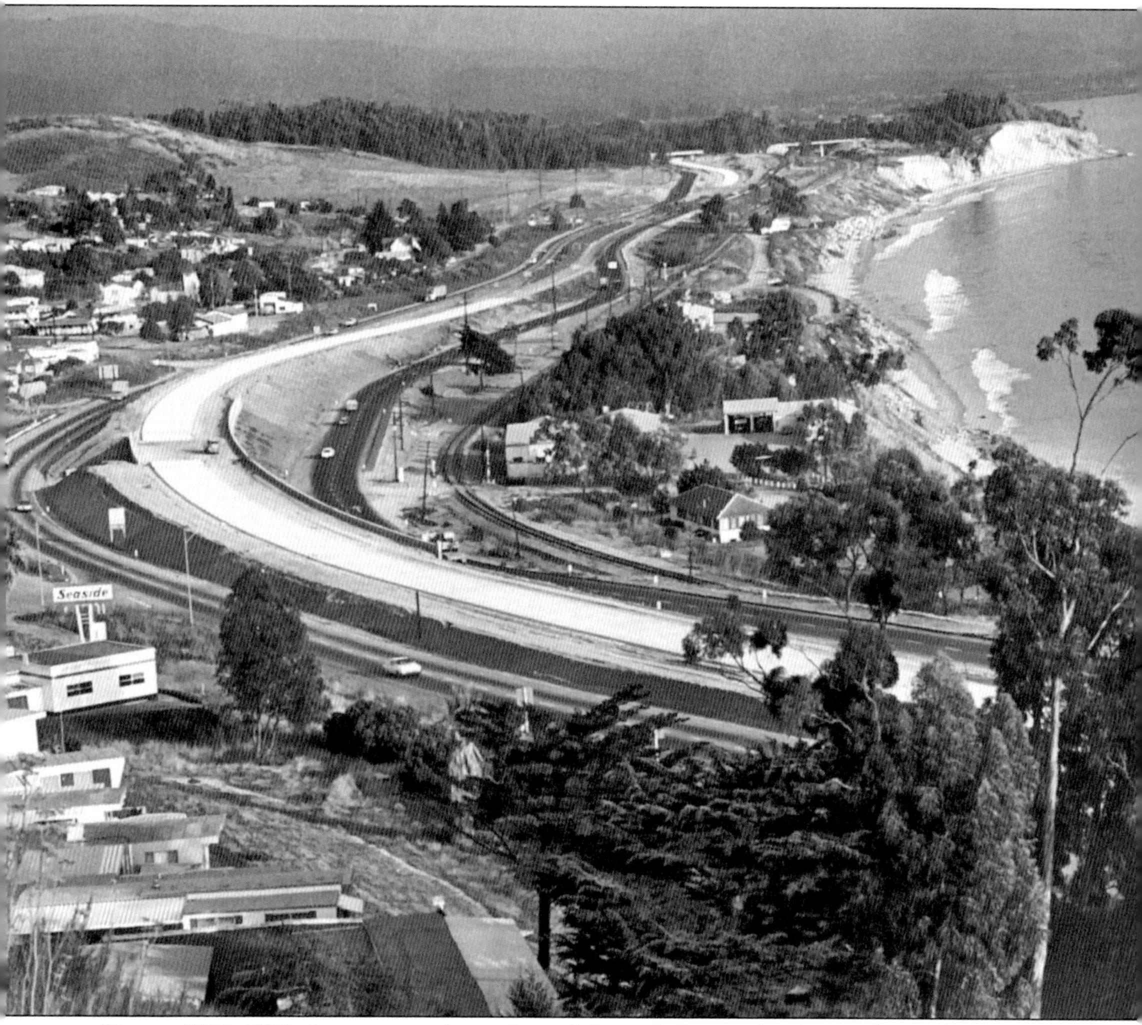

During 1925–1926, the main north-south road through Summerland was relocated from Wallace Avenue to Lillie Avenue and became part of U.S. 101. Lillie Avenue thus became the main thoroughfare in Summerland, as Wallace Avenue was effectively cut off, dividing the town into two parts. A tunnel was built near the Seaside station on Lillie Avenue at Valencia Road providing access to the beach. In 1950, the highway was moved again back to its original location through Wallace Avenue, eliminating the avenue and most of the buildings along it. Access to the beach was restored in the 1960s, when the freeway was elevated, as shown in this 1967 aerial photograph, allowing an underpass at Evans Avenue. Note the Seaside station on the left. It was relocated near Ortega Hill in the 1960s to make way for the freeway project. (Courtesy Carpinteria Valley Museum of History.)

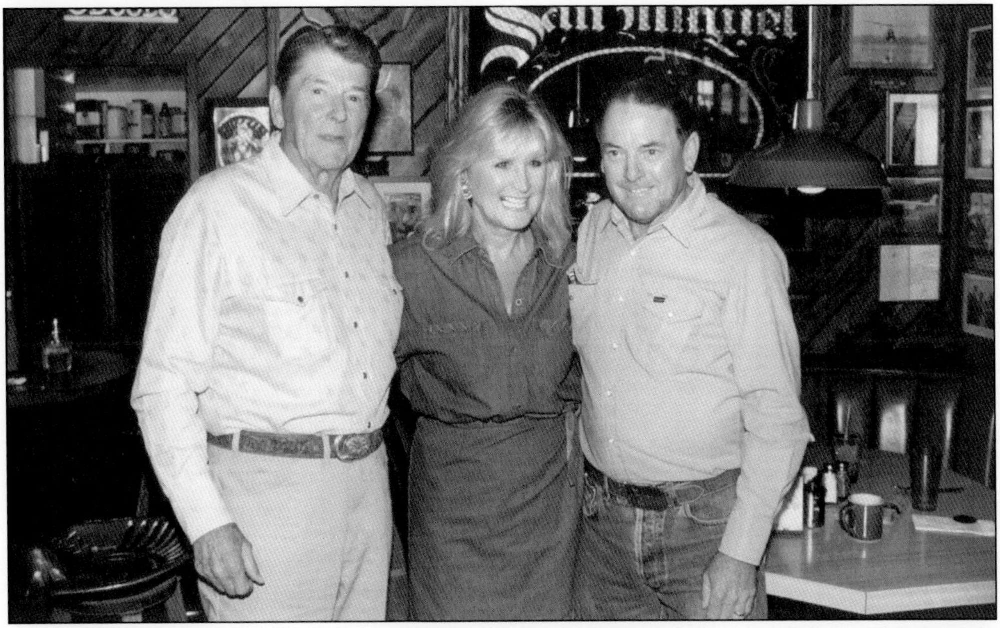

The Nugget restaurant was the successor to a few hamburger joints on the same location in Summerland under different names. Roland Trombley began to make a name for the Nugget in the 1970s, but it was under the proprietorship of Doug and Sally Taylor that the Nugget hit its stride, bringing the rich and famous to this establishment. Pres. Ronald Reagan made a visit in the 1980s and is pictured next to Sally and Doug Taylor. (Courtesy the Nugget.)

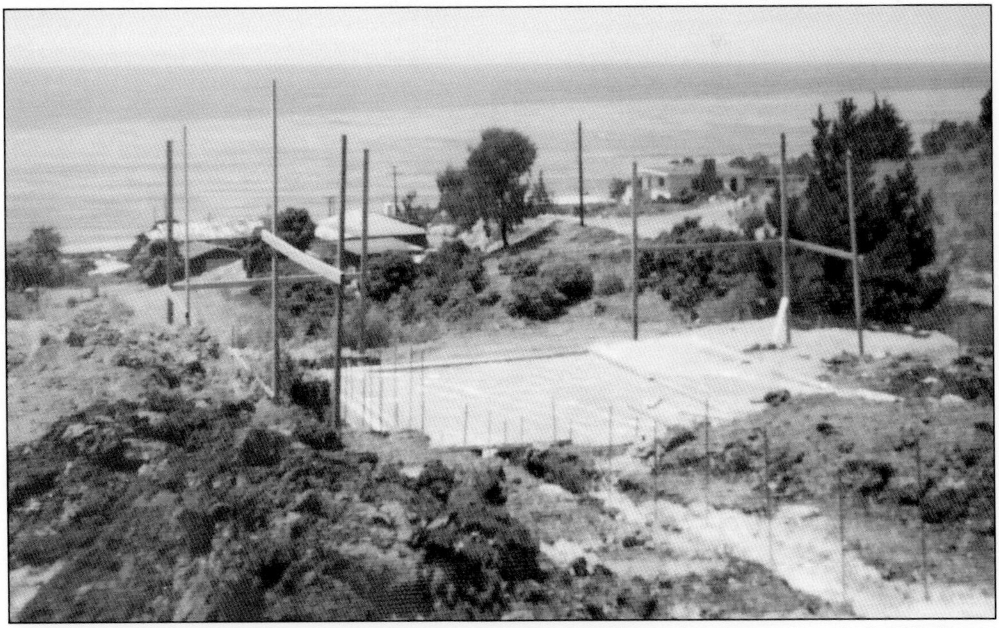

The Summerland Water Board solved the town's water problem when water from Lake Cachuma became available in 1984. A new water board installed just after this event, however, mandated owners of undeveloped parcels to build on them or risk losing their newly acquired water rights. This caused a building explosion of about 200 houses. The c. 1988 photograph shows the construction of a house with a view of the ocean on Whitney Avenue. (Courtesy Fran Vos.)

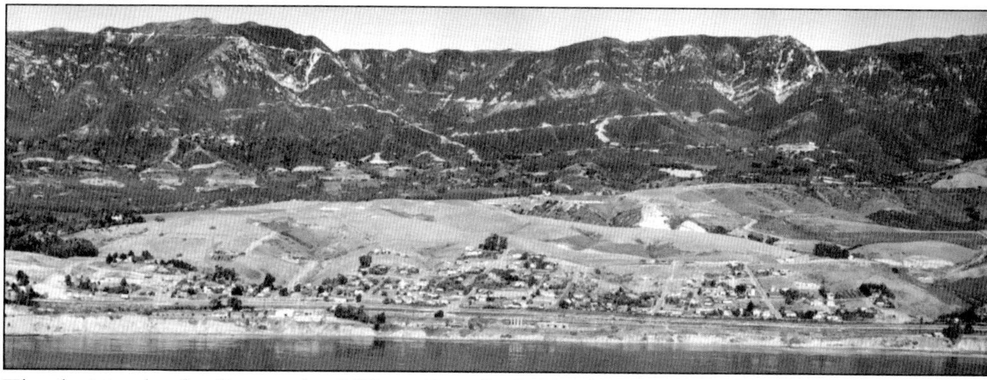

The decision by the Summerland Water Board of 1988 that property owners build or lose their water meter rights was not popular with the long-standing community, as evidenced by the board's ouster in the next election. This decision, however, turned Summerland into its current configuration, a quaint upscale village of residential housing, antique shops, and boutiques. This c. 1940 aerial photograph shows a panorama of the Summerland hillside as it was and largely still is to this day. (Courtesy the Duncan family.)

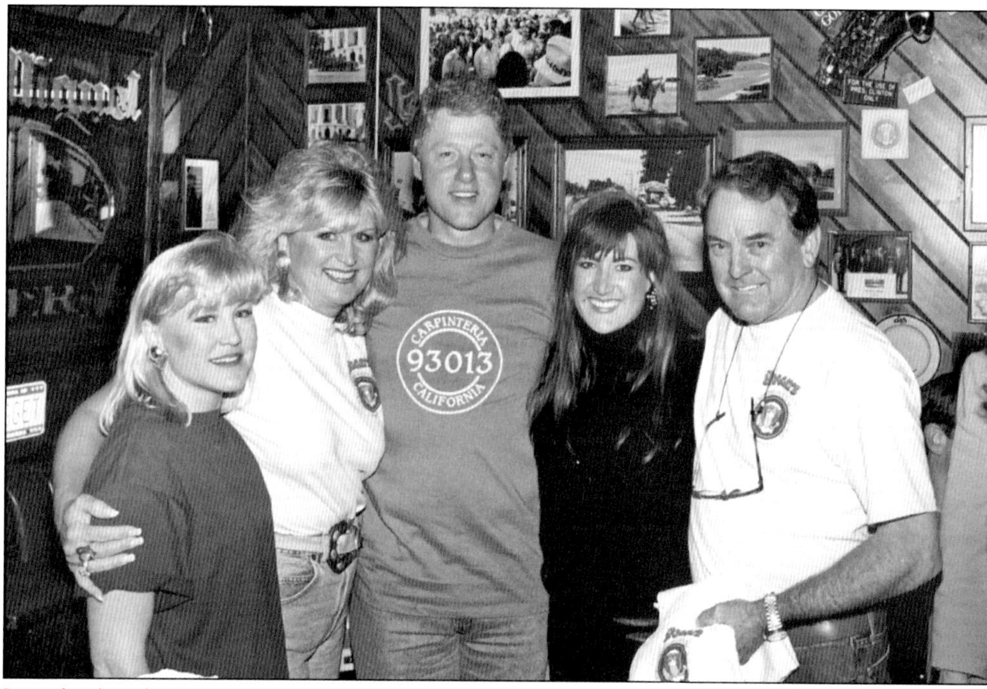

Just after his election in 1992, Pres. Bill Clinton visited the Nugget. Pictured from left to right are Jenny, Sally, President Clinton, Julie, and Doug Taylor. Note that President Clinton is wearing a Carpinteria T-shirt. On the wall, under the saxophone, is inscribed on a plaque, "For the use of Pres. Clinton only." President Clinton did not play the saxophone on his visit to the Nugget that day, but it is still there in 2009, waiting to come down into the hands of our country's 42nd president. (Courtesy the Nugget.)

Six

La Conchita and the Rincon

The history of the community of La Conchita has always been closely tied to the Rincon area of Greater Carpinteria, despite the appearance of the Ventura County line, which separated them in 1873. *La Conchita*, Spanish for "little shell," was first used as the name of a spur on the Southern Pacific Railroad line in the 1880s, and it designated a much broader area than the present-day village now known by that name. Up through the 1930s, the area from Bates Road down to Mussel Shoals (then known as Mussel Rock) was referred to as La Conchita (essentially following the La Conchita section of the railroad line) and included Rincon Point. "Punta" was the original name of the small beach settlement founded in 1880, and its immediate coastal area was called *Punta Gorda*, Spanish for "massive point," which referred to its large rock promontory. From 1880 to 1916, a U.S. post office in Punta served as a stop for both the stagecoach and the railroad. In 1890, the first Punta Gorda School, a one-room schoolhouse covering grades one through six, was built in the village. It was replaced by a more substantial building in 1935. Innovative and progressive for its time, Punta Gorda School had a major impact on the development of La Conchita.

It was through the failed beachfront resort development of 1923 that Punta was renamed La Conchita del Mar and promoted as a seaside paradise. But La Conchita was destined to become a different kind of paradise. Abandoned by investors, it was settled by farmhands, railroad workers, and oil workers and became a unique multicultural, working-class, coastal neighborhood. A rich mix of Pacific Islander, Mexican, and Anglo cultural elements shaped the character of the community. Today La Conchita continues to have a distinct sense of place. It's a community of multigenerational friendships, one that welcomes cultural difference, appreciates individuality, and embraces creative eccentricities. It's a place where one is likely to see an incongruous variety of dwellings on the same block. In this tiny 10-block-long, 1-block-deep enclave, stark succulent-covered lots meet wild abundant tropical foliage, and banana plants can spring up anywhere.

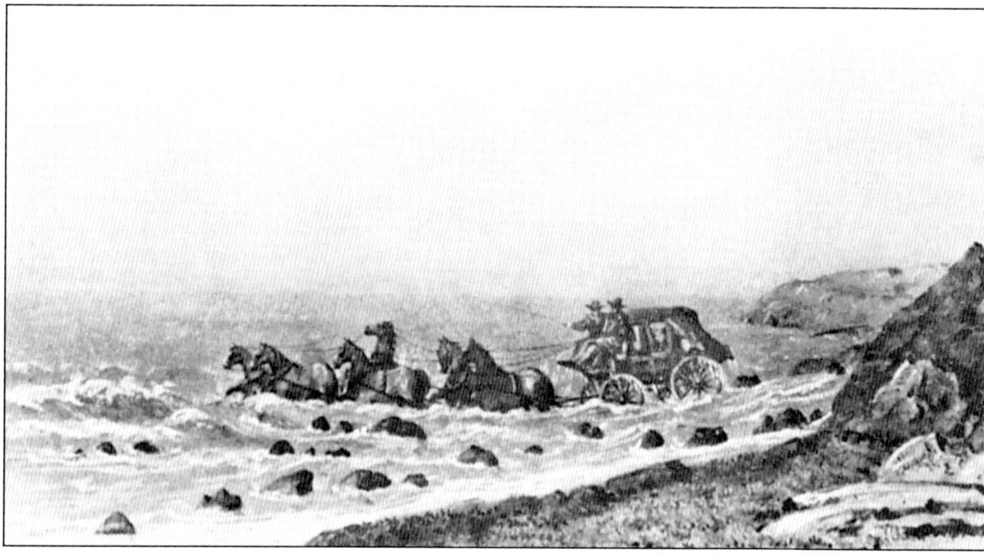

Driving a stagecoach on the coastal route was a hazardous occupation in the early years, when the idea of a road around the steep cliffs of the Rincon seemed impossible. There are many dramatic stories of horses and coaches with terrified passengers aboard being swept away during high tides, as illustrated by Edward Vischer's much reproduced sketch, *Stagecoach Crossing the Rincon during High Tide, 1871.* (Courtesy Bonnie Kelm.)

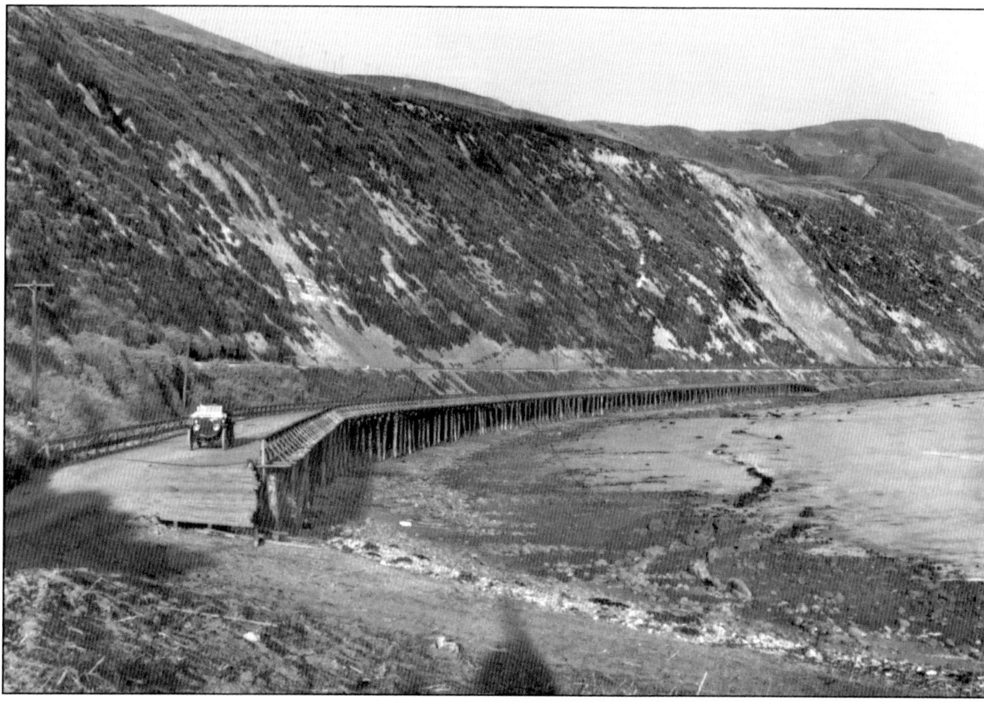

Narrow ledges were blasted to create the track bed for the Southern Pacific Railroad in 1887. A series of wooden causeways around the cliffs was first developed in 1910 from European models in Monte Carlo. The causeway was a timber pile trestle with a 16-foot-wide roadway. By 1912, Rincon Road (Camino Real) became part of the state highway system. Pictured above is the Rincon Causeway from the north end. (Courtesy Jeff Ross.)

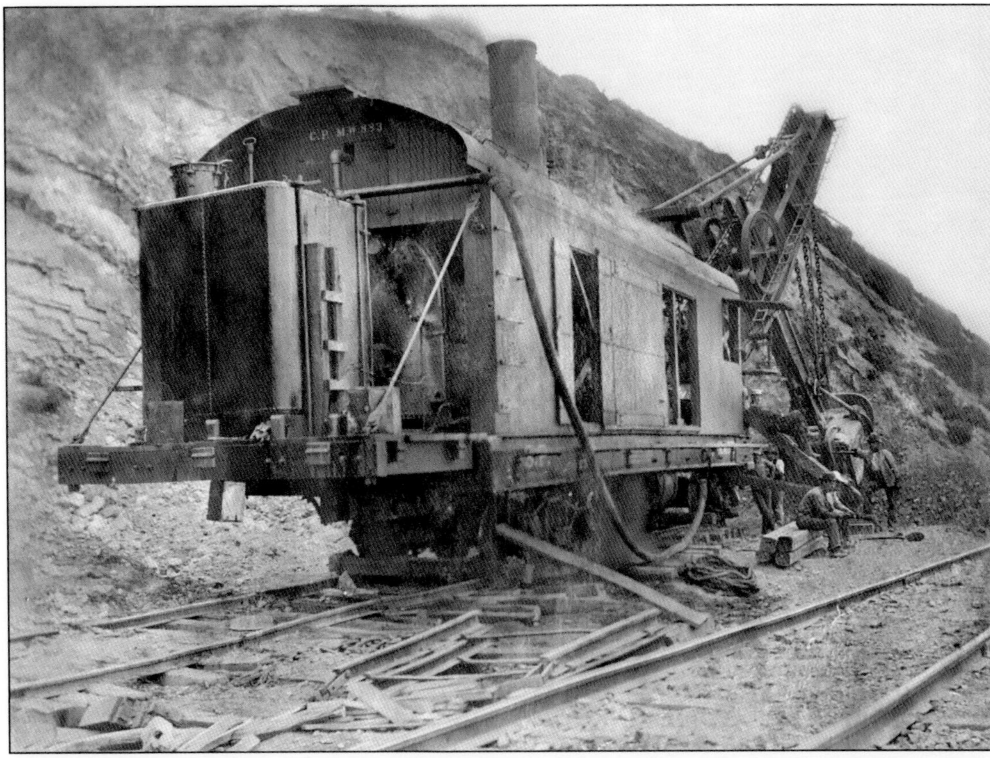

The section of the railroad tracks hugging the steep cliffs around the bend between Rincon Point and the village of Punta frequently had to be cleared of rockslides. In 1909, one such rockslide took on tragic proportions with the loss of six lives. (Courtesy Doug Treloar.)

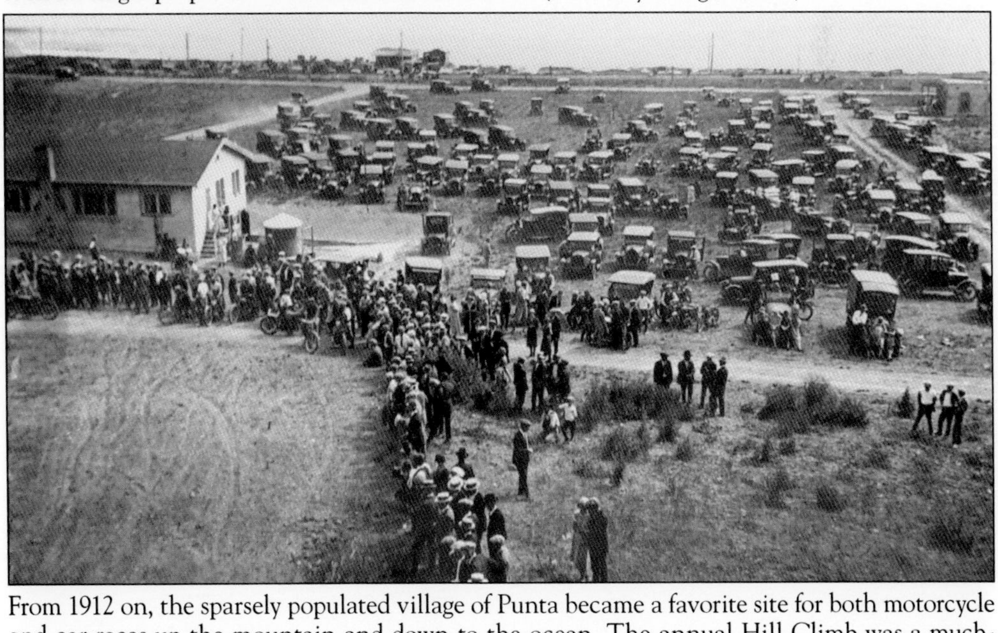

From 1912 on, the sparsely populated village of Punta became a favorite site for both motorcycle and car races up the mountain and down to the ocean. The annual Hill Climb was a much-anticipated event that continued to be held into the 1920s. Pictured above is the Hill Climb of 1918. (Courtesy Jeff Ross.)

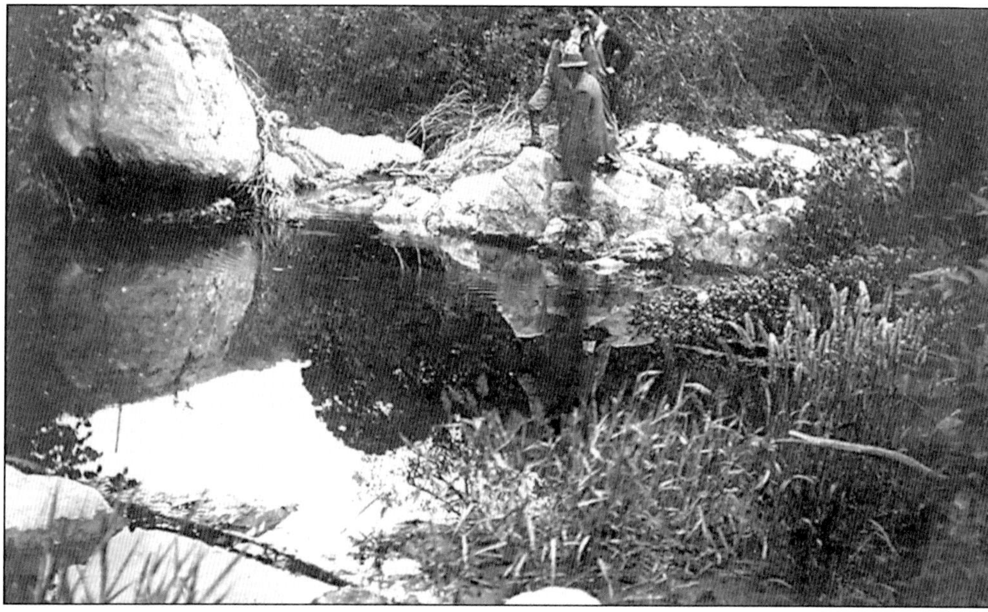

Pictured above are members of the Hill family at Rincon Creek around 1912. La Conchita and the Rincon were originally part of the Rancho El Rincon, a Spanish land grant received by Teodoro Arrellanes in 1840. Dr. C. E. Bates and Dr. Benigno Gutierrez jointly owned the ranch until late 1903. In 1889, the Hill family inherited 50 acres at Rincon Point and made their homestead on the west side of the creek. (Courtesy Robbie Hutto.)

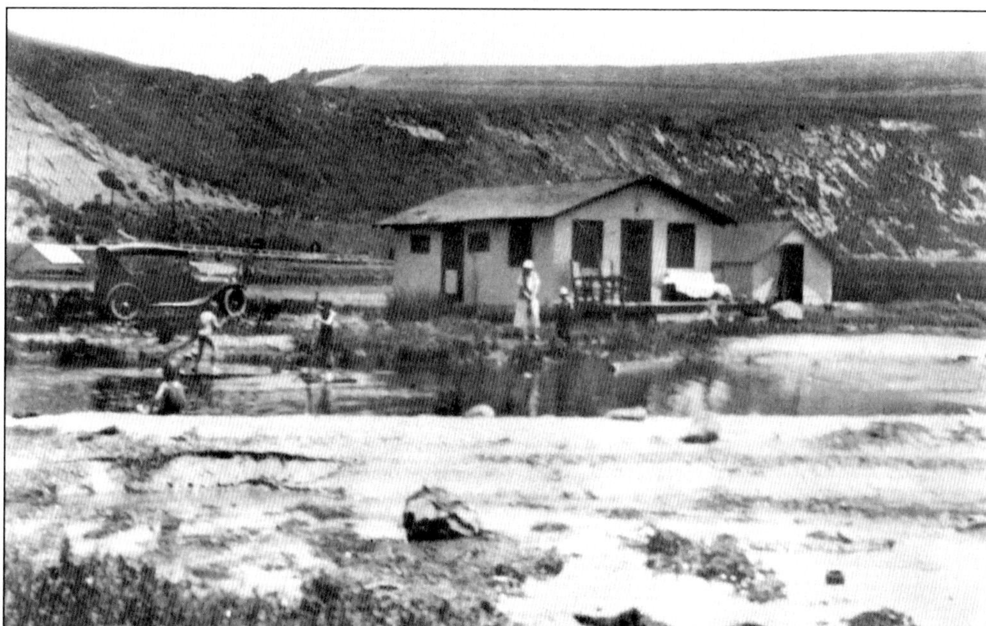

The descendants of Dr. C. E. Bates retained and purchased additional property around the creek at Rincon Point from the Hill family in 1923. Robert W. Bates and his wife, Juliette Marchand Bates, built their first family home on that site. Above, the four Bates children—Juliette, Bobette, Bobby, and Fleurette—play in Rincon Creek while mother Juliette keeps a watchful eye around 1930. (Courtesy Robbie Hutto.)

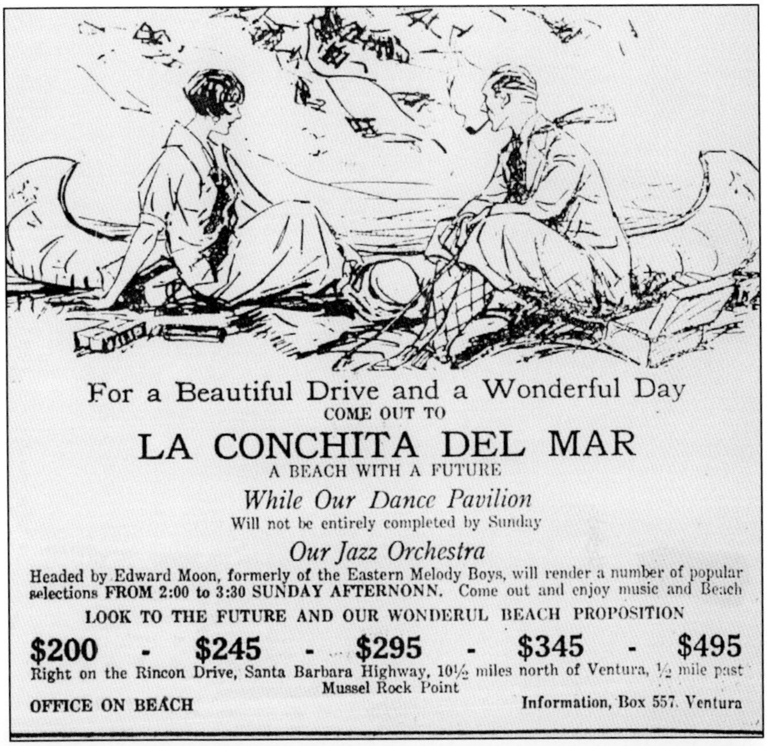

A parcel map of La Conchita was first recorded in the 1920s. Edward C. Ramelli purchased the Mussel Rock Inn and property in La Conchita in 1923. His brother, Milton, a civil engineer and surveyor, laid out the community plan. Promoted as "La Conchita del Mar," an affordable seaside paradise with lots starting at $200 including oil rights, the development proved to be a financial disaster. (Courtesy Jeff Ross.)

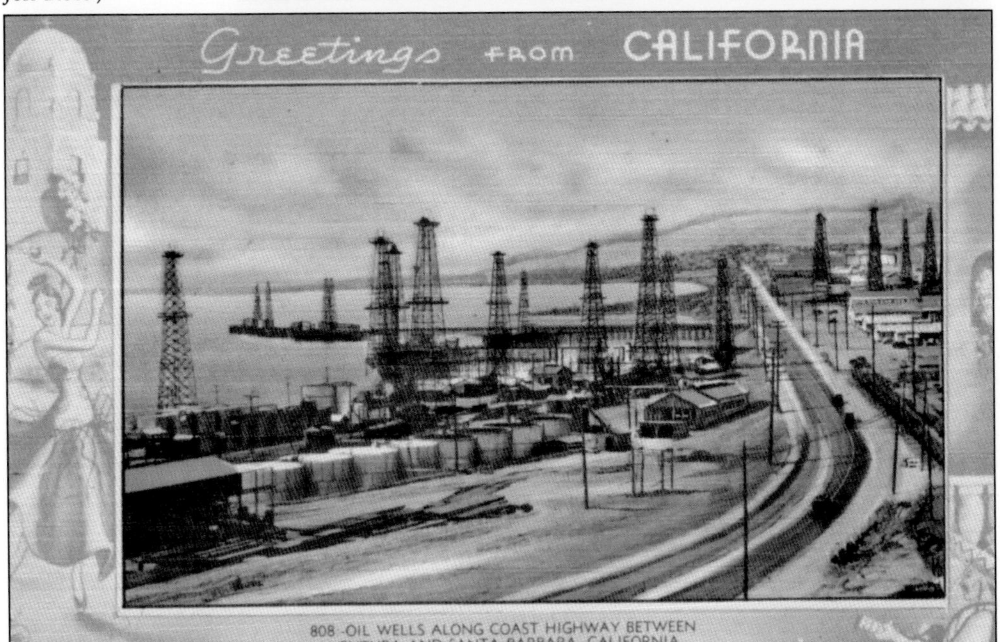

The Punta Gorda Land and Oil Company was established in 1900. Robert Bates and Andrew Bailard purchased land in La Conchita in the 1920s in hopes of finding oil. Successful oil drilling off Mussel Rock began in 1927. However, despite oil fields producing in Sea Cliff and elsewhere on the Rincon, no oil was ever discovered in La Conchita. The fresh water promised to all lots also never materialized. (Historic postcard courtesy Jeff Ross.)

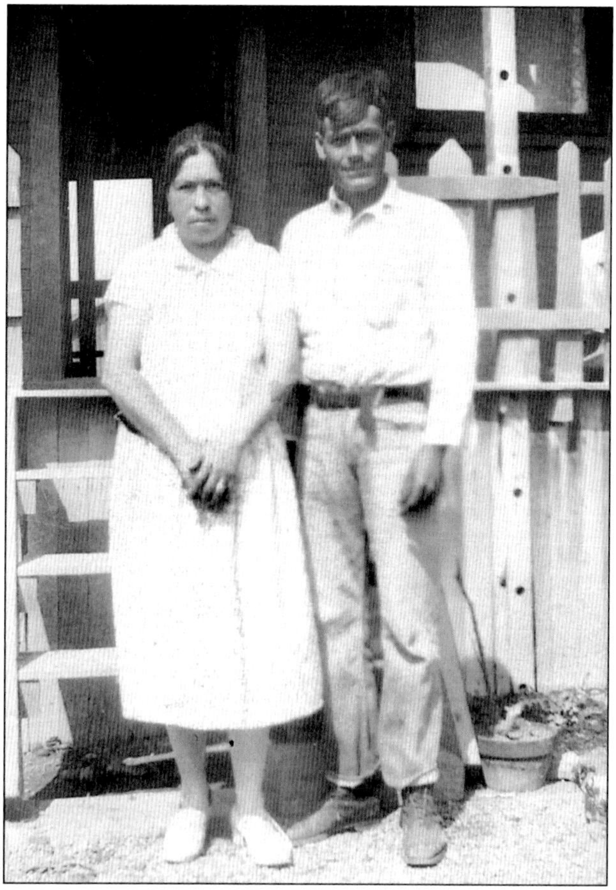

Although the resort development failed, a unique multicultural community took root in its place. La Conchita became a haven where people lacking economic means could fulfill their dreams of having property of their own. Joseph Gallardo and his wife, Jesse, came to La Conchita from Mexico in 1925, when Joseph went to work for the Southern Pacific Railroad as a watchman. At the time, the Gallardos were among the few families to live year-round in La Conchita. The house they built in 1927 still stands on Sunland Avenue (then known as Ventura Avenue). It is the oldest existing house in La Conchita. (Both courtesy Eleanor G. Ramey.)

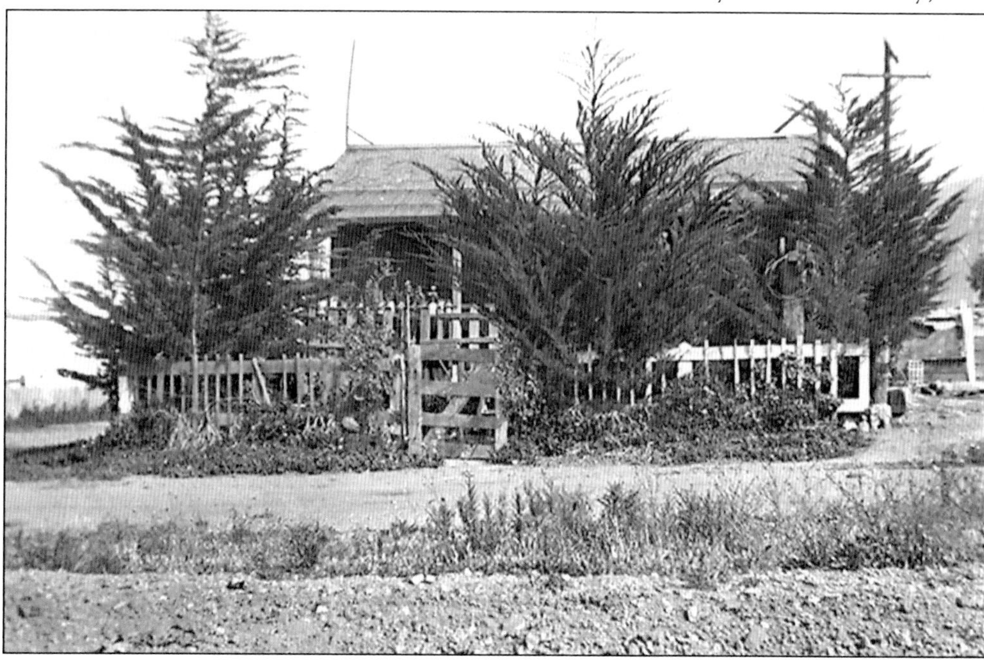

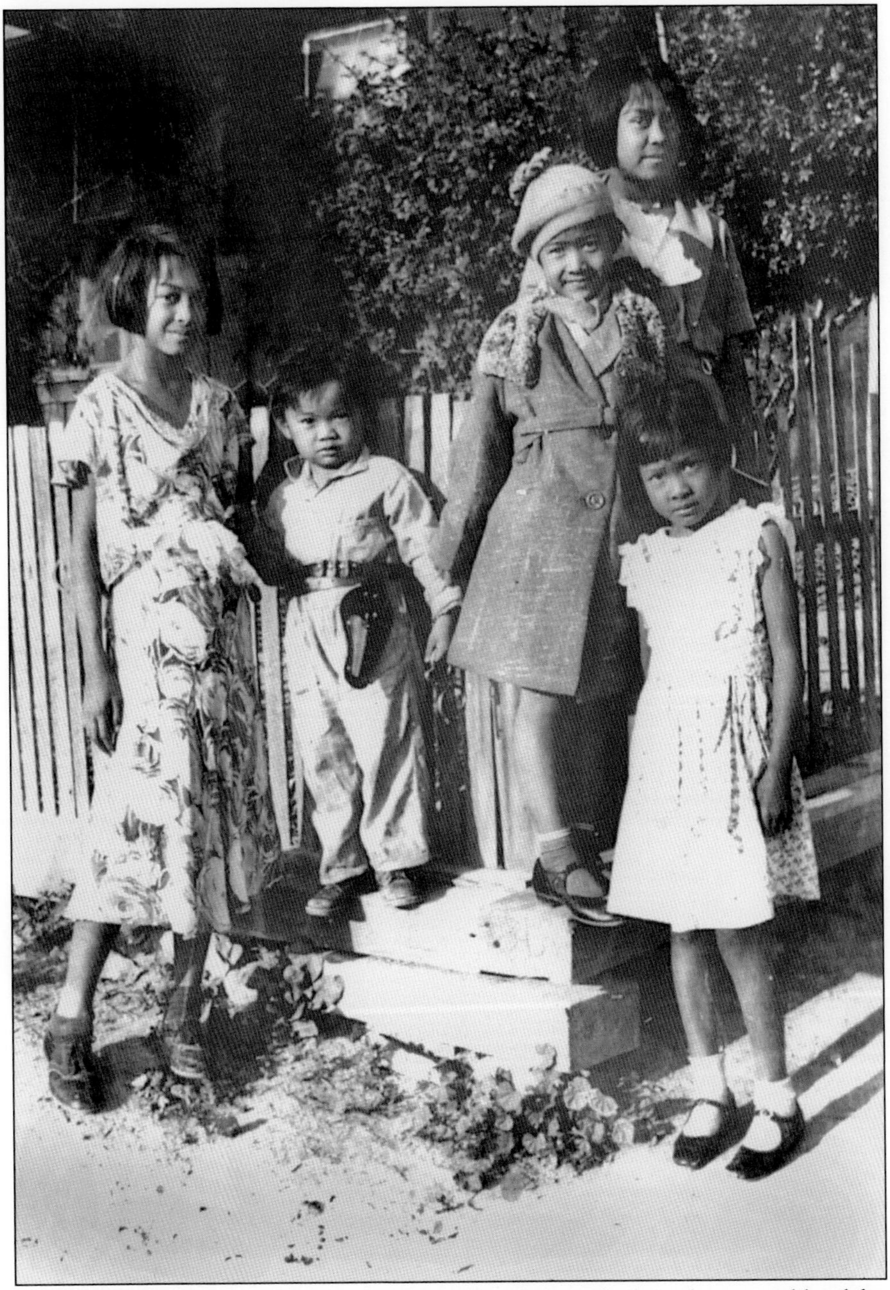

Federico Talaugon, his wife, Asuncion, and their family leased a large house and land from the Gaynor family ranch between La Conchita and the Rincon. They moved there in 1932 and became part of a growing Pacific Islander community in the La Conchita area. Many leased land to farm from the large ranches of the region. Federico Talaugon and his three brothers, Andres, Severo, and Paulino, worked on the Gaynor property until around 1950, when most of the family either moved to neighboring La Conchita or Carpinteria. Pictured above are children and relatives of the Talaugon family in 1935: from left to right are (first row) Gloria Talaugon, Dick Talaugon, and Marcy Jacoby; (second row) Pacita Montayre and Clara Montayre. (Courtesy Federico Talaugon Jr.)

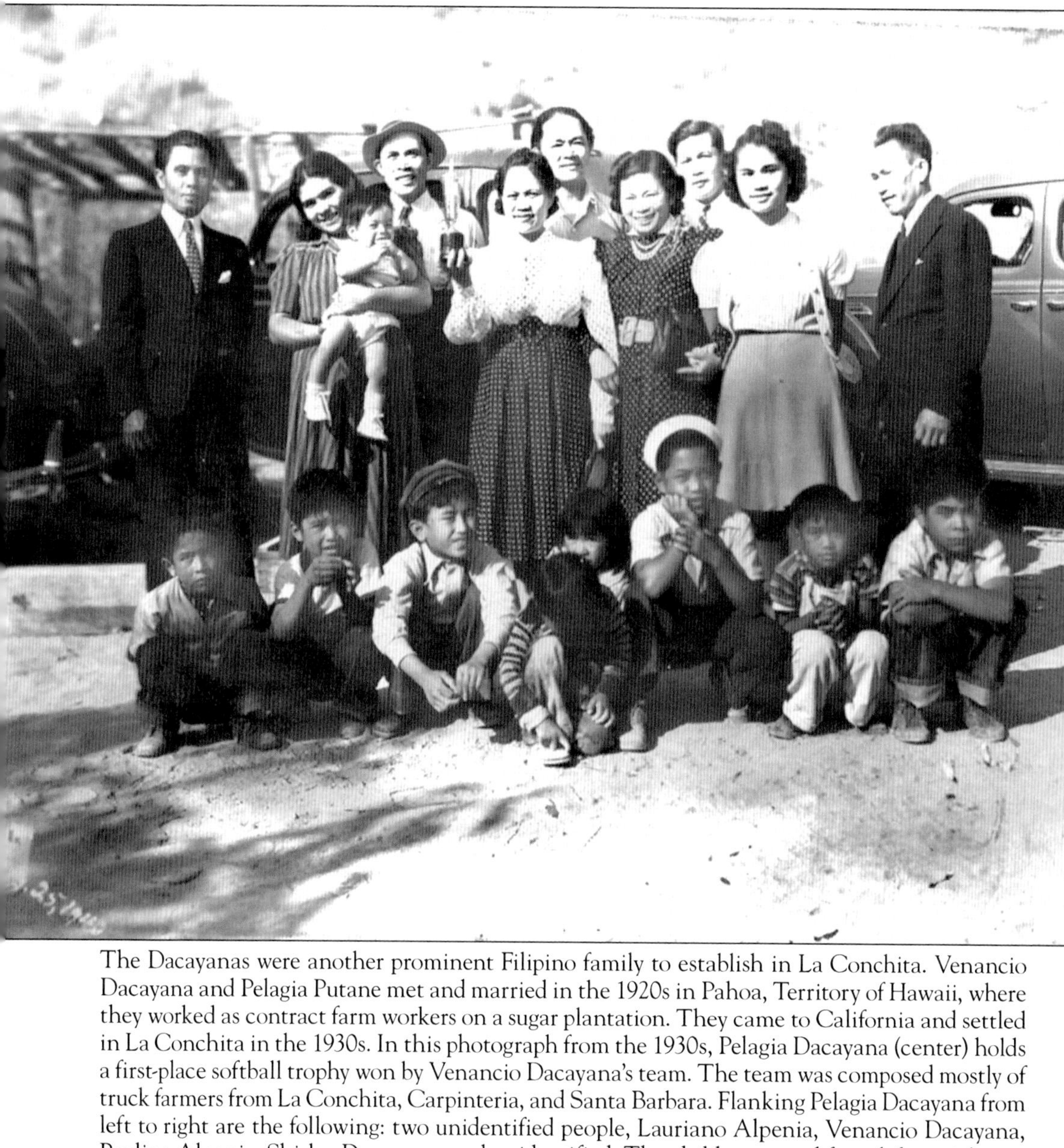

The Dacayanas were another prominent Filipino family to establish in La Conchita. Venancio Dacayana and Pelagia Putane met and married in the 1920s in Pahoa, Territory of Hawaii, where they worked as contract farm workers on a sugar plantation. They came to California and settled in La Conchita in the 1930s. In this photograph from the 1930s, Pelagia Dacayana (center) holds a first-place softball trophy won by Venancio Dacayana's team. The team was composed mostly of truck farmers from La Conchita, Carpinteria, and Santa Barbara. Flanking Pelagia Dacayana from left to right are the following: two unidentified people, Lauriano Alpenia, Venancio Dacayana, Pauline Alpenia, Shirley Dacayana, and unidentified. The children seated from left to right are two unidentified, Jackie Alpenia, Josie Dacayana, Archie Alpenia (in front of Josie tying his shoe), Chester Dacayana, Bobby Dacayana, and unidentified. (Courtesy Chet Dacayana.)

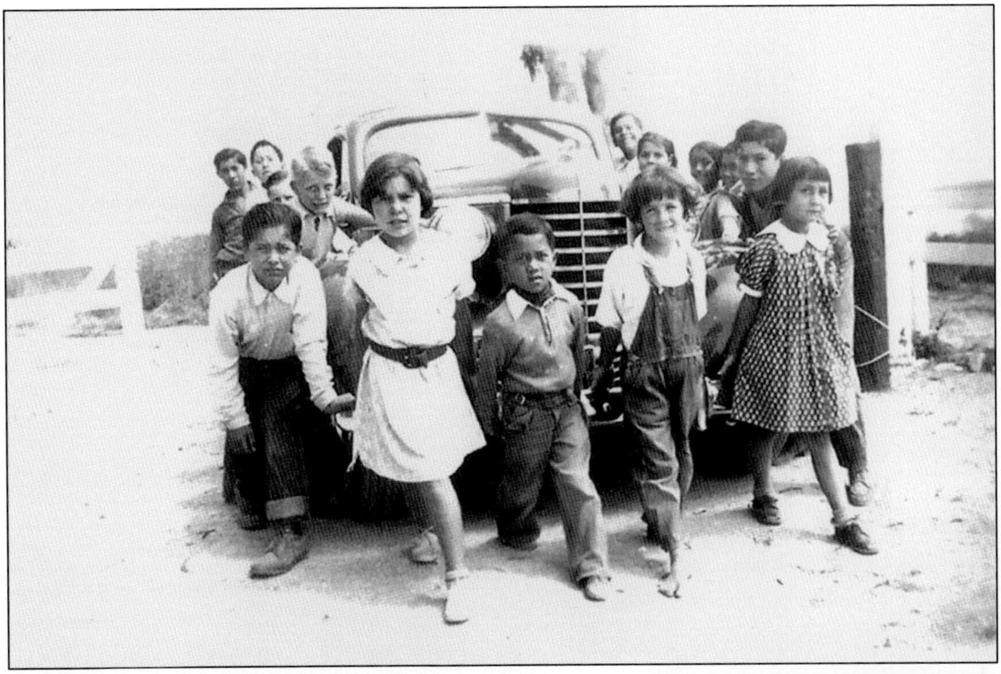

Outstanding among the memories of La Conchita residents past and present is the story of the Punta Gorda School, where Bessie Davison taught for many years. Above, students surround Miss Davison's car in the 1930s. From the rear left to right are Chester Wilson, Tom Gallardo, Edward Musick, Francis Hughes, Billy Ayala, Jesse Wilson, Chester Dacayana, Dorothy Musick, Mary Ruano, Louie Gallardo, Eleanor Gallardo, Dorothy Ruano, and Eugene Ayala. (Courtesy Eleanor G. Ramey.)

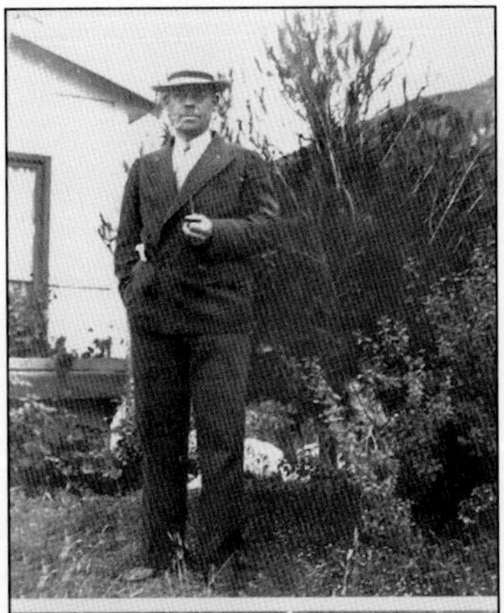

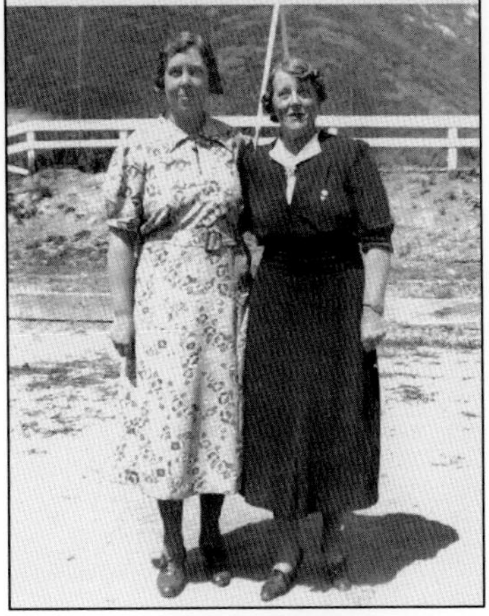

The guardian angels of Punta Gorda School were the president of the school board, Robert W. Bates (top right around 1935); teacher Bessie Davison (bottom right on the left around 1939); and school board member Margaret Hughes (bottom right on the right). Despite its humble size, Punta Gorda School left an amazing legacy of documentation testifying to its unique place in La Conchita history. (Courtesy Eleanor G. Ramey.)

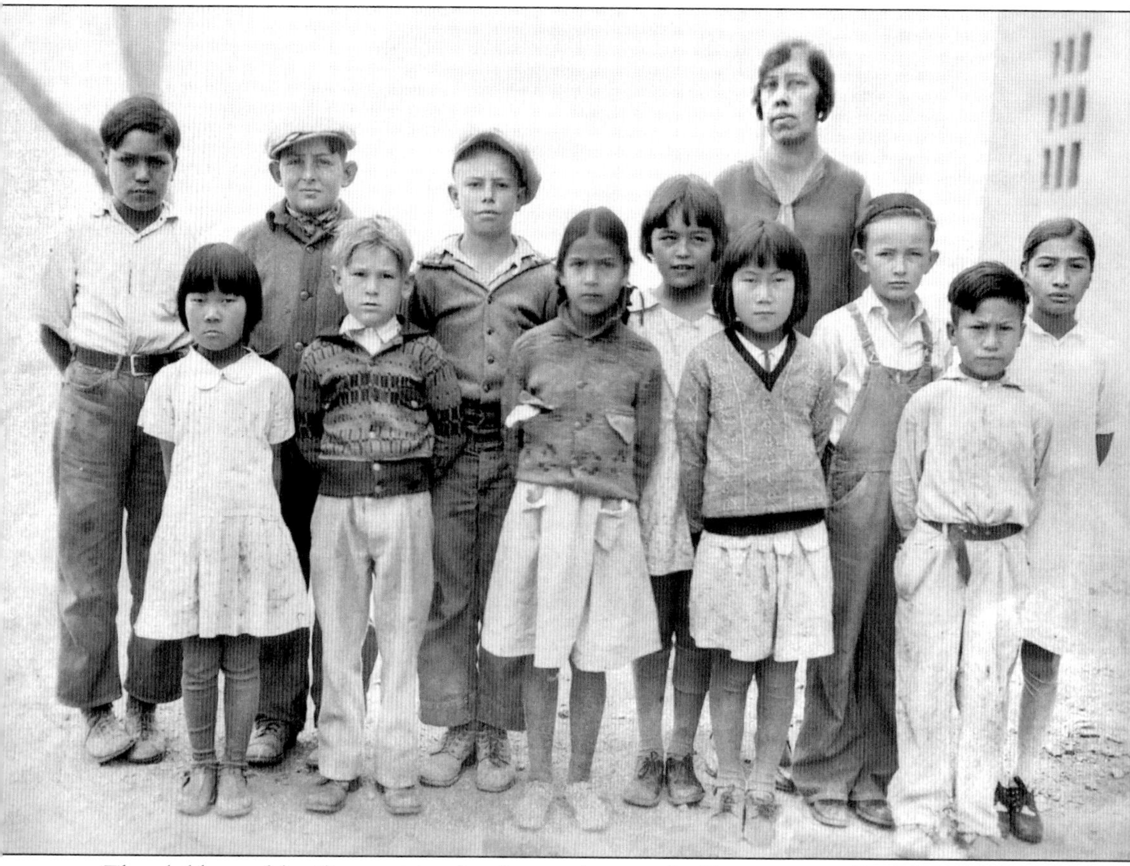

The children of families working for the ranches on the Rincon, as well as those living in La Conchita, attended Punta Gorda School. In the 1930 class picture, on the far left of the second row, is Ignacio "Nash" Gallardo, the oldest son of Joseph and Jesse Gallardo. On the far right in the first row is the Gallardos' second son, Abel. In the first row, on the left and second from the right are the Ota girls, Hanei and Masai, whose father, Kijuro Ota, worked as a foreman and leased land to farm from the Bates family's Rincon del Mar Ranch. On the far right in the second row is Teresa Ramirez, whose father worked for the Southern Pacific Railroad as a trackwalker. The railroad provided housing for the Ramirez family at Rincon Point. The Ota and Ramirez children walked to school along the wooden causeway that connected Rincon Point to La Conchita. Teacher Bessie Davison stands in the rear right of the class group. (Courtesy Eleanor G. Ramey.)

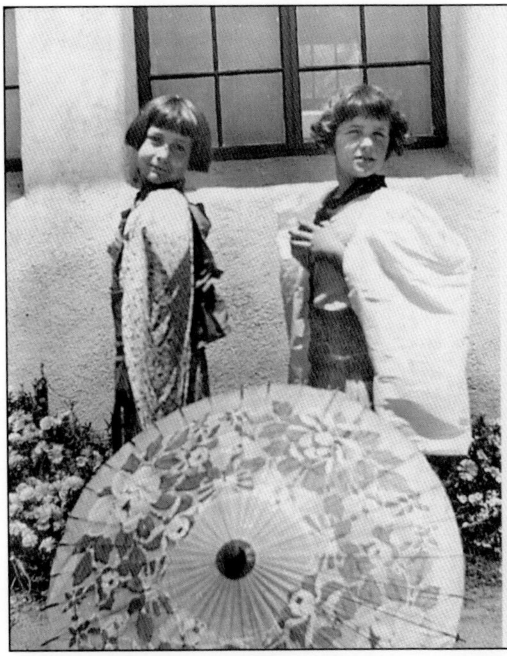

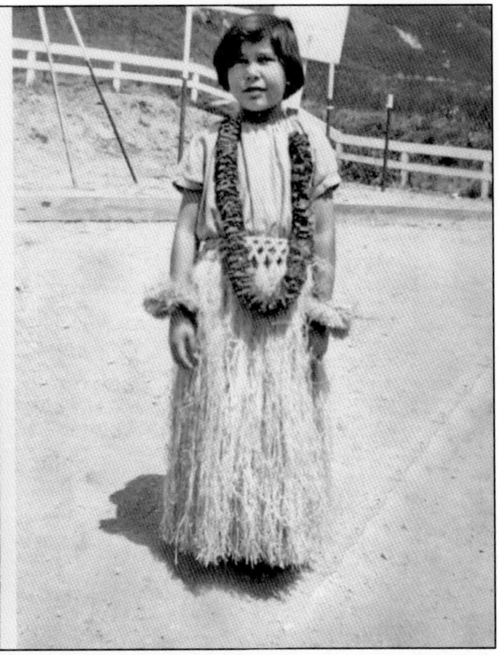

Punta Gorda School children had international costume pageants as part of their studies. In 1938, the pageant was "Our Pacific Playmates," which is described in one of the handwritten reports included in *Whisperings*, a student-created yearbook. Pictured above from left to right, Mary Ruano and Dorothy Musick participated as Japanese ladies, and Jesse Wilson performed as a Hawaiian dancer. Below, Francis Hughes (left) and Edward Musick appear costumed as Chinese men. As president of the school board, Robert W. Bates was particularly interested in the students' international education. He made generous contributions, providing opportunities that would have never been imaginable at a tiny school in a poor community. Among other cultural enrichments, R. W. Bates provided the funds for overnight trips to the World's Fair in San Francisco from 1939 to 1941. (Both courtesy Eleanor G. Ramey.)

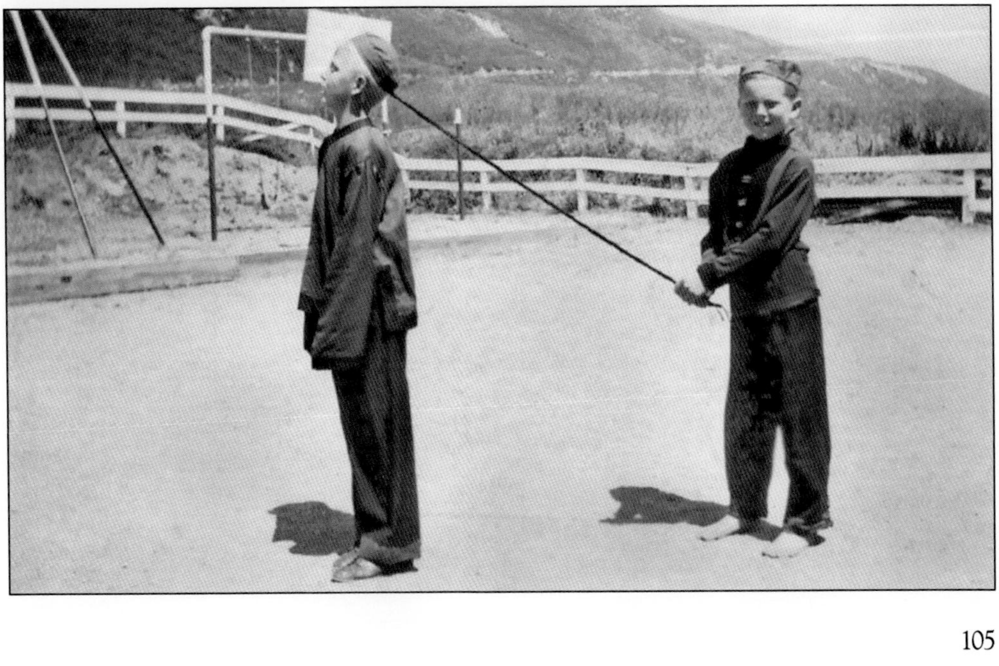

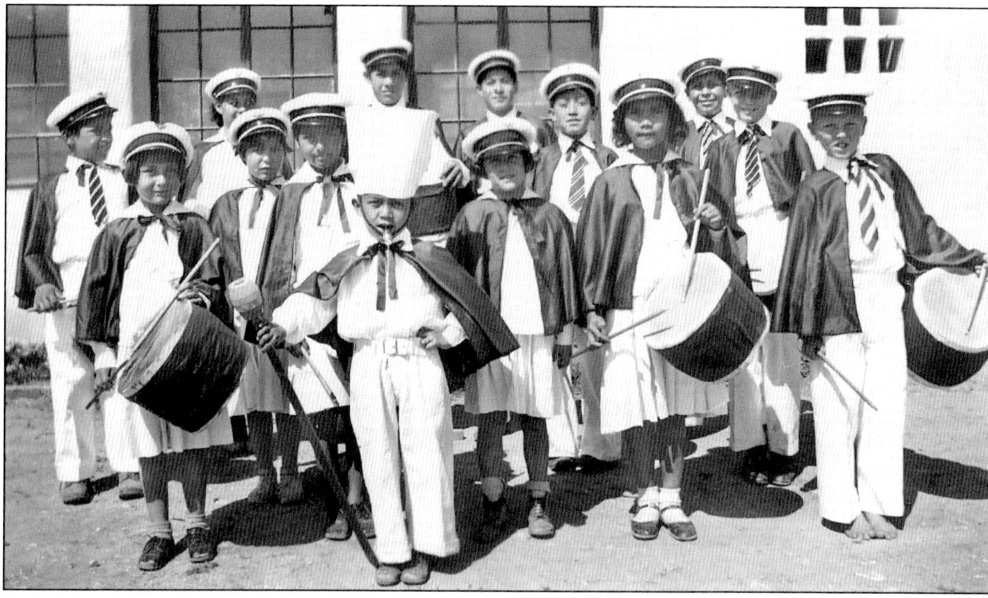

The drum corps was the pride of Punta Gorda School. The uniforms were made by student Dorothy Ruano and Miss Davison. In this c. 1938 picture, drum major Chester Dacayana is front and center. From left to right are (second row) Mary Ruano, Eleanor Gallardo, Dorothy Musick, Shirley Dacayana, and Edward Musick; (third row) Jesse Wilson, Tom Gallardo, and Francis Hughes; (fourth row) Billy Ayala, Dorothy Ruano, Chester Wilson, Louie Gallardo, and Eugene Ayala. (Courtesy Ben Dacayana.)

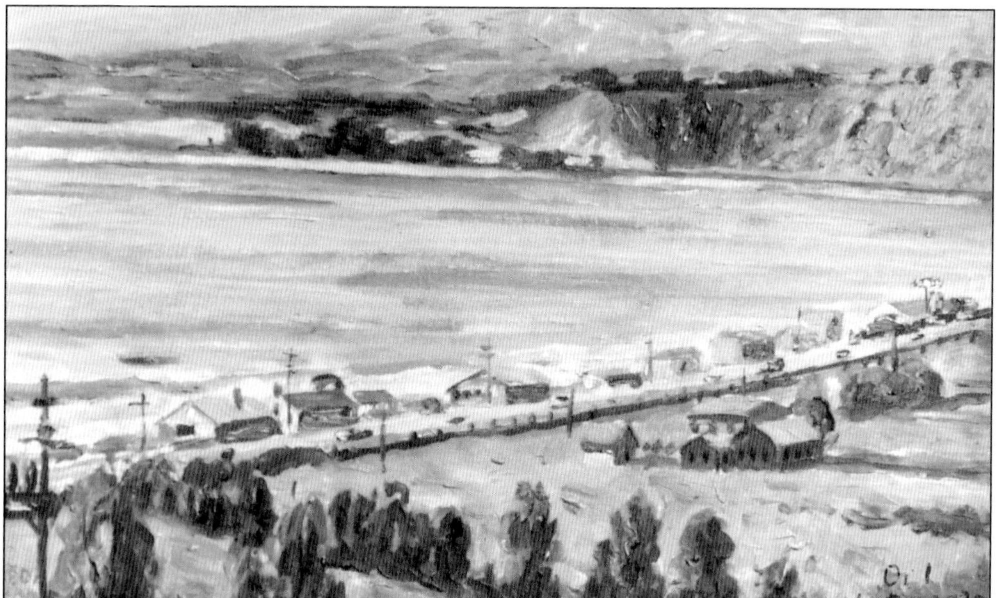

By 1930, approximately a dozen families lived year-round in La Conchita in small cottages at the foot of the hill. The beachfront properties included a restaurant, tavern, and a short fishing wharf. In the 1930s, Rudy Scheidman commissioned artist Victor Nikol to paint La Conchita. The painting gives an overall view of cottages and beachfront amenities in this thriving seaside community prior to World War II. (Courtesy Jeff Ross.)

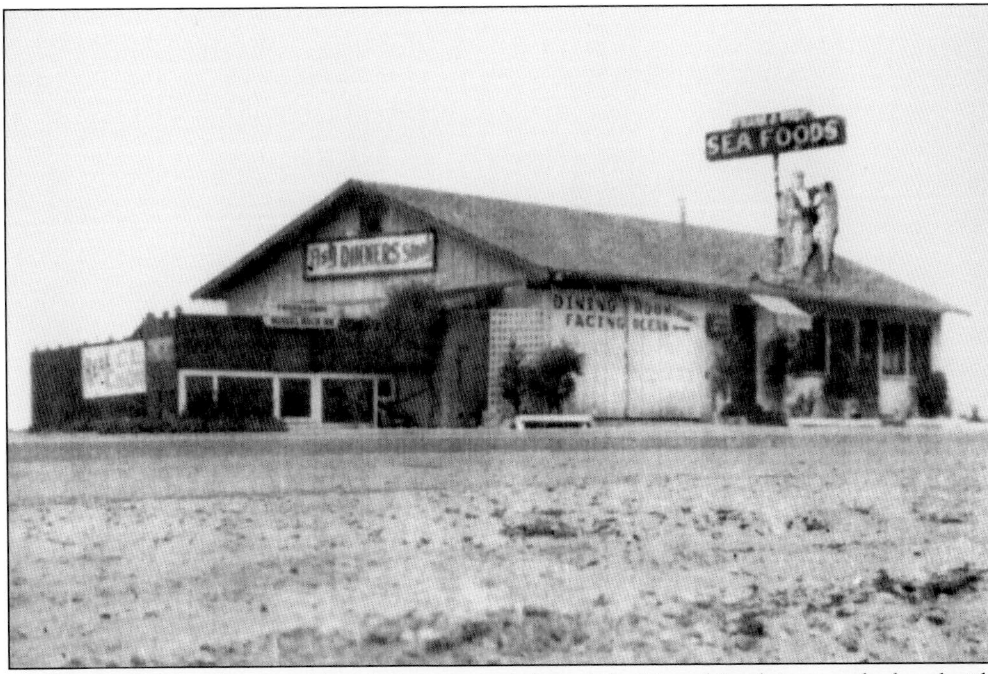

In 1931, Rudy Scheidman and Frank Regamey purchased the Mussel Rock Inn on the beach side of the railroad track at Mussel Shoals. It once had a glass-enclosed dance floor over the water that attracted such Hollywood celebrities as Warner Oland (the best-known Charlie Chan character) and opera singer Lotte Lehmann. When the highway was widened to three lanes in 1935, the restaurant was moved to the beach at La Conchita and renamed Frank and Rudy's (pictured above). During World War II, travel through La Conchita all but stopped, forcing the restaurant to close in 1942. Below is a Frank and Rudy's postcard by artist Victor Nikol. (Both courtesy Jeff Ross.)

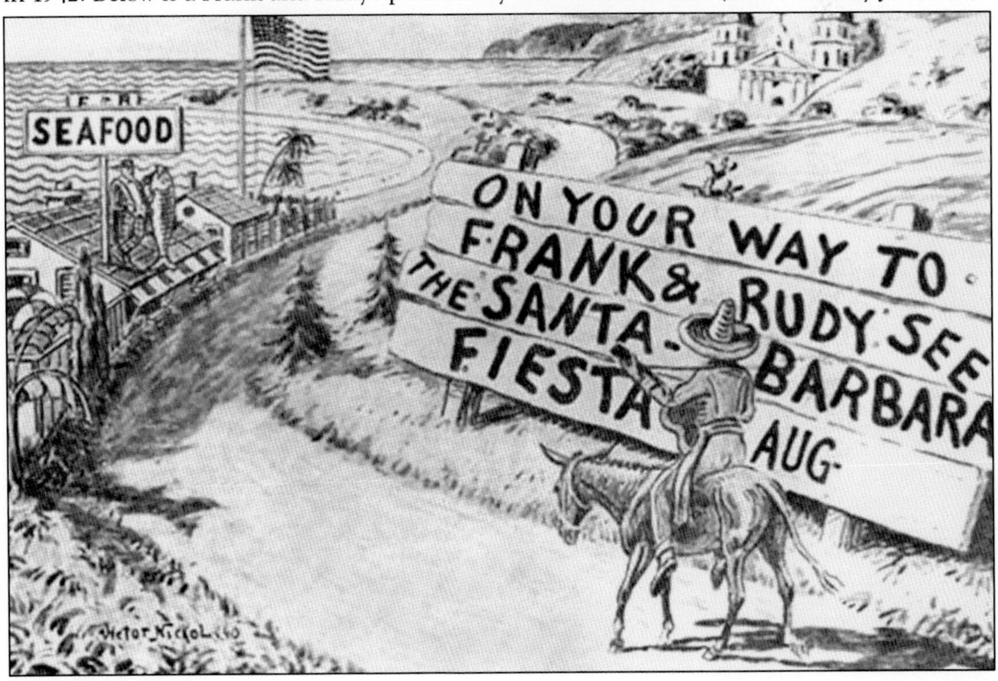

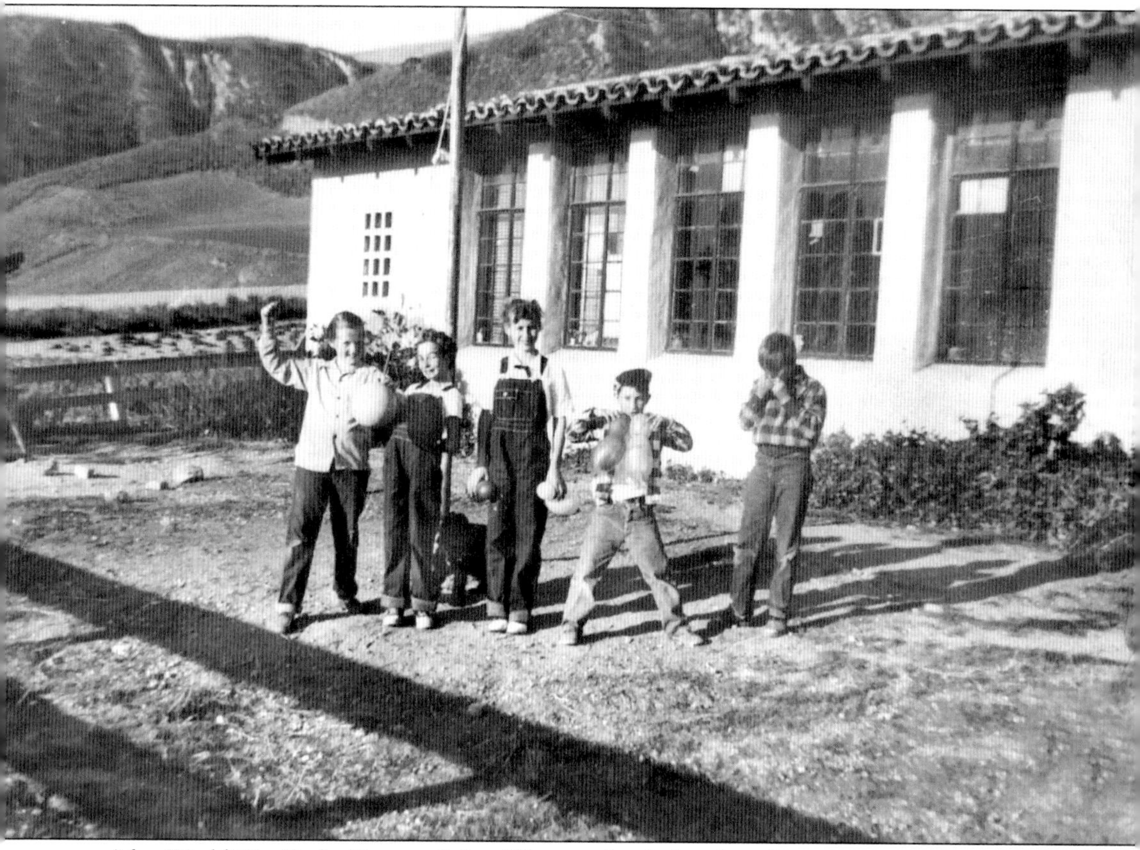

After World War II, the Ventura School District decided to close down Punta Gorda School, thus ending an extraordinary 60-year tradition. After the school officially closed in 1948, Madeline Giles and her two young daughters, Janet and Mary, moved into the vacant building, because they had no place else to live. In 1949, the building was moved from its foundation and relocated in Ventura, leaving the family again without shelter; local railroad workers helped them build a redwood-framed dwelling on the school site. After Madeline Giles remarried, the cabin was moved to Santa Barbara Street in La Conchita, where it later became the home of Janet Giles and her husband, Chet Dacayana. Pictured in the middle, both in coveralls, are the Giles girls—Mary on the left and Janet on the right—playing with three unidentified friends in front of Punta Gorda School around 1946. (Courtesy Chet Dacayana.)

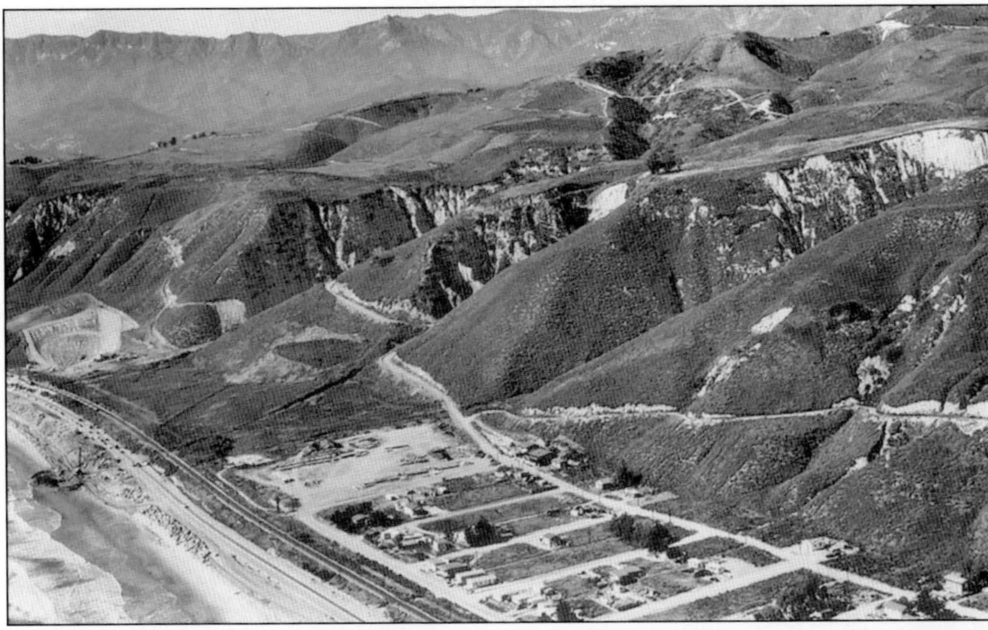

In 1949, the Coast Highway was widened to four lanes. The seawall was protected by a riprap of boulders weighing up to 10 tons brought by rail from Riverside County. The widening of the highway separated La Conchita from its seashore. Most of the cottages on the beach at La Conchita and Mussel Rock (now Mussel Shoals) were either moved to a new location or demolished. (Courtesy Ray Blackwell.)

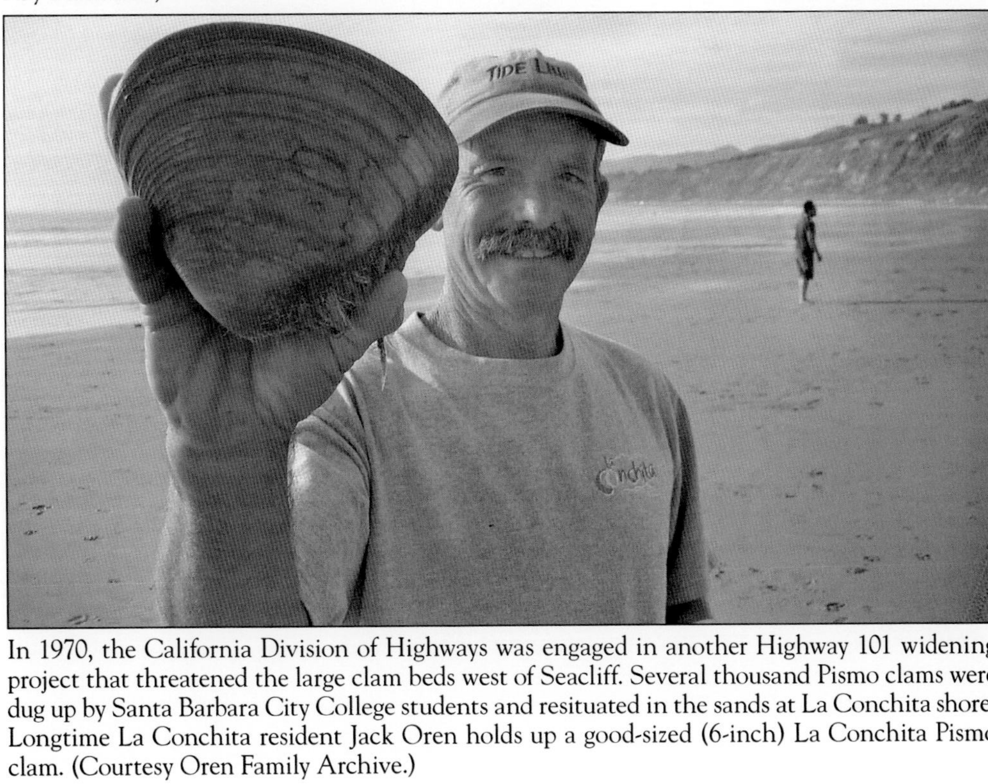

In 1970, the California Division of Highways was engaged in another Highway 101 widening project that threatened the large clam beds west of Seacliff. Several thousand Pismo clams were dug up by Santa Barbara City College students and resituated in the sands at La Conchita shore. Longtime La Conchita resident Jack Oren holds up a good-sized (6-inch) La Conchita Pismo clam. (Courtesy Oren Family Archive.)

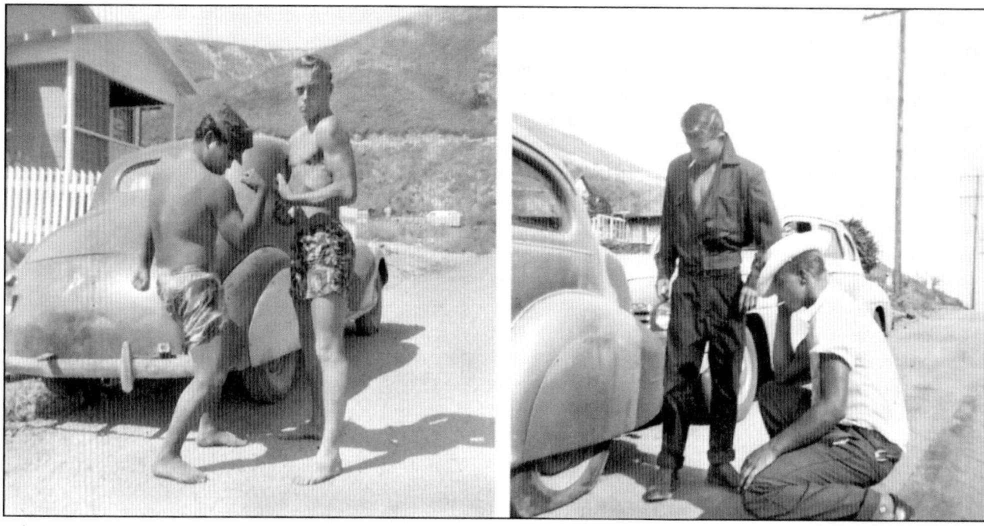

The 1950s were well remembered by those who lived in La Conchita, despite the lack of running water and the material things Los Angeles and Santa Barbara had to offer. Pictured in the left photograph are Archie Alpenia (left) and Stanley Sawyer (right), teenagers playing tough guys. In the photograph on the right, Bill Mingus and Stanley Sawyer invoke a cool James Dean sense of style while inspecting a flat tire. (Courtesy Bill Mingus.)

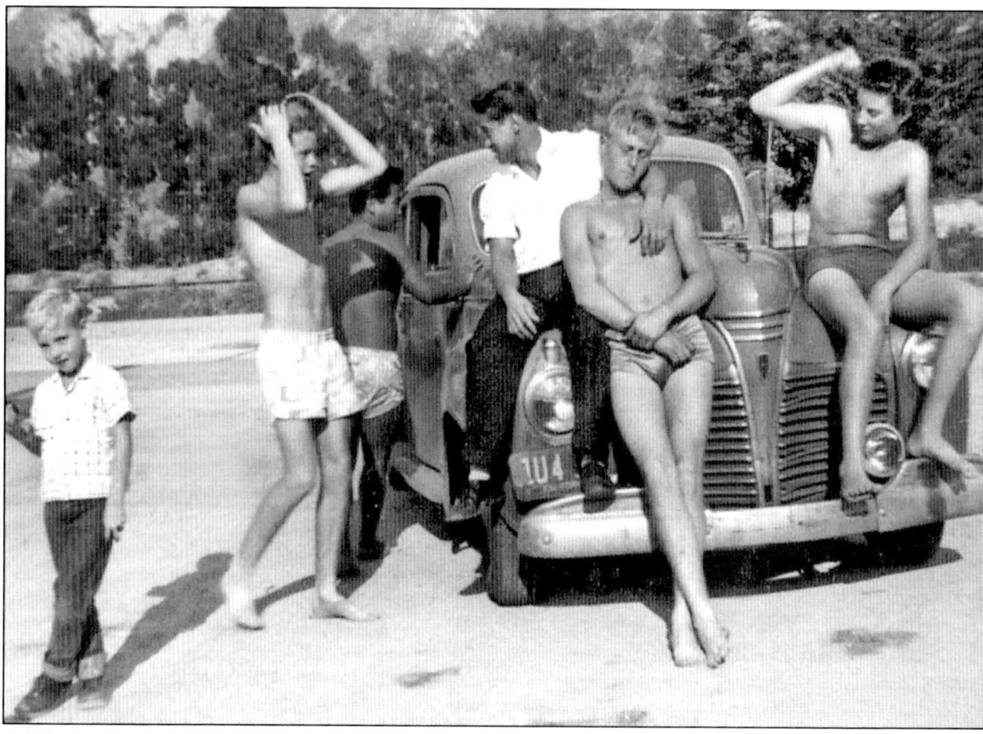

Bill Mingus remembers, "We were a close group of kids sharing the life style of a small community. I thought that everybody had similar bonding experiences. It wasn't until later that I realized that was not the case at all, ours was unique especially for the time." Pictured above from left to right are unidentified, Bill Mingus, unidentified, Bobby Dacayana, Stanley Sawyer, and Allen Blackwell. (Courtesy Bill Mingus.)

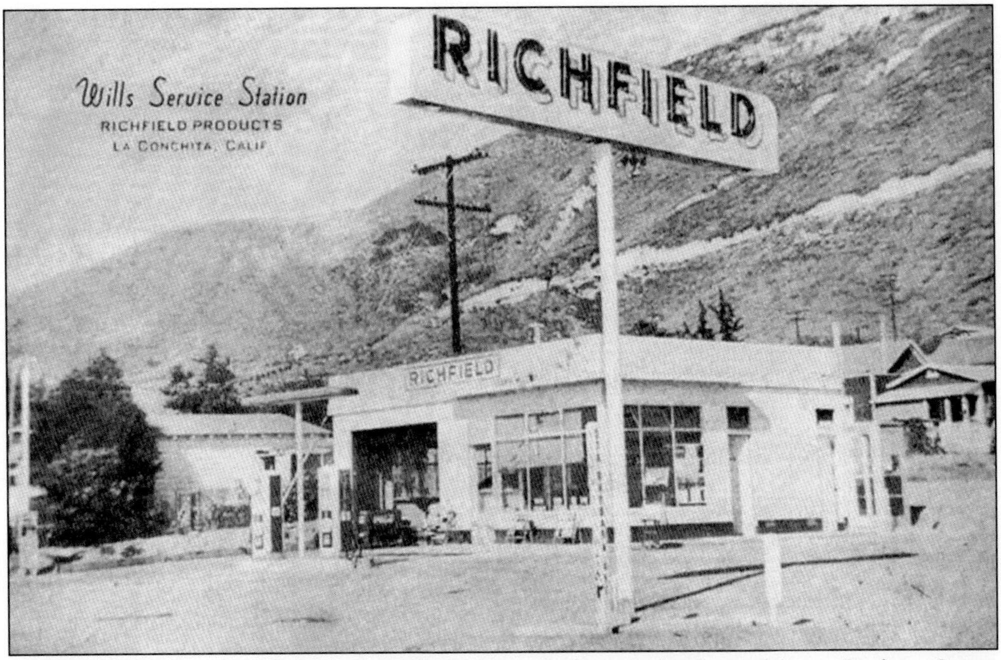

A landmark during the 1950s was Wills Service Station at the foot of Santa Barbara Street in La Conchita. It became something of a celebrity spot, since Frank Wills, a member of the western swing family of Bob Wills and His Texas Playboys, operated it. In the 1940s and early 1950s, Bob Wills and His Texas Playboys were the No. 1 country-western group in America. (Courtesy Ray Blackwell.)

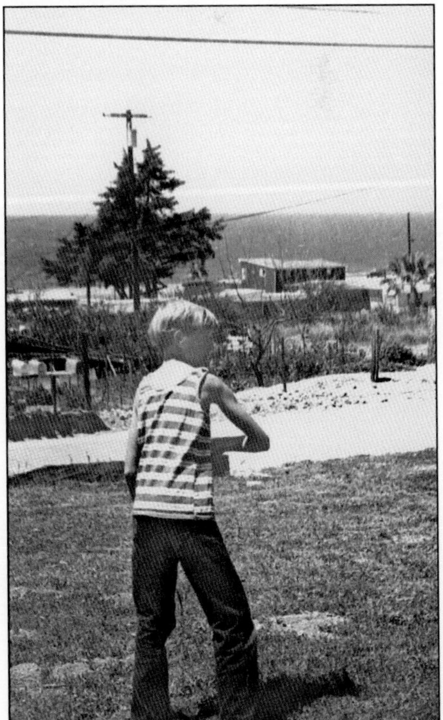

With the completion of Casitas Dam in 1959, running water finally came to La Conchita. Although separated by the highway, La Conchita still has an accessible beach and an ocean view. On the left, Jim Hazlewood, whose family has lived in La Conchita since the 1960s, throws a Frisbee on an empty lot above Vista del Rincon around 1974. (Courtesy Ken M. Hazlewood.)

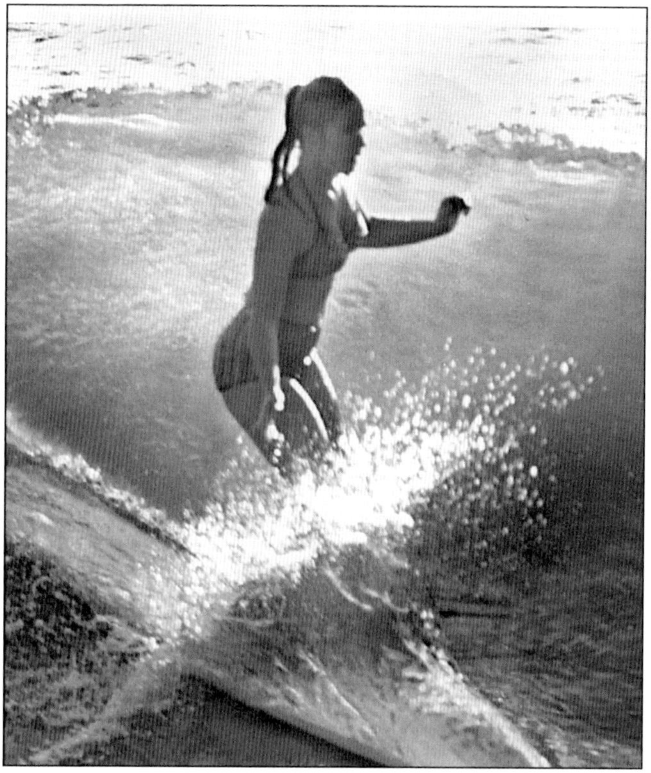

Among La Conchita's notable people is surfing legend Linda Merrill. She was the first woman to be featured on the cover of *Surfer* magazine in 1964. Her unique surfing style was highlighted by ballet-like artistry as she danced from tail to nose of her surfboard on the waves of Hawaii and California in the early 1960s. (Courtesy Linda Merrill.)

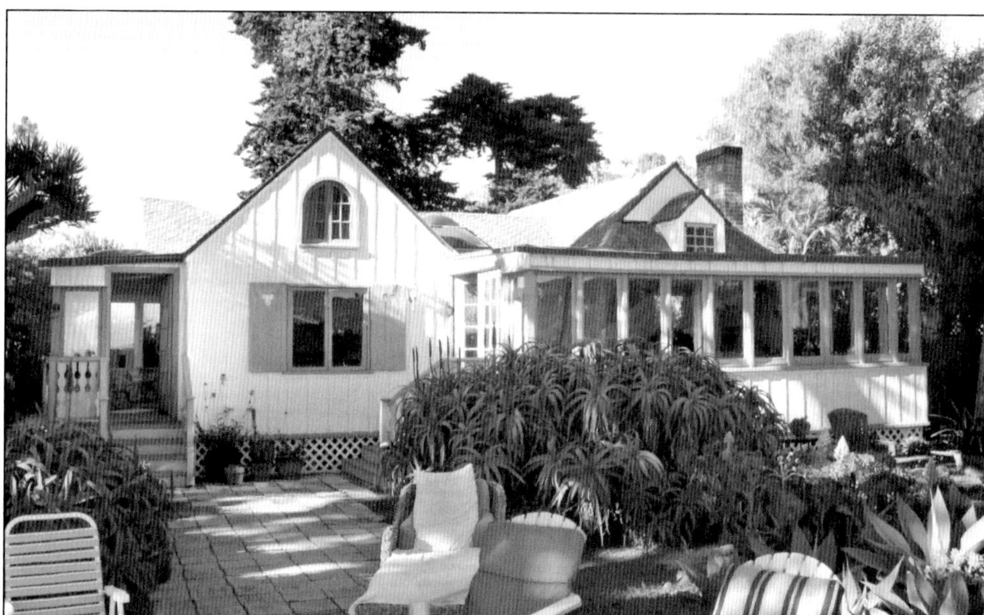

Warner Oland owned a cottage on the beach at Mussel Rock. He was a Swedish-born veteran actor destined to be remembered as the actor who first popularized the movie character Charlie Chan. Oland played the inscrutable detective in some 16 movies. When the highway was widened, Oland's cottage was moved to Rincon Point, where much of the original structure remains. (Courtesy the Lindley Institute.)

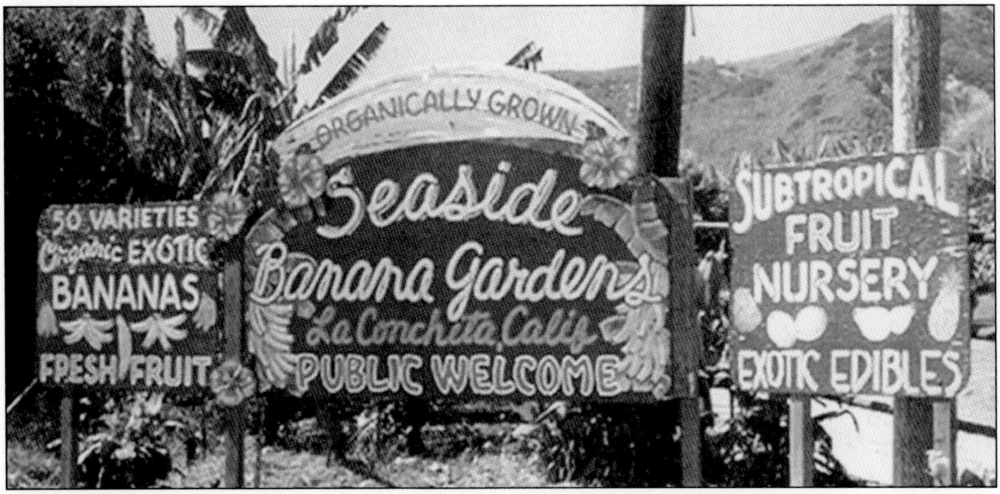

The Seaside Banana Gardens operated by Doug Richardson and Paul Turner was the most famous attraction in La Conchita from its opening in 1985 until it closed in 1996. The gardens were featured in major publications and defied the experts' opinions that bananas could not be commercially grown in California by cultivating over 50 exotic varieties. La Conchita's unique microclimate was ideal for this purpose. (Courtesy Jeff Ross.)

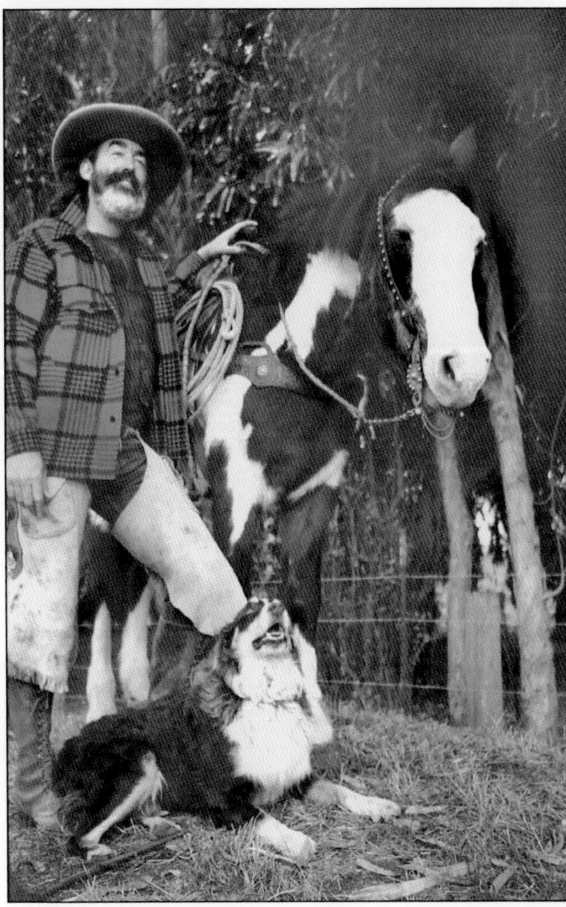

The tragic La Conchita mudslide of 2005 took the life of one of the community's most unique and beloved individuals. Tony Alvis was the founder of the Los Padres Wilderness Outfitters, the mountain guide service that enabled visitors to experience the Sespe Wilderness backcountry of the Los Padres National Forest. Pictured on the left is Tony Alvis with his dog Otis and his horse Mutah. (Courtesy the Alvis family.)

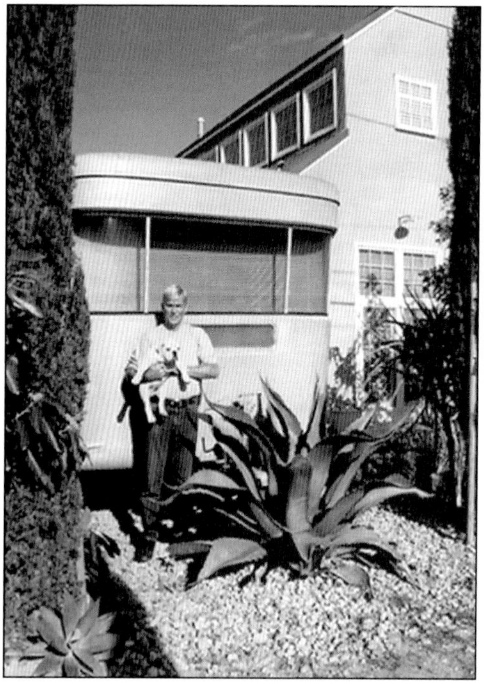

Internationally recognized artist Roger Brown (1941–1997) lived in La Conchita from the late 1980s until his untimely death in 1997. The community inspired many of Brown's paintings during that period. His works are in major museums throughout the country. The artist and his dog Elvis are pictured on the left in their La Conchita backyard. (Courtesy © Roger Brown Study Collection at the School of the Art Institute of Chicago.)

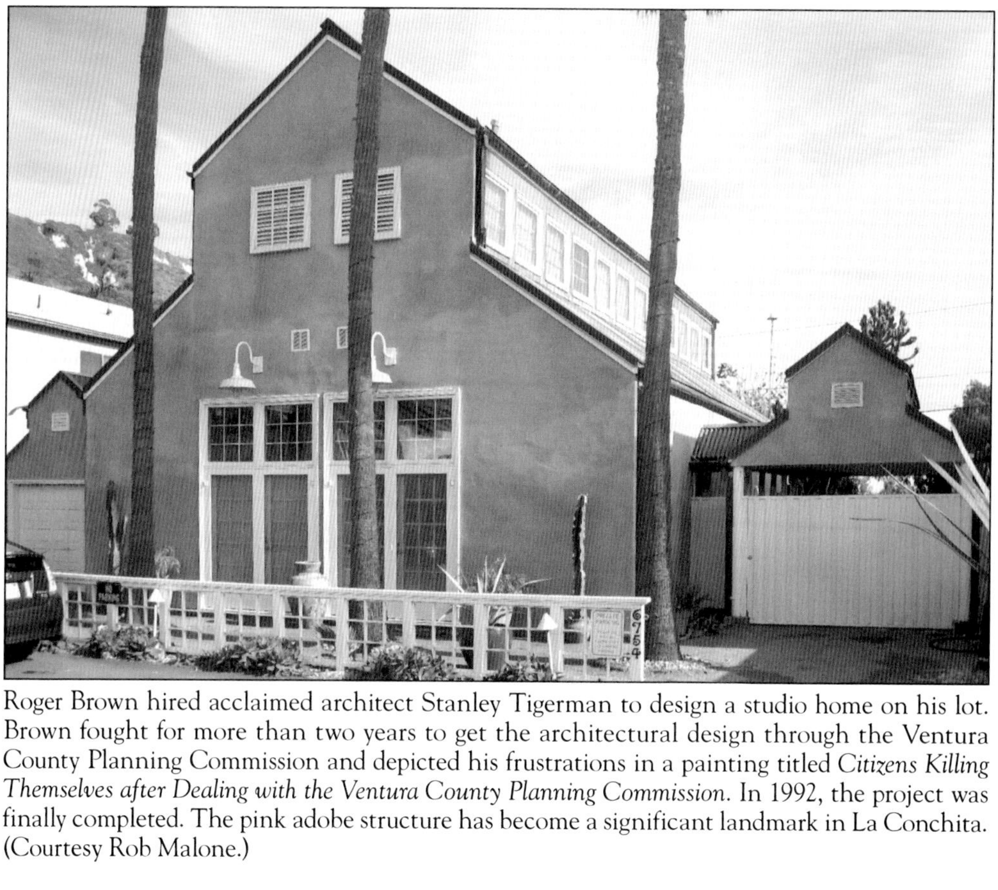

Roger Brown hired acclaimed architect Stanley Tigerman to design a studio home on his lot. Brown fought for more than two years to get the architectural design through the Ventura County Planning Commission and depicted his frustrations in a painting titled *Citizens Killing Themselves after Dealing with the Ventura County Planning Commission*. In 1992, the project was finally completed. The pink adobe structure has become a significant landmark in La Conchita. (Courtesy Rob Malone.)

Seven

Flyboys and Girls, Miners, and Then Some

Diversity, a continuing theme in Carpinteria's remarkable history, joins the Carpinteria schools, the asphalt industry, Carpinteria's aviation pioneers, and a downtown blacksmith shop as the focus of chapter seven.

The valley's aviation history more than made up in breadth what it lacked in length. The Bauhaus brothers were major players in American aviation's formative years. They were joined in Carpinteria during this era by numerous legendary pilots.

The Chumash Indians' use of asphaltum deposits in waterproofing their remarkable plank canoes established, early on, that there were practical applications for the tar that seeped out of the bluffs on Carpinteria's beaches. During the 1880s, clever entrepreneurs picked up the Chumashes' sticky baton and began extracting the gooey black substance to pave roads nationwide. The pictures included here are intriguing for a number of reasons, not the least of which is the photographic framing of the age-old dilemma of the ecological debit and credit columns. Are the costs of harvesting natural resources from a pristine landscape too exorbitant? The debate, as of 2009, rages on.

Hopefully, these stories will inspire the reader to pursue the innumerable narratives and photographs that remain hidden in the valley's attics, closets, and garages. A visit to the Carpinteria Valley Museum of History, a remarkable resource, is also highly recommended for anyone who's interested in Carpinteria's past.

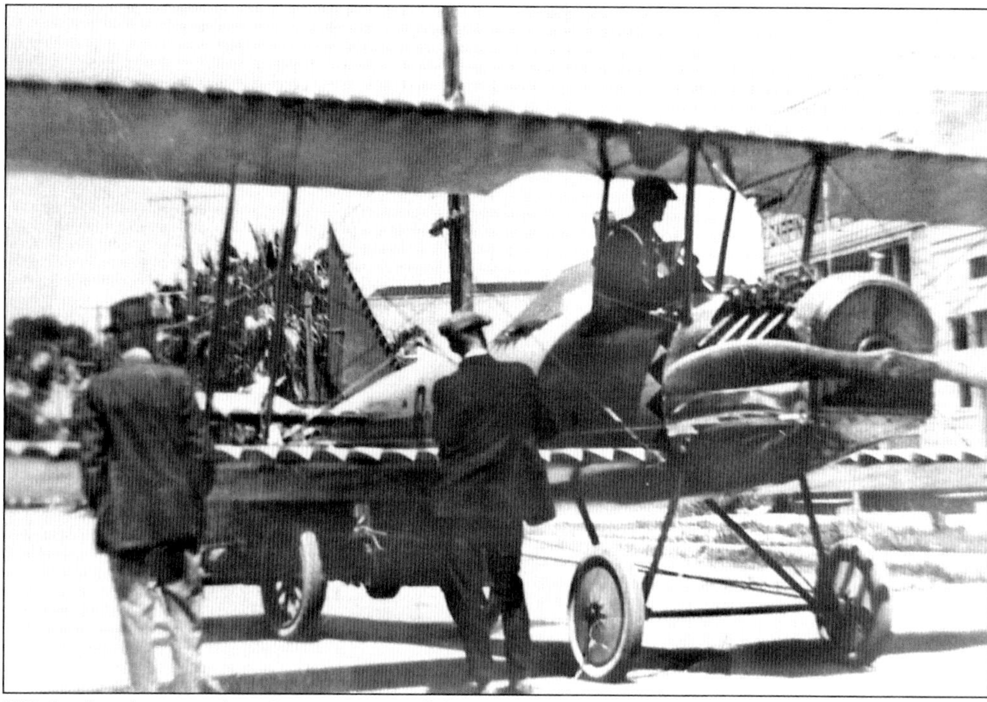

While the chances that Carpinteria will be confused with Kitty Hawk, North Carolina, are remote, Carpinteria does have an impressive aviation history. This plane is being towed along Linden Avenue to be fueled at Arthur Hebel's garage in 1920, a common occurrence during the aviation years. The Bauhaus brothers were Carpinteria's most noteworthy aeronautical innovators. In fact, elements of a Bauhaus-inspired design were appropriated for use in Charles Lindbergh's *Spirit of St. Louis.* (Courtesy Carpinteria Valley Museum of History.)

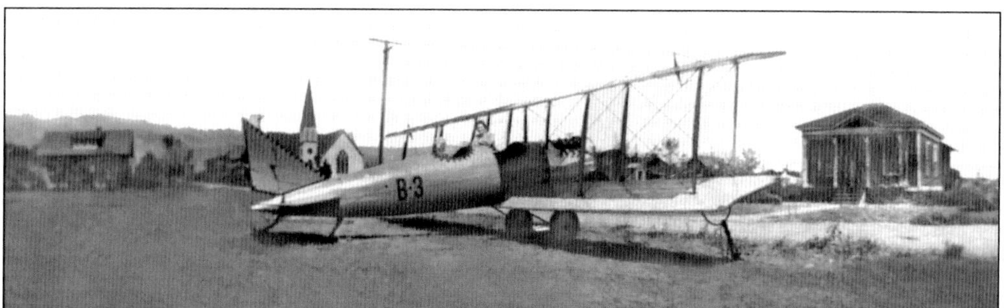

This B-3 is parked in a field at the corner of Seventh Street and Maple Avenue. That's today's Carpinteria Valley Baptist Church in the background. The small house at the right was rented by the Bauhaus family around 1920. (Courtesy Carpinteria Valley Museum of History.)

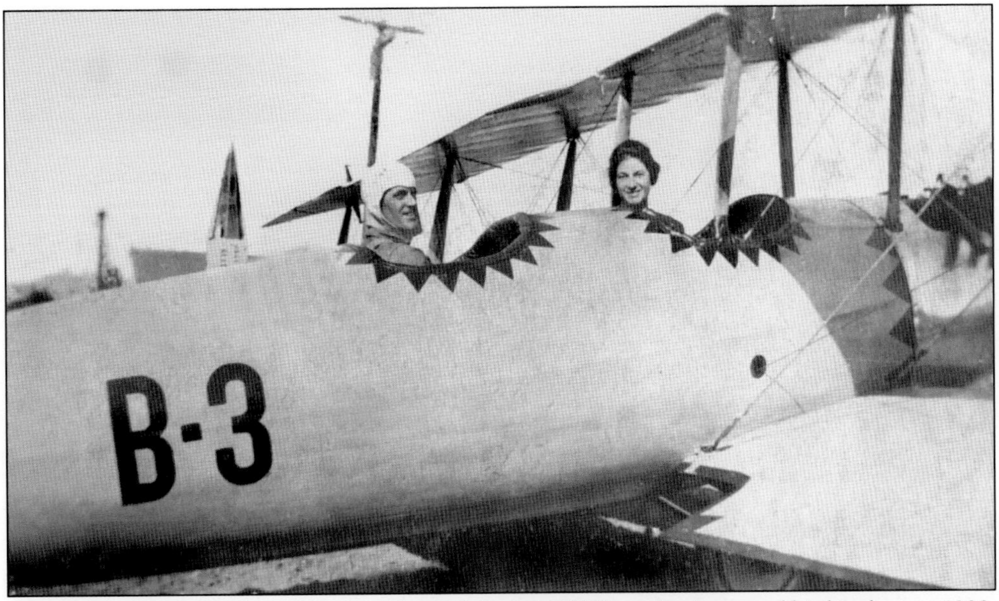

The pilots pictured in the cockpits of this B-3, built by William Bauhaus and his brothers in 1920, are Mr. and Mrs. William K. Bauhaus. (Courtesy Carpinteria Valley Museum of History.)

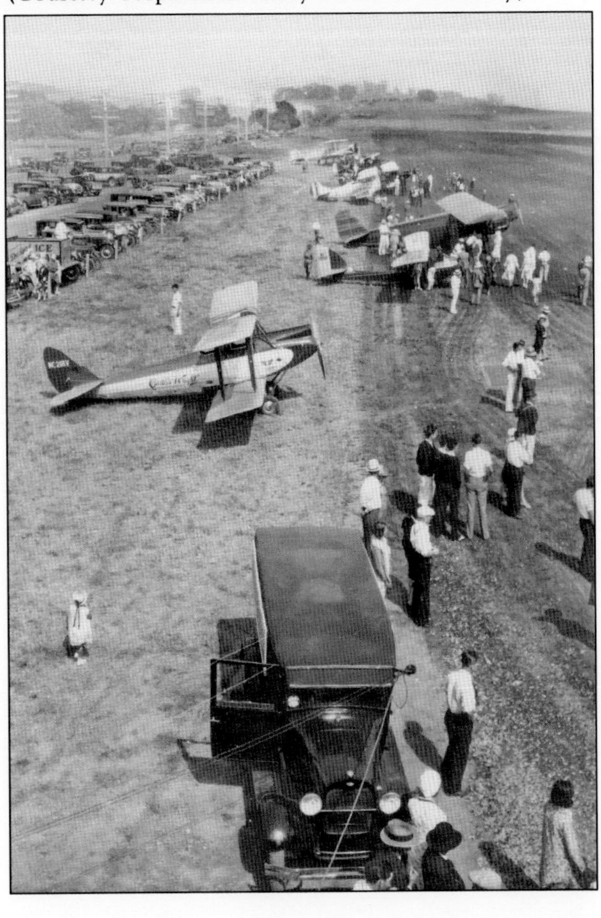

Carpinteria has never been shy about drawing a crowd, be it to an early celebration of the automobile, singing the praises of the avocado, or sponsoring an air show like this one in the 1920s. (Courtesy Carpinteria Valley Museum of History.)

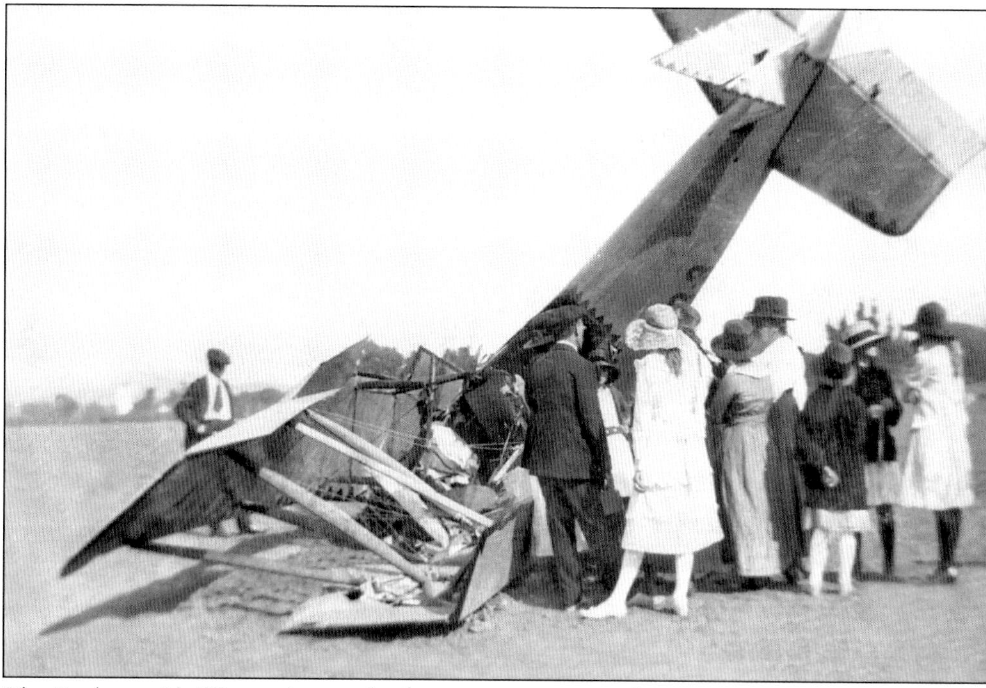

The Bauhauses' brilliance during the formative moments of American aviation was mirrored by tragedy. William Bauhaus, a passenger during this ill-fated flight in the 1920s, died in the crash pictured above. The velocity of the B-3 buried its engine 4 feet deep in a local bean field. Triumphs in early flight often went hand in hand with tragedies. (Courtesy Carpinteria Valley Museum of History.)

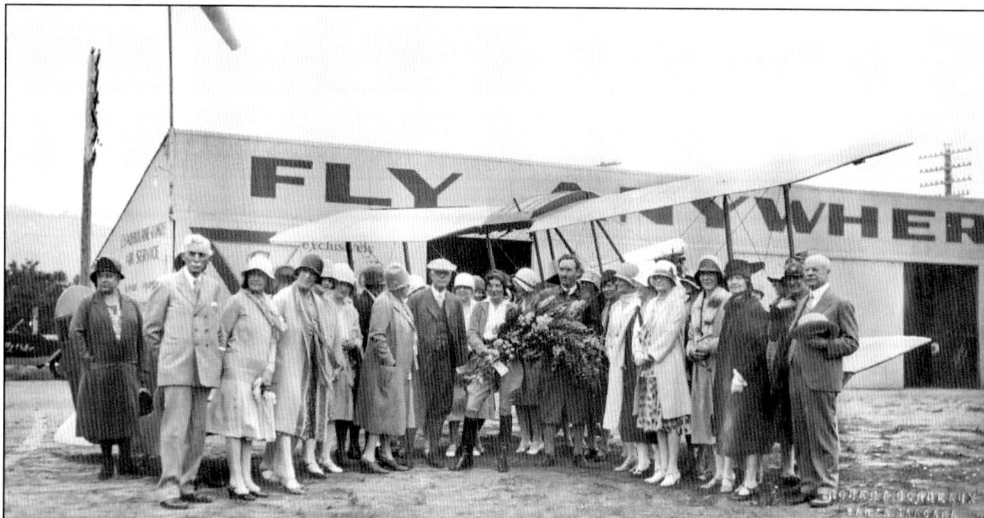

That's noted aviatrix Ruth Elder with an armful of flowers in the middle of a crowd of local admirers around 1927. Elder was but one of a number of aviation legends who set their planes down at Carpinteria's Chadbourne-Donze Airport over the years. Others included Charles Lindbergh, Florence "Pancho" Barnes, Evelyn "Bobbi" Trout, Wiley Post, Howard Hughes, and Will Rogers. The signage on the front of the hangar reads, "Fly Anywhere—Speed and Safety." (Courtesy Carpinteria Valley Museum of History.)

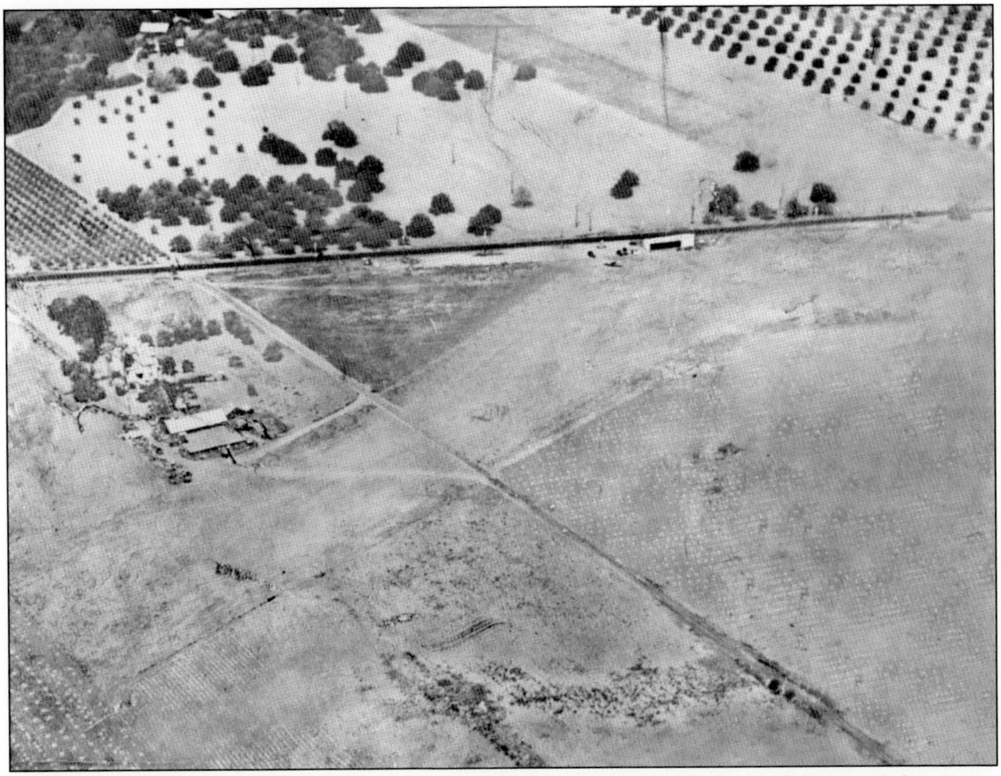

This late 1920s aerial view of Chadbourne-Donze Airport includes a glimpse of the Coast Highway, which would become Carpinteria Avenue, running in front of the hangar at top right; a diagonal dirt runway; and, at middle left, the Higgins Ranch, which was located in the field bounded by today's Carpinteria Avenue and Dump Road. (Courtesy Carpinteria Valley Museum of History.)

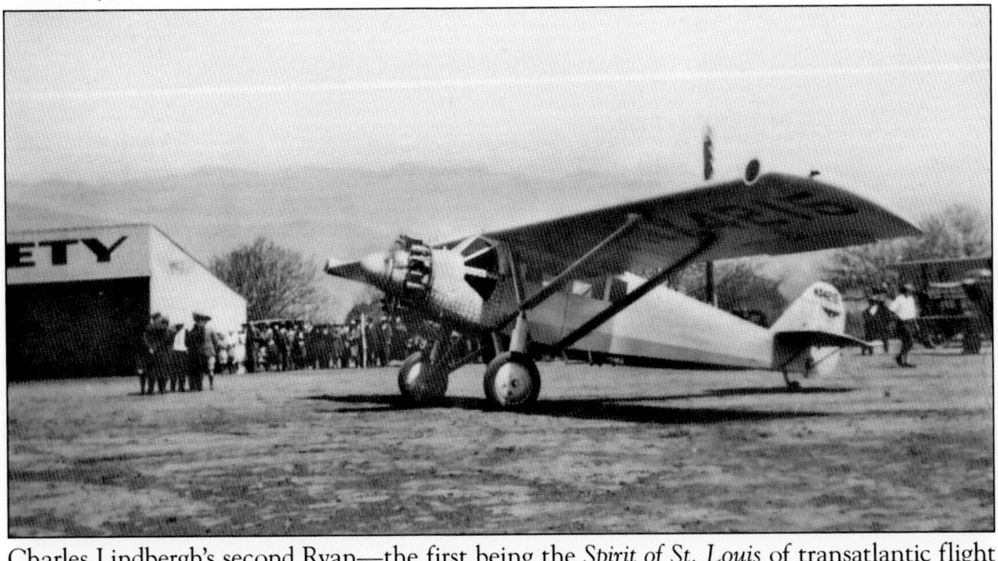

Charles Lindbergh's second Ryan—the first being the *Spirit of St. Louis* of transatlantic flight fame—was captured in this photograph taken at Chadbourne-Donze in 1928. (Courtesy Carpinteria Valley Museum of History.)

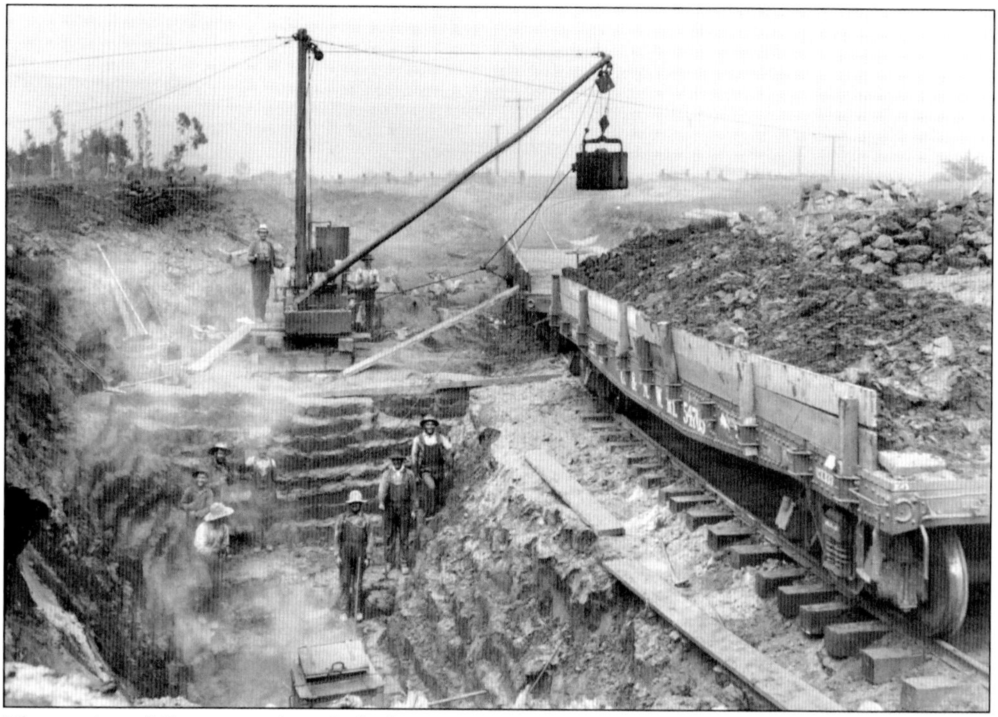

The residue of Carpinteria's asphalt deposits continues to make its presence felt in local seeps, much to the chagrin of numerous Carpinteria Park residents. The scope of one of the early asphalt operations is shown here around 1912. (Courtesy Carpinteria Valley Museum of History.)

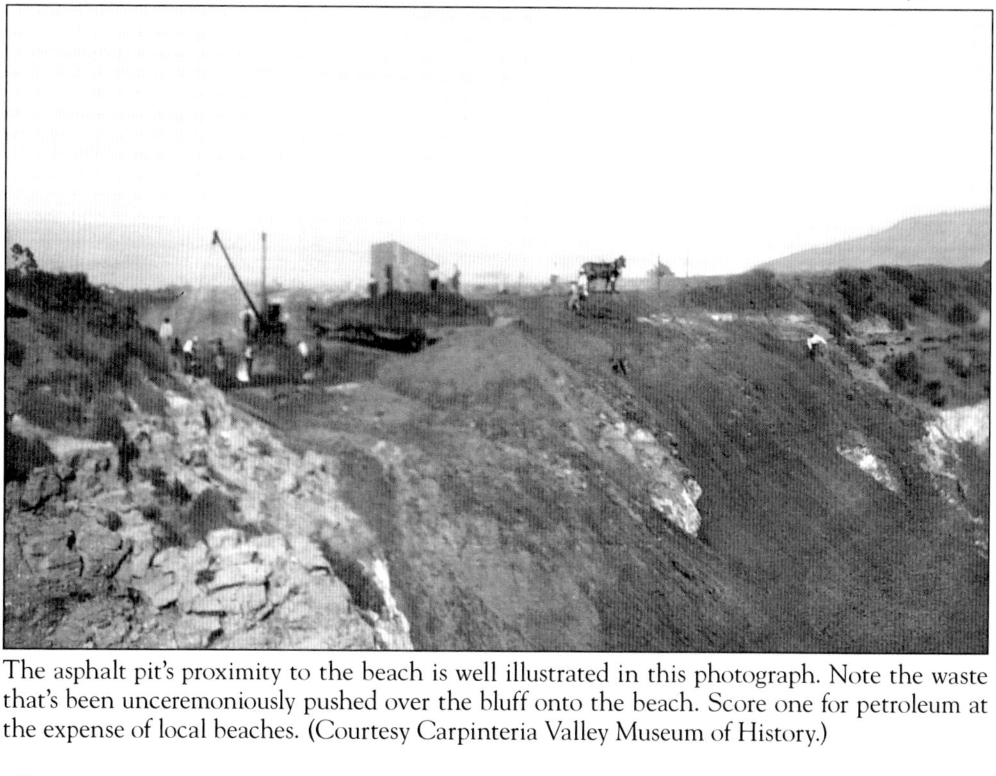

The asphalt pit's proximity to the beach is well illustrated in this photograph. Note the waste that's been unceremoniously pushed over the bluff onto the beach. Score one for petroleum at the expense of local beaches. (Courtesy Carpinteria Valley Museum of History.)

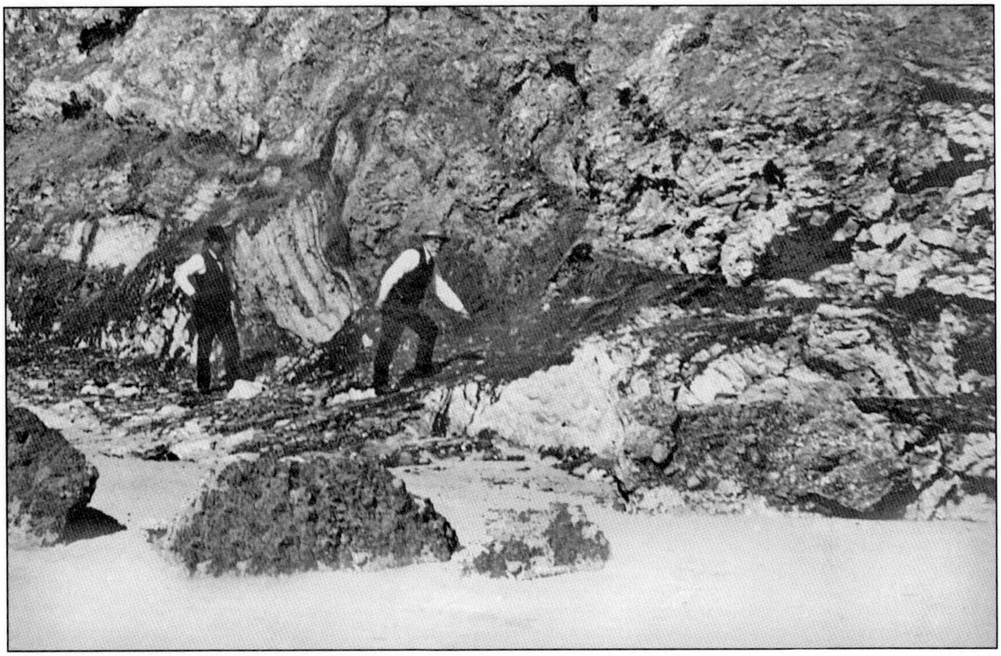

These two men, pictured around 1900, are examining liquid asphaltum seepage on Higgins' Beach, today's Jellybowl. (Courtesy Carpinteria Valley Museum of History.)

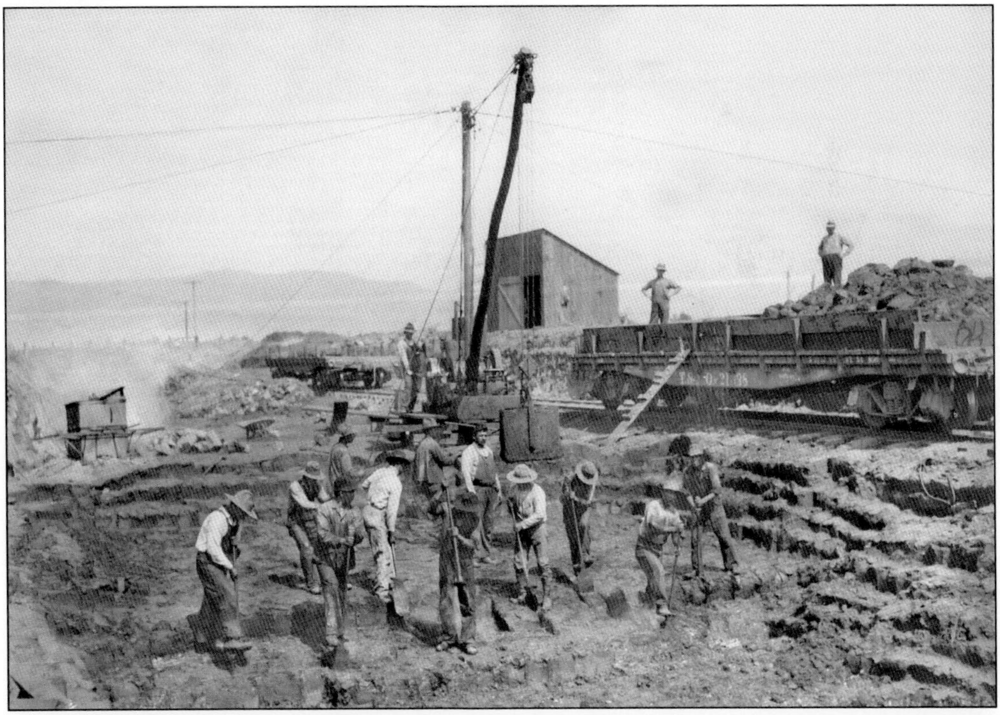

While the toll paid for doing exhausting work in the asphalt mines of Carpinteria was partially subsidized by Carpinteria's mild climate and the ocean breezes that wafted over the bluff that was only yards away, a day in the pits in 1912 would never be confused with a day at the beach. (Courtesy Carpinteria Valley Museum of History.)

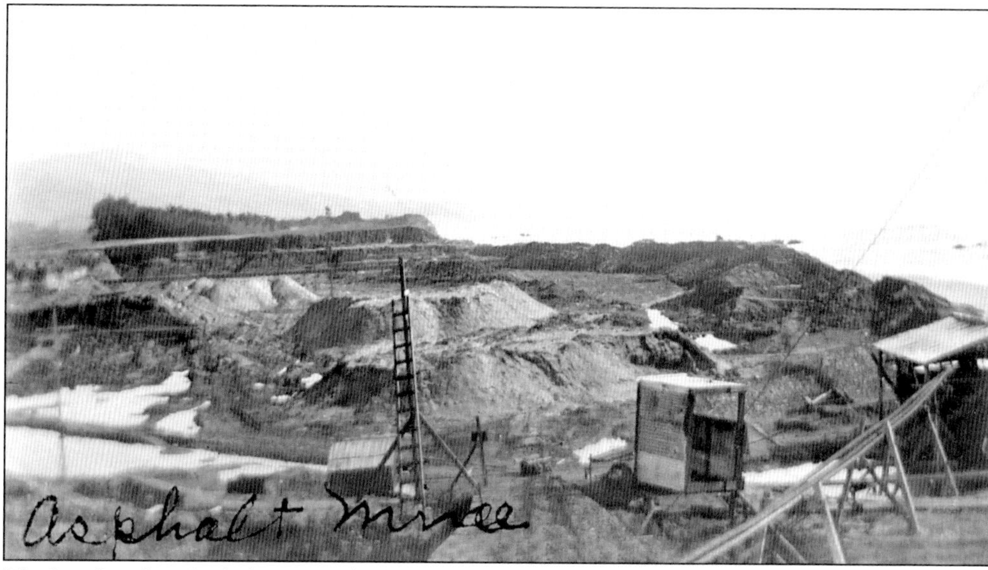

The Las Conchas Asphalt Mine, which operated from the 1880s through 1903, was a large open-pit operation. Decades later, it was filled in, and it now serves as a campground at Carpinteria State Park, quite a contrast from the 1880s. (Courtesy Carpinteria Valley Museum of History.)

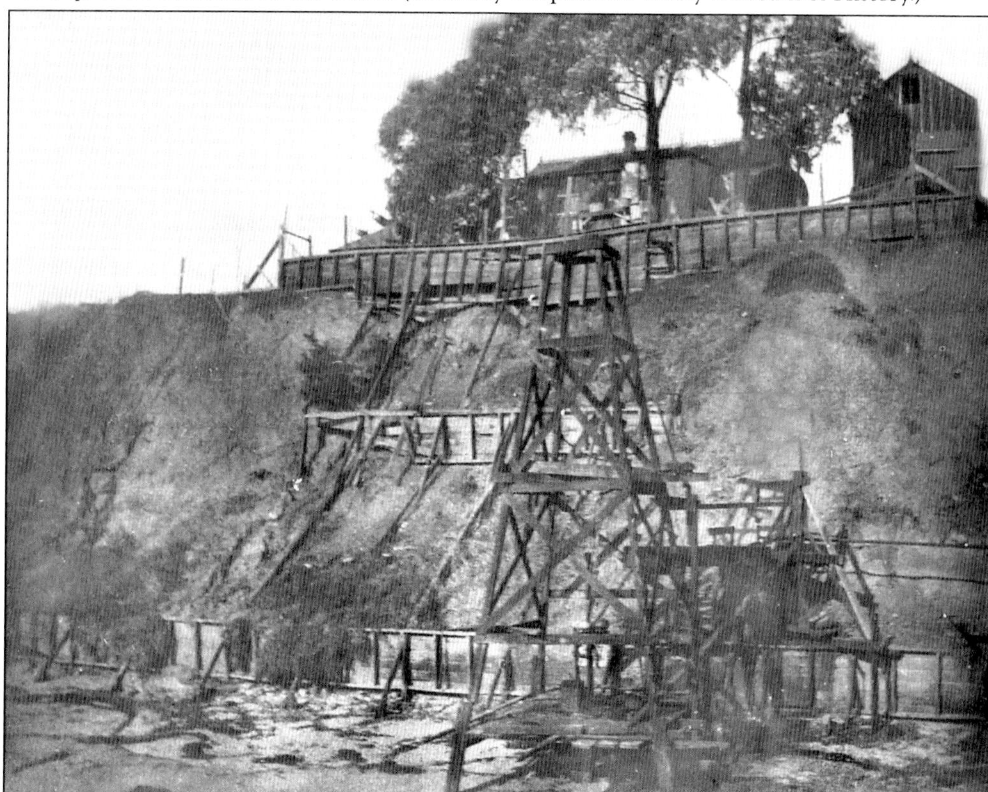

The ongoing debate over local petroleum continues unabated in 2009. This c. 1915 photograph of an oil derrick on the beach epitomizes the citizenry's ongoing concerns about the ultimate cost of drilling for oil. (Courtesy Carpinteria Valley Museum of History.)

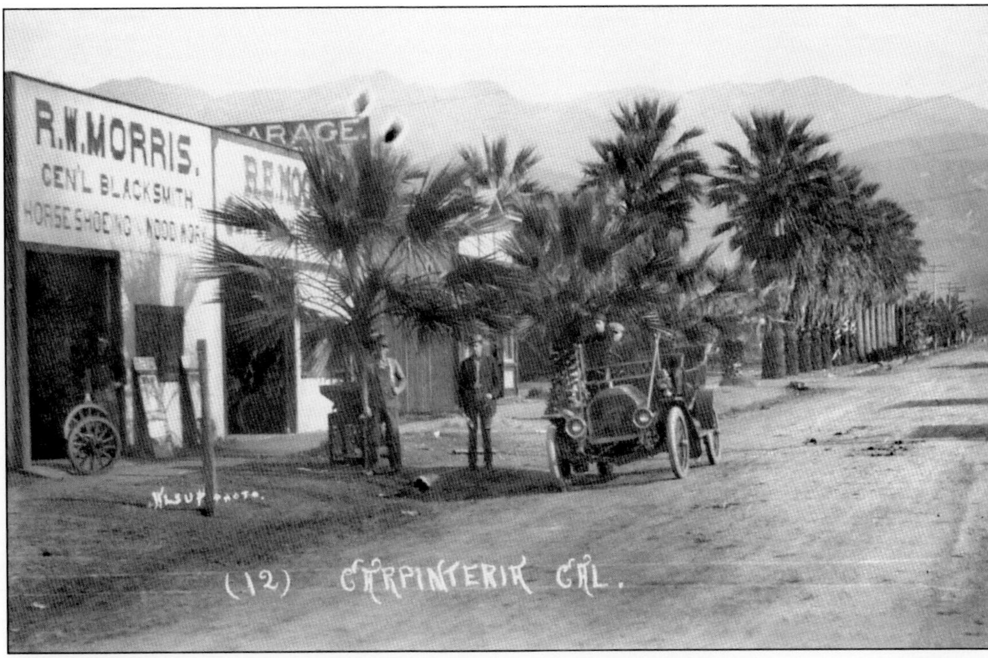

The R. W. Morris blacksmith shop was one for the ages. Started by Dick Morris in 1908, it is the oldest business establishment in Carpinteria. He provided the Carpinteria Valley with his welding services until 1945 and then sold the business to Joe Wullbrandt. Wullbrandt in turn operated the shop for an even longer period of time, into the 21st century. Two owners provided a century's worth of service to the Carpinteria community! (Courtesy Carpinteria Valley Museum of History.)

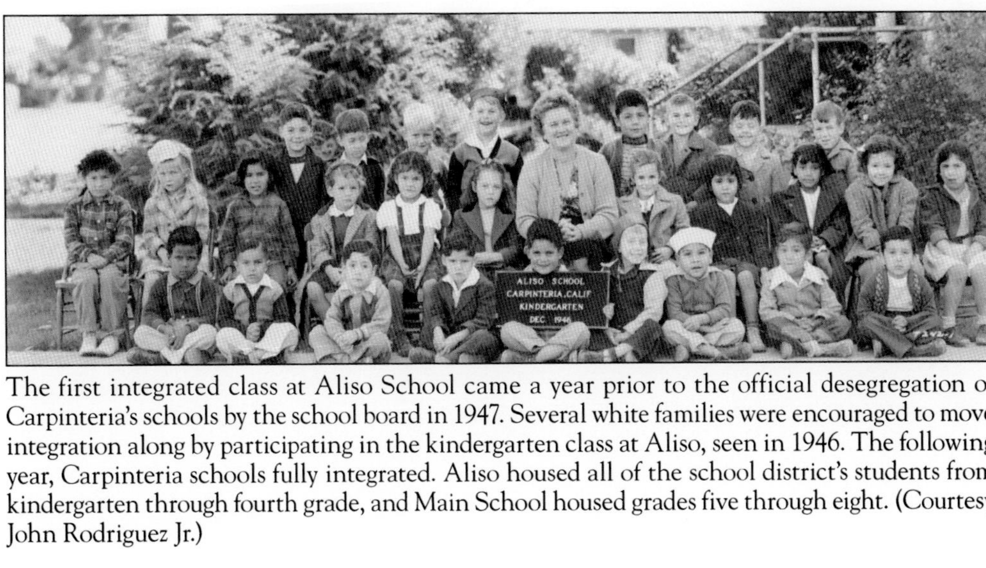

The first integrated class at Aliso School came a year prior to the official desegregation of Carpinteria's schools by the school board in 1947. Several white families were encouraged to move integration along by participating in the kindergarten class at Aliso, seen in 1946. The following year, Carpinteria schools fully integrated. Aliso housed all of the school district's students from kindergarten through fourth grade, and Main School housed grades five through eight. (Courtesy John Rodriguez Jr.)

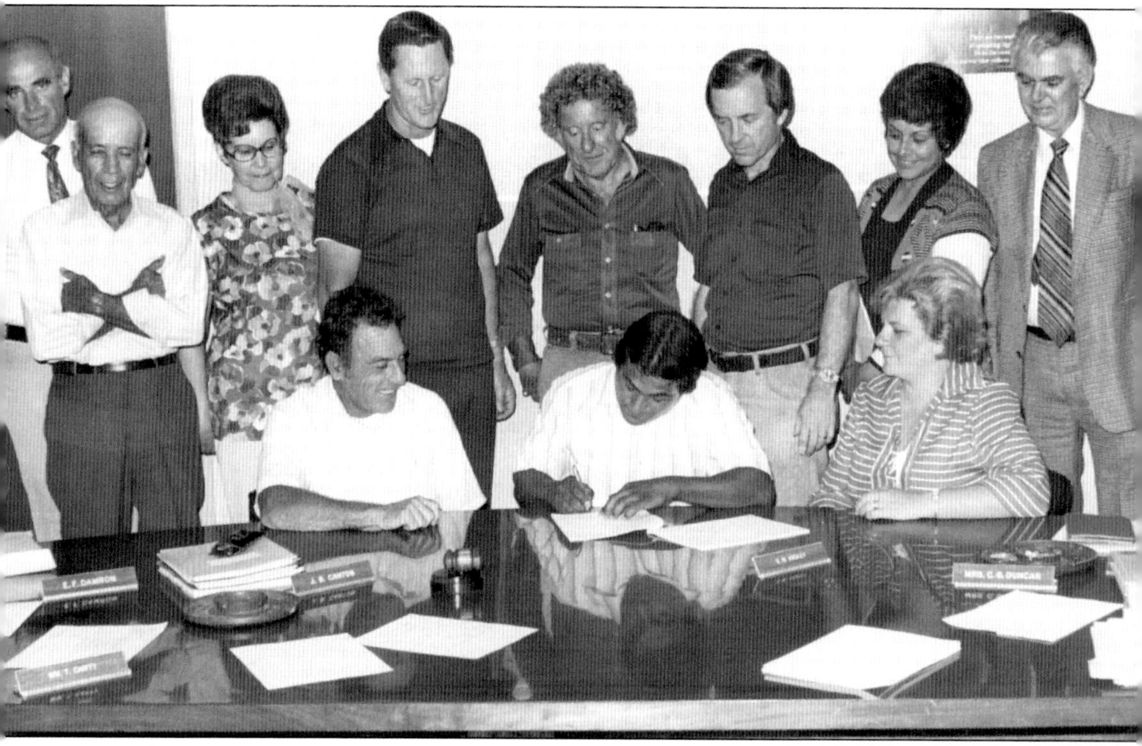

Dr. William Carty, on the extreme left of this photograph, was the first superintendent of the Carpinteria Unified School District (CUSD), beginning in 1960. Prior to his selection as superintendent, there were two school boards in Carpinteria, one for elementary school and another for secondary, each with a principal/superintendent. In 1961, the two boards were combined, and Summerland joined the new configuration. With the opening of a new high school on Foothill Road in 1967 and the completion of a state-of-the-art Early Childhood Learning Center wing on the Canalino Elementary school site soon thereafter, a complete education system was achieved in the valley. In this 1977 picture, the CUSD Board of Education is signing a contract with its classified employees. From left to right are (seated) are Glen Hickey, Tom Villa, and Carole Duncan; (standing) Dr. Carty, Jess Franco, Evelina Toth, Bert Goebel, J. B. Canton, Buddy Reeves, Lucy Diaz, and district business manager Robert Duff. (Courtesy Sal and Delia Campos.)

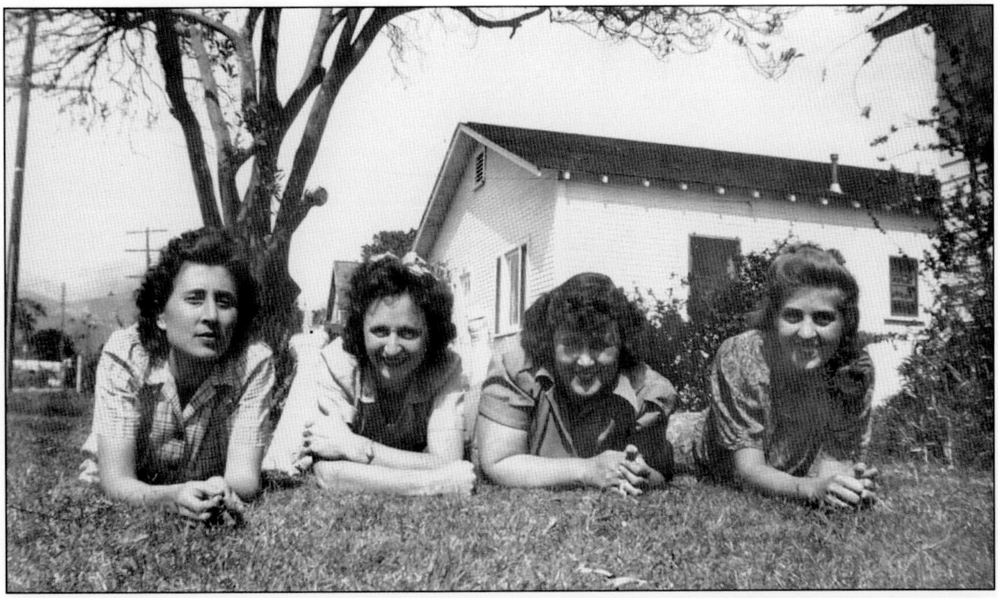

Tipton, Oklahoma, provided upwards of a dozen new families to Carpinteria around the time of the Great Depression. They were looking for a more prosperous way of life than their home state could provide. Other groups of working-class families came from states like Arkansas, Kansas, Nebraska, and Texas. The young women from Oklahoma pictured here around 1946 are, from left to right, Dorothy Whitmore, Edna McCafferty, Gladys Minyard, and Norene Rollins. (Courtesy John McCafferty.)

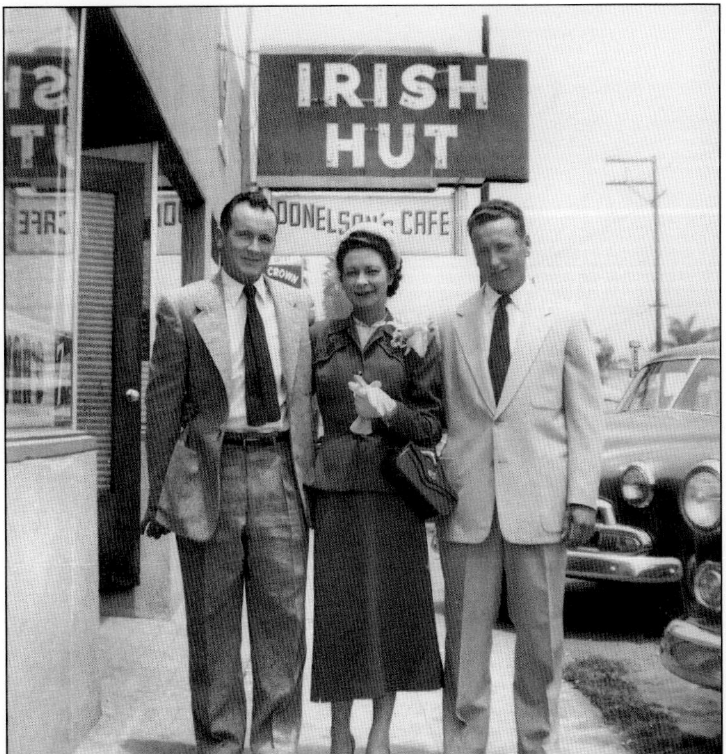

The Irish Hut, pictured here on Linden Avenue in 1954, offered Irish cuisine, as the name states. The hut was divided into two sections. On one side it was a restaurant serving Irish fare. On the other side, it was an Irish pub. The owner, Peggy Donovan, is flanked by her sons, Jack (left) and Larry (right). Later in the afternoon on the day this photograph was taken, Larry married his bride, Bonnie. (Courtesy Larry and Bonnie Donovan.)

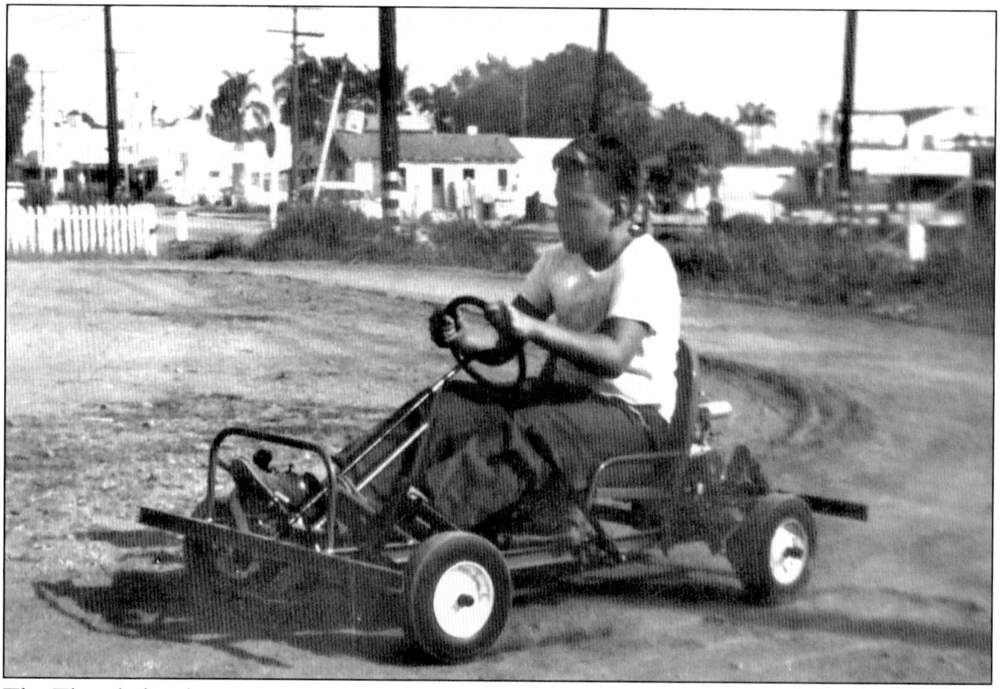

The Thunderbowl was not the only race car attraction in Carpinteria. Ray Rollins landscaped a go-cart track on the Rosebro Garage site at Carpinteria Avenue and Sawyer Lane. In this 1959 photograph, Lonnie Johnson puts his go-cart into high gear. (Courtesy Jimmy Rosebro.)

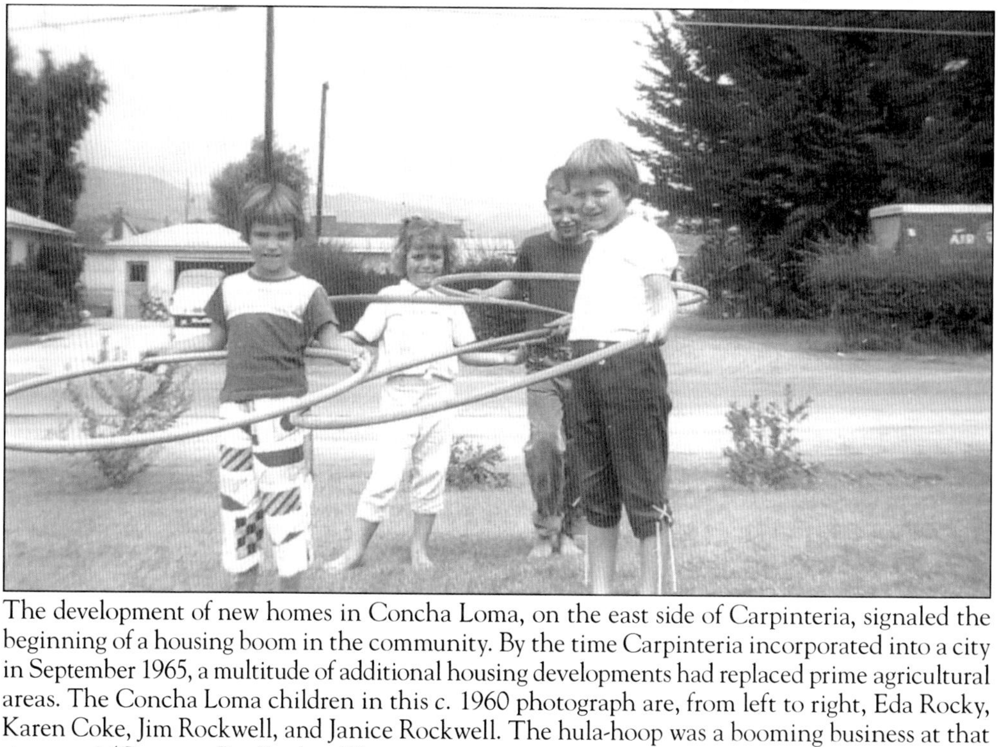

The development of new homes in Concha Loma, on the east side of Carpinteria, signaled the beginning of a housing boom in the community. By the time Carpinteria incorporated into a city in September 1965, a multitude of additional housing developments had replaced prime agricultural areas. The Concha Loma children in this c. 1960 photograph are, from left to right, Eda Rocky, Karen Coke, Jim Rockwell, and Janice Rockwell. The hula-hoop was a booming business at that time, too! (Courtesy Jim Rockwell.)

Bibliography

"A Battle to Preserve Solitude." *Ventura Star Free Press*, December 4, 1983.

Bates, Edward. *A Brief, Factual History of the Rincon Del Mar Ranch*. Unpublished, April 22, 1979.

Caldwell, Jayne C. *Carpinteria as It Was*. Carpinteria, CA: Carpinteria Valley Historical Society, 1979.

———. *More about Carpinteria as It Was*. Carpinteria, CA: Papillon Press, 1982.

Clark, Arthur M. *From Grove to Cove to Grove: A Brief History of the Carpinteria Valley, California*. Carpinteria, CA: Self-published, 1962.

Dacayana, Chet. *Growing up in La Conchita*. Unpublished, 2009.

Davis, Myrna and Mary Holzhauer. *Almost Heaven: A Walk through Old Summerland*. Santa Barbara, CA: McNally and Loftin, 1997.

Hollenhorst, Linda. "Growin' Bananas." *Organic Gardening* (September 1989): 54–60.

Kleine, Henry. "Ride With Seaside." *Noticias* 34 (Winter 1988): 104–111.

Lambert, May. *Growing up with Summerland*. Carpinteria, CA: Carpinteria Valley Historical Society, 1975.

Lambert, Opal, Eleana Darling, and Earle Taylor. *Historic Buildings of Summerland, California*. Research project, 1976.

Lathim, Kim and Rod Lathim. *The Spirit of the Big Yellow House: A History of Summerland's Founding Family*. Santa Barbara, CA: Emily Publications, 1975.

Mingus, Bill. *Growing up in La Conchita*. Unpublished, 2009.

Myrick, David. "Summerland: The First Decade." *Noticias* 34 (Winter 1988): 65–103.

Reynolds, Christopher. "La Conchita: The Town at the End of the Tunnel." *Los Angeles Times*, August 22, 1991, J10–11.

Summerland Advance Courier. *Southern Santa Barbara County and Its Resources*. Souvenir Edition. Summerland, CA: W. H. Smith, Publisher, February 1900.